DR JOHNSON'S WOMEN

Dr Johnson's Women

Norma Clarke

Hambledon and London
London and New York

Hambledon and London

102 Gloucester Avenue
London, NW1 8HX

838 Broadway
New York
NY 10003-4812

First Published 2000

ISBN 1 85285 254 2

A description of this book is available from the
British Library and from the Library of Congress.

Typeset by Carnegie Publishing,
Lancaster LA1 4SL

Printed on acid-free paper and bound in
Great Britain by Cambridge University Press

Contents

Illustrations

Preface

'I dined yesterday at Mrs Garrick's, with Mrs Carter, Miss Hannah More, and Miss Fanny Burney. Three such women are not to be found; I know not where I could find a fourth, except Mrs Lennox, who is superior to them all.'

Samuel Johnson to James Boswell, 15 May, 1784

This book is an attempt at collective biography which is also, in part, collective criticism. It is exploratory, speculative, selective in its choice of materials. It begins with a moment in Boswell's *Life of Samuel Johnson* where a tantalising conversation about women writers fails to happen. Johnson's friendships with literary women barely feature in Boswell's account of his life; and on the one occasion when Boswell did record a remark by Johnson revealing his pleasure in the company of 'three such women' the conversation went nowhere. In *Dr Johnson's Women* I have taken up the thread, convinced not only that a rich and detailed conversation could have been had in 1784, but that Johnson, at the end of a long life spent in the heart of literary London, had things to say about female authorship which would have been of great interest to us today. Even in a short exchange he managed to be provocative.

What follows is a study of relationships between individuals who suc-ceeded in becoming successful writers. It is at the same time an enquiry into the conditions of female authorship at a particular time, the mid eighteenth century, and in a particular place, England, meaning mostly London. I have taken up the names Johnson listed to Boswell, and added some more: no book called *Dr Johnson's Women* would be complete without Hester Thrale, and there are others, such as Hester Mulso Chapone, Ca-therine Talbot and Laetitia Hawkins who demanded walk-on parts. As readers will discover, the chapter divisions look more orderly than they are: the person named in the chapter title is rarely allowed undisputed possession of the territory. There is much popping in and out. I have made no attempt to be fair or balanced in the amount of attention given to the different subjects. Some, like Fanny Burney and Hannah More, are relatively well known and there is a substantial literature available about their lives and works. Others, like Elizabeth Carter, Elizabeth Montagu and Charlotte Lennox, are not. My choices have been governed to some extent by the raw materials but my underlying question has been the same throughout: what did it mean to this individual living this specific life to be a woman and a writer?

Acknowledgements

Much of this book was written while I held a three-year Research Fellowship in the department of English at Kingston University. I am pleased to record my gratitude to Gail Cunningham, John Ibbett, Gabriele Griffin and David Rogers for their support. At Kingston I have found an environment – thanks to colleagues, students, and administrative staff – where it remains a pleasure to teach. In the wider academic community, I owe a great deal to the stimulus of the international Feminism and Enlightenment project. The Women's History Network invited me to speak, as did the Eighteenth Century Studies Centre at the University of York. My fellow editors on *Gender & History* have been patient with my absences over the past year. I particularly thank Keith McClelland, Myna Trustram and Megan Doolittle.

Staff at the British Library have been helpful as always. The London Library remains an essential resource. I am grateful to the librarians at Deal County Library for making available the Stebbing Collection and books by Elizabeth Carter.

Amongst friends who have provided much appreciated help at key moments, I would like to single out Catherine Hall, Cora Kaplan and Jenny Uglow. Judith Hawley read and commented on a draft of the Elizabeth Carter chapter. Tom Betteridge gave me helpful feedback on *The Female Quixote*. Sarah Prescott kindly sent draft chapters from her book on early women writers which helped me think about Elizabeth Rowe. Conversations with Sally Alexander, Monica Bolufer, Leonore Davidoff, Konstantin Dierks, Elizabeth Eger, Harriet Guest, Frances Harris, Carla Hesse, Sarah Knott, Clarissa Campbell Orr, Ruth Perry, Adam Phillips, Jane Rendall, Jacqueline Rose, John Tosh and Dror Wahrman have nagged productively at my mind for one reason or another. The many others who know they contributed but whose names I have omitted, please consider yourselves thanked. Alison Light has given me untold encouragement: when the work gets gruelling, we walk in the park and remind each other that it is a privilege to be able to write the book one wants to write. Jenny Uglow, combining scholarship with publishing expertise, and bringing her own blend of warm iconoclasm to both, was the ideal reader. Martin Sheppard at Hambledon and London has been an exacting editor in the best sense, and the book has gained from his suggestions.

My sons, Nick Tosh and William Tosh – adults now, with intellectual passions of their own – bring a special scrutiny to my work which I want them to know I appreciate. Barbara Taylor, with her unrivalled knowledge of feminist history and thought, has extended my understanding of the period more than I can say. She read the manuscript at various stages and helped me think and feel differently in ways that were always strengthening. This book is for the family, with love.

Tottenham, May 2000

1

At Mrs Garrick's

On Saturday 15 May 1784 Samuel Johnson spent the evening with James Boswell and other members of the Essex Head club. This club, instituted the previous winter, was the latest in a series of dining and discussion clubs which Johnson relied on for conversation and company. In membership, it was a pale echo of the Literary Club (or The Club) which had flourished from the mid 1760s and which had included Joshua Reynolds, Edmund Burke, Oliver Goldsmith, Charles James Fox, Edward Gibbon and Richard Brinsley Sheridan among others. But like The Club it was dedicated to the extension of knowledge. Johnson's ideal since boyhood had been to possess, as he put it, the 'general principles of every science', to 'grasp the Trunk' of knowledge and 'shake all the Branches'. This meant not only literature in many languages, philosophy, psychology, theology, medicine and history; but also the law, science, and such practical arts as brewing, coining, tanning, the making of gunpowder or butter, and even, in spite of his 'horror of butchering', the slaughter of cattle for the table – a subject Boswell discovered him to be proficient in explaining. Such knowledge he had got, he said, by 'running about the world with my wits ready to observe, and my tongue ready to talk'.

There was pleasure in this but it was also work. Knowledge of every kind was capital to be intelligently deployed; it was the means by which an 'author by profession' gained credit. As Johnson admitted: 'a fellow shall have strange credit given him, if he can but recollect striking passages from different books, keep the authors separate in his head, and bring his stock of knowledge artfully into play'.[1]

The newly established club met three times a week at a tavern called the Essex Head in Essex Street off the Strand, run by an old servant of the brewer Henry Thrale. (The club was a way of providing him with business.) Members, who had to be proposed, were bound by club rules which Johnson had drawn up: membership was limited to twenty-four, though members could bring one guest per week; attendance was insisted upon and absence punished by fines. This 'assembly of good fellows' was, like the more famous club before it, a men only affair.

On the evening of Saturday 15 May, Johnson was in 'fine spirits'. Boswell describes him at that time as being particularly 'able and animated in conversation, and appearing to relish society as much as the youngest man'. Certainly, Johnson's social energy was undimmed by age and illness. However, his 'fine spirits' at the Essex Head on 15 May were connected with his enjoyment of another and very different gathering which he had been at the evening before, an account of which he was eager to share with the club. Boswell reported it thus in *The Life of Samuel Johnson*:

> He told us, 'I dined yesterday at Mrs Garrick's with Mrs Carter, Miss Hannah More, and Miss Fanny Burney. Three such women are not to be found; I know not where I could find a fourth, except Mrs Lennox, who is superior to them all.' BOSWELL. 'What! Had you them all to yourself, Sir?' JOHNSON. 'I had them all, as much as they were had; but it might have been better had there been more company there.' BOSWELL. 'Might not Mrs Montagu have been a fourth?' JOHNSON. 'Sir, Mrs Montagu does not make a trade of her wit; but Mrs Montagu is a very extraordinary woman: she has a constant stream of conversation, and it is always impregnated; it has always meaning.' [2]

If Johnson meant to surprise, he certainly succeeded. Momentarily at a loss, Boswell could think of no intelligent response. His roguish, 'What! Had you them all to yourself, Sir?' seems to be a reflex, and rather meaningless; and the suggestion, 'Might not Mrs Montagu have been a fourth?' earned him nothing but a reproof. Johnson's stern encomium on Mrs Montagu's virtues carried more than a hint that Boswell would do well to try to follow her example: she was 'a very extraordinary woman' with a remarkable ability to talk. Johnson had once said to Mrs Thrale of Mrs Montagu: 'She diffuses more knowledge than any woman I know, or indeed almost any man.' And on another occasion he commented: 'That lady exerts more *mind* in conversation than any person I ever met with.' Unlike Boswell's, her conversation was 'always impregnated; it has always meaning'.

For the reader who has followed Boswell through his thousand-plus pages to 1784, the final year of Johnson's life, this exchange is an arresting one, made all the more so by its setting. At the formally constituted club of men, Johnson testified to the merits of certain distinguished women writers of his time. All were praised, blanket-fashion, though one – Mrs Lennox – was praised above the rest. The men of the club probably shared Boswell's sense of surprise but neither they nor Boswell asked Johnson to elaborate on his remarks. Establishing the cause of surprise – Boswell's 'What!' – is not straightforward. Was it the fact that Johnson had dined with these women? Was it his evident relish of their company, such as a younger man might have been expected to enjoy, the being amongst 'three such women'? Was it the critical opinion laid down like a gauntlet: that Mrs Lennox was 'superior to them all'? We don't know. The conversation, beginning so intriguingly with praise of women, goes on to discuss praiseworthy men. Five extraordinary women (six if we include Eva Garrick) flash suddenly into view in *The Life of Samuel Johnson* and just as suddenly out of it.

The vanishing acts of women writers make a familiar theme in the annals of literature. Women celebrated in their own times become hidden from history and must be rediscovered by later generations. The work of rediscovery has gathered pace in recent decades, but it is still the case that eighteenth-century women writers are relatively unknown to the general reader. Furthermore, the conditions of the activity – what it was like to *be* a woman writer, what the credit of female authorship consisted in and how it might be maintained – are little understood, in spite of the fact that the eighteenth century witnessed the establishment of the professional woman writer as a recognised and respected figure in the culture. Indeed, Britain prided itself as a nation on its ability to produce such women. In 1752 George Ballard published a biographical collection, *Memoirs of Several Ladies of Great Britain: Who Have Been Celebrated for their Writings or Skill in the Learned Languages, Arts and Sciences*, in which he declared: 'it is pretty certain that England hath produced more women famous for literary accomplishments than any other nation in Europe'.

Such a declaration was characteristic of the mid eighteenth century. Johnson, in an essay of 1753, coined the phrase 'The Age of Authors' for his own time: 'there never was a time', he wrote, 'in which men of all degrees of ability, of every kind of education, of every profession and employment, were posting with ardour so general to the press'. Previous ages had devoted themselves to warfare, and just as in warlike times there had been illustrious women warriors, so the mid eighteenth century, committed to prosperity and letters, had produced 'a generation of Amazons of the pen, who with the spirit of their predecessors have set masculine tyranny at defiance, asserted their claim to the regions of science, and seem resolved to contest the usurpations of virility'. Similarly, Mary Scott, in her introduction to *The Female Advocate* in 1774, somewhat tartly reminded readers: 'facts have a powerful tendency to convince the understanding, and of late, *Female Authors*, have appeared with honour, in almost every walk of literature'.[3]

Samuel Johnson's dinner companions at Mrs Garrick's in May 1784 were among those female authors who had appeared with honour in several walks of literature. All had been successful, all could be said to have reached the top of the profession; and as a group they represented the literary establishment of the day. What then was Boswell surprised about? Not that Johnson had been dining with these women. They were friends – each individually a friend of Samuel Johnson – and fellow professionals. Boswell knew them, though he had offended Hannah More by getting drunk at Bishop Shipley's. Her first impression of him, that he was 'a very agreeable and good-natured man' had been spoiled by his behaviour on their second meeting: 'I was heartily disgusted,' she wrote, 'with Mr Boswell, who came upstairs after dinner, disordered with wine, and addressed me in a manner which drew from me a sharp rebuke, for which I fancy he will not easily forgive me.' Whether Boswell forgave her or not is one question; another is how posterity has responded, posterity being generally more indulgent to the drunken male writer than to the offended woman delivering a rebuke. The anecdote has come down to us as an encounter between prude and profligate; a comic juxtaposition, especially if we add our knowledge of Boswell's use of street prostitutes and Hannah More's piety. But there is another consideration. Hannah More's asperity, her sense of entitlement to deliver rebukes to men who addressed her disrespectfully, signalled a social confidence that was more than merely personal. At Bishop Shipley's the young, unmarried, female writer rested comfortably on her rights. Those rights – to bring herself into largely male literary company and be addressed appropriately – had been earned by an earlier generation. They were not spoken of as rights but they were in use, and they had been achieved by some resolute women.[4]

Like Boswell, the men of the Essex Head club would have been familiar with the names and reputations of the women with whom Johnson had dined, and they too might have been intimidated at the thought of 'three such women'. Dr Johnson, however, the man who, in Fanny Burney's words was, 'the acknowledged Head of Literature in this kingdom', was at ease in their company. His friendship with Elizabeth Carter went back almost fifty years. He had known Eva Garrick, the widow of actor-manager David Garrick, since at least the mid 1740s. David Garrick had been Johnson's pupil at the ill-starred school at Edial which Johnson had set up in 1735 with his wife Tetty's money, most of which was lost in the venture.

The younger women, Fanny Burney and Hannah More, were more recent friends and favourites, brilliant women who looked up to Johnson, and had a profound respect for what he had achieved and what he represented, and whose affection for him was sincere. Fanny Burney had become Johnson's special pet after the publication of her first novel, *Evelina*, in 1778. Nothing like *Evelina* had been seen before and Samuel Johnson – perhaps surprisingly – was as enthusiastic a reader of the adventures of this particular 'Young Lady's Entrance into the World' as the next person. Introduced to the author by Hester Thrale, he adored the mixture of shyness and slyness, diffidence and self-determination he discovered in her. The elderly man and the young woman spent hours together tête-à-tête at

Streatham, after which Fanny would return to her room and write up their conversations at great length in her diary.

All Johnson biographers have drawn on Fanny Burney's diary as raw material for their accounts of Samuel Johnson. It is, like Boswell's *Life of Samuel Johnson*, a primary source, vivid, immediate and intensely personal. Boswell made no secret of his determination to capture the talk of the greatest talker of his age and preserve it for posterity. He would take his notebook out in public and openly take notes, a practice Mrs Thrale, for one, took offence at. It was ill-mannered, in her view, to sit 'steadily down at the other end of the room to write at the moment what should be said in company, either *by* Dr Johnson or *to* him'. This was not Fanny Burney's style and she avowed no such agenda. Ostensibly, her diary was a 'private journal', begun at the age of fifteen and serving as the repository of her secret thoughts, private wishes, fears and dislikes. It was where she could freely tell her 'wonderful, surprising and interesting adventures'.

These included the interesting adventures of literary success, first with *Evelina* and subsequently, in 1782, with *Cecilia*. In its playful irony, the diary entry announcing *Evelina* reveals an unusual preoccupation with public fame:

> This year was ushered in by a grand and most important event! At the latter end of January, the literary world was favoured with the first publication of the ingenious, learned and most profound Fanny Burney! I doubt not but this memorable affair will, in future times, mark the period whence chronologers will date the zenith of the polite arts in this island!

Becoming an intimate of Samuel Johnson was itself a significant yardstick of literary success. Writing down her conversations with him was another way for Fanny Burney – the 'morbidly timid', 'the very cowardly Writer' – to convey to posterity the achievements of her own 'wonderful, surprising and interesting' self.[5]

In this respect, Fanny Burney's motives were much like Boswell's. Both were tireless diarists. The young Scot, James Boswell, had come to London determined to make his way; or, to use his own formulation, longing for 'the company of men of Genius' whose wisdom he could absorb and whose example he could emulate. Considering himself 'a man of singular merit', he had written to the French writer and philosopher Jean-Jacques Rousseau, requesting an interview; he had pressed himself on Voltaire, Wilkes and Horace Walpole. Those he admired he sought to become: when the streets of London evoked for Boswell the literary world of the early eighteenth century, the world of Swift and Pope and Addison and Steele's *Spectator*, he confessed to his diary that he felt 'strong dispositions to *be a Mr Addison*'.

On another occasion he 'was in such a frame to *think myself an Edmund Burke*'. But mostly it was Johnson he wanted to become: '*Resemble Johnson ... your mind will strengthen*'; or, as he wrote in one entry when commending his own conversational performance, 'Was *powerful* like Johnson, and very much satisfied with myself'. Samuel Johnson had been Boswell's target when he came to London and in 1763, at the age of twenty-two, he achieved his ambition and was introduced to him in the back parlour of Tom Davies's Covent Garden bookshop:

> At last, on Monday the 16th of May, when I was sitting in Mr Davies's back-parlour, after having drunk tea with him and Mrs Davies, Johnson unexpectedly came into the shop; and Mr Davies having perceived him through the glass-door in the room in which we were sitting, advancing towards us, – he announced his aweful approach to me, somewhat in the manner of an actor in the part of Horatio, when he addresses Hamlet on the appearance of his father's ghost, 'Look, my Lord, it comes.'

Such theatricality was to be expected from an ex-actor like Davies, who may also have been sending up his intense young guest. Boswell proceeded to blunder his way through the meeting, being twice snubbed and feeling 'much mortified' at what he considered a rough reception. His first mistake was to disparage Scotland in an attempt at pleasantry: 'I do indeed come from Scotland, but I cannot help it.' Johnson's reply was crushing: 'That, Sir, I find, is what a great many of your countrymen cannot help.' The second was puppyish presumption: cutting in on Johnson's conversation with Davies and brushing aside the very object of Johnson's visit. Boswell recalls the moment in painful and honest detail:

> He then addressed himself to Davies: 'What do you think of Garrick? He has refused me an order for the play for Miss Williams, because he knows the house will be full, and that an order would be worth three shillings.' Eager to take any opening to get into conversation with him, I ventured to say, 'O, Sir, I cannot think Mr Garrick would grudge such a trifle to you.' Sir (said he, with a stern look), I have known David Garrick longer than you have done: and I know no right you have to talk to me on the subject.[6]

Johnson had come to Davies's shop expressly to vent irritation at Garrick for his disrespect to a female author. Miss Williams, who lived in Johnson's house and under his protection, had neither wealth nor power. The question, 'What is Miss Williams worth?' lay behind Johnson's anger at Garrick, a component of the larger question: what was Johnson worth, what credit did he have with Garrick? If Boswell knew little about Garrick and Johnson and had no right to offer his opinion, he knew less and cared nothing for Miss Williams.

Boswell's interest in Johnson was unapologetically self-promoting. Sincerely ambitious after literary fame, he attached himself to the man whose words could carry his own name down to posterity. This element in Boswell is well recognised in the vast literature that has since grown up about Boswell and Johnson. The same cannot be said about Fanny Burney, whose presentation of herself as a timid, modest, awe-struck female child, properly obedient and deferential, who would *naturally* want her diary to be a secret because it was merely an outlet for her feelings, has been endorsed by critics infatuated with the image of 'little Burney'. Fanny Burney's characteristics, we learn, are 'self-effacement' and 'sensitivity'; her writing is 'unpremeditated', without 'any trace of self-consciousness'. But even a scholar committed to this point of view is forced to acknowledge some contradictions. Chauncey Brewster Tinker, the editor of an early compilation of all the passages about Samuel Johnson which appeared in Fanny Burney's diary, *Dr Johnson and Fanny Burney*, reflecting on Burney's 'modesty', observed:

> These meek young women who are for ever retiring to their 'chambers,' to escape the voice of the flatterer or to record his words in interminable letters, seem at times possessed of a remarkable sanity which detects the market value of this favorite virtue. They exhibit a surprising facility in contracting successful engagements, in publishing novels ... or an almost Boswellian faculty for scraping acquaintance with the most distinguished folk of their time. It is all very innocent ...[7]

Or perhaps it is not so very innocent, or no more innocent than Boswell's 'faculty for scraping acquaintance with the most distinguished folk'. Young Boswell could pass himself about in his forthright way, displaying his self-regard and declaiming his admiration of men of genius and his desire to be of their company. What could young women do? How were they to get knowledge and get on? Ready as they might be with wit and tongue, they were not for the most part encouraged to go 'running about the world' in the way Johnson had done. Fanny Burney recognised the market value of meekness. It served her purposes. To read it as innocent is a form of chivalry rather like the old-fashioned habit of holding open doors for ladies.

Certainly, she was afraid: 'I am frightened out of my wits, from the terror of being attacked *as an author*, and therefore *shirk*, instead of *seeking*, all occasions of being drawn into notice.' She feared ridicule. She was obsessed with the need for privacy, an obsession that was at least matched by the compulsion towards self-display. This ambivalence is clear in her response to the success of *Evelina*, which quickly became the craze of provincial circulating libraries: 'I have an exceeding odd sensation,' she wrote,

> when I consider that it is now in the power of *any* and *every* body to read what

I so carefully hoarded even from my best friends, till this last month or two, – and that a work which was so lately lodged, in all privacy in my bureau, may now be seen by every butcher and baker, cobbler and tinker, throughout the three Kingdoms, for the small tribute of three pence.[8]

All these responses were part of the adventure of going into print. Women writers were by no means new in the 1770s and 1780s, but the market value of meekness was.

In *The Life of Samuel Johnson* Boswell's intense excitement in the presence of the older man communicates itself as an excitement about the *idea* of Johnson, which is also about the idea of the famous writer Boswell himself wanted to become. Inevitably, the picture Boswell gives us is a partial one, idealising and romanticising and oddly weighted: a full half of this huge biography is devoted to the last eight years of Johnson's life. It favours the Johnson of the masculine clubs and taverns over the domestic Johnson, placing him amongst groups of men rather than groups of women. Women tend to appear in *The Life of Samuel Johnson* in the footnotes, relating an anecdote or confirming one. The fact that many of them were active participants in the literary world, celebrated and made much of by their contemporaries, is easy to overlook.

Emulation was considered a virtue in the eighteenth century. Young people were encouraged to model themselves on worthy older figures; anybody with a public identity understood that they had a responsibility to behave in ways that contributed to the common good when emulated. But young men like Boswell were not exhorted to emulate women. Boswell would not write in his diary: 'Think myself a Hannah More. Resemble Elizabeth Carter ... your mind will strengthen. Be meek like Fanny Burney.'

It is not surprising that Boswell's identifying impulses were directed towards male models. But reading *The Life of Samuel Johnson* as history is misleading in many particulars, not least in its representation of women in the literary world of the eighteenth century. Boswell's response to Johnson's conversational gambit on the evening of 15 May 1784, his inability to do anything with the pleasurable recollections of dinner at Mrs Garrick's the night before, his failure to take up a provocative critical judgement and his haste to move the conversation on to the familiar ground of men's affairs, is symptomatic. It is a moment which reminds us that life stories are not told but made. Boswell's consciousness of his own 'singular merit', his urge to identify with those he admired, his fantasy of being 'a man of letters' and his possessive appetite for the territory, inclined him not just to disregard women but in rivalry to elbow them out. In doing so, this most 'clubbable' of men did more than most to reinforce the idea of literature as a club of men.

Nevertheless, the literary world in the eighteenth century was very far
from being a club of men. All the women amongst whom Johnson had
dined so contentedly had found places for themselves in this world with
remarkable ease. Admittedly, they were extraordinary women. They had
talent and energy and self-belief. But without any special advantages of birth,
wealth or marriage, without formal schooling such as a similarly situated
boy would have received (for better or worse), each of them had directed
their ambitions towards literary success. And each of them had succeeded:
writing words people wanted to read and talk about, and gaining entry
into social circles that would otherwise have been closed to them. Even
the younger ones, Hannah More and Fanny Burney, were already part of
the literary establishment in 1784. It had opened its arms and welcomed
them in.

In this world the sexes mixed on relatively equal terms. To say this is
not the same as saying that women had equal opportunities with men,
nor that social structures did not discriminate against them. Women's
lives were different from men's, and how they imagined their lives – the
mix of personal desire with social expectation – was also different. But
many imagined themselves as writers and received confirmation of the
acceptability of that sense of self from family, friends, teachers, booksellers
and readers. Women of every degree, single, married, widowed, wealthy
and poor, educated and semi-literate, leisured and labouring, sought the
realm of print. Some became celebrated; most did not. Books were status
symbols. To be a successful writer was to reach the top of a hierarchy of
status open to talent. Elizabeth Carter, Hannah More and Fanny Burney
occupied such positions. So did Elizabeth Montagu, and so too, at an earlier
period – during the 1750s – did Charlotte Lennox.

Johnson's manners were notoriously rough. His social behaviour was much
commented on and variously described. He was considered uncouth, irritable, violent-tempered, ill-mannered, and brusquely indifferent to the
feelings of those around him. His attempts at gentility were laughable.
Arthur Murphy, in his *Essay on the Life and Genius of Dr Johnson* (1792),
admitted that 'self-government, or the command of his passions in conversation, does not seem to have been among his attainments ... he has been
known to break out with violence, and even ferocity'. Boswell's first encounter with him illustrated the point. 'Dr Johnson', he was later to write,
'did not practise the art of accommodating himself to different sorts of
people.' Slovenly, ugly, huge, scrofulous and squinting, he was grotesque
to look upon. His body was never still. He suffered from obsessive compulsive disorders, twitching and performing ritual motions whilst walking

or before going through a door. The painter Hogarth, calling on Samuel
Richardson, 'perceived a person standing at a window in the room, shaking
his head and rolling himself about in a strange ridiculous manner. He
concluded that he was an idiot, whom his relations had put under the care
of Mr Richardson as a very good man.' That was Johnson soon after he
came to London in 1737. Many years later, Fanny Burney said he had 'a
face the most ugly, a person the most awkward, and manners the most
singular that ever were or ever can be seen'.

Boswell raised the subject of Johnson's 'forcible spirit, and impetuosity
of manner' with him a number of times, suggesting that his habit of harsh
contradiction was a trial to people with weak nerves. 'I know no such
weak-nerved people', he reports Johnson replying. And on another occasion,
when it was suggested to Johnson that he might have done more good if
he had been gentle, he defended his own harsh manners on the grounds
that they produced better manners in others: 'I have done more good as I
am. Obscenity and impiety have always been repressed in my company.'

It is unlikely that the female company at Eva Garrick's on the evening
of 14 May 1784 experienced difficulty in repressing their impulses towards
obscenity and impiety in his presence. In contrast to Johnson they were
models of mannerly behaviour, women whose lives were rooted in the
centrality of perfect self-command and self-government. Johnson's physical
and temperamental difficulties caused him great problems. They were
balanced by qualities that also made him loved: he was a 'virtuous bully'
as one writer puts it, who became 'the idol of the club, the tavern and the
drawing-room – the perfect companion at once of the profligate, the toper,
the scholar, and the fashionable lady'.[9]

Perfect he may have been but easy he was not. Yet women of all kinds,
but especially those with intellectual interests or literary aspirations,
sought him out. His situation at dinner at Mrs Garrick's – a single man
in the company of women – was not particularly unusual for him. Indeed
the image of Johnson holding forth among 'the ladies' was so common
and for different reasons had such currency that it has circulated as one
of the many definitive images of Samuel Johnson. In its most sentimentalised version, Johnson is a grizzly bear and the ladies are tinkling visions
of elegance. Eva Garrick, Elizabeth Carter, Hannah More and Fanny Burney
did not tinkle and, with the exception of Eva Garrick who had been on
the stage and understood the importance of self-presentation, they were
not inclined to elegance. But neither were they inky-fingered slatterns. And
whatever difficulties an evening with Samuel Johnson might entail, their
nerves were evidently equal to it.

By 1784 Johnson was in his mid seventies; it was to be the last year of his life. He was in poor health. A paralytic stroke the summer before had affected his speech. In the autumn of 1783 he had suffered so badly with the dropsy that his whole body had swollen from head to foot. He was sleeping even less well than usual, and in terror of death and judgement. Arthur Murphy, who had first introduced Johnson to Henry Thrale and who knew him well, tells us:

> The contemplation of his own approaching end was constantly before his eyes; and the prospect of death, he declared, was terrible. For many years, when he was not disposed to enter into the conversation going forward, whoever sat near his chair, might hear him repeating, from Shakespeare,

> > Ay, but to die, and go we know not where;
> > To lie in cold obstruction and to rot;
> > This sensible warm motion to become
> > A kneaded clod, and the delighted spirit
> > To bathe in fiery floods –

The powerful and moving words of Claudio in *Measure for Measure* at once frightened and comforted.[10] Johnson's love of literature was a passion. But being 'an author by profession' had been far from easy. For almost fifty years he had been at the centre of London literary life. His periodical, the *Rambler*, which ran twice weekly from the summer of 1750 to the summer of 1752, following on the favourable reception of the *Life of Savage* of 1744, established him as an authoritative voice, and the *Dictionary* of 1755 confirmed his high standing. But if his reputation was secure, his material existence was not. He had never recovered the loss of his wife's money, sunk in his attempt at schoolmastering. In London, she had lived uncomfortably with him in a series of lodgings until the space was gradually taken over by the papers, books and assistants required for work on the dictionary. Increasingly ill and discontented, secretly drinking heavily, Tetty had moved out to Hampstead. She was almost sixty and did not live to see her much younger husband become celebrated. She died in 1752. Johnson was grief-stricken to a degree that surprised his closest friends, most of whom thought the marriage a disaster or a joke. (Garrick occasionally mimicked the 'tumultuous and awkward fondness' of Johnson and Tetty making love, having spied on them through the keyhole of their bedroom when he was a boy at the Edial school.) Some of Johnson's grief had its origins in guilt, but although the life he shared with Tetty had deteriorated through the difficult years of the 1740s it had been based on a real affection.[11]

Money continued to be a problem throughout the 1750s. In 1759 he struggled to raise sufficient to travel to Lichfield to visit his dying mother – this was the prompt which led to the writing of *Rasselas* during the evenings of one week; and he gave up his house in Gough Square because he could no longer afford to maintain it. Murphy's comment, that he 'removed to chambers in the Inner Temple-lane, where he lived in poverty, total idleness, and the pride of literature', hint at the bitterness Johnson felt.

The year 1759 marked the beginnings of a severe depression during which Johnson feared the complete loss of his reason and which was to maintain its hold until the late 1760s. Instrumental in the relief of this depression was the patronage of the wealthy brewer and MP Henry Thrale and his young wife, Hester. Concerned about 'the horrible condition of his mind', the Thrales more or less adopted Johnson, making their homes at Southwark and Streatham available to him as his home. He ceased to be a middle-aged waif and became the centre of an admiring circle. Hester Thrale undertook 'the care of his health'. This was no small matter. It included listening to an endless litany of complaint about his condition in general and his mental condition in particular and sitting up with him until the small hours. Mrs Thrale reported that Johnson's doctor had declared he would rather Johnson came and beat him once a week, since 'to hear his complaints was more than *man* could support'. She added caustically: ''Twas therefore that he tried, I suppose, and in eighteen years contrived to weary the patience of a *woman*.' Her patience was certainly tested in those eighteen years:

> Mr Johnson loved late hours extremely, or more properly hated early ones. Nothing was more terrifying to him than the idea of retiring to bed, which he never would call going to rest, or suffer another to call so. 'I lie down (said he) that my acquaintance may sleep; but I lie down to endure oppressive misery, and soon rise again to pass the night in anxiety and pain.' By this pathetic manner, which no one ever possessed in so eminent a degree, he used to shock me from quitting his company, till I hurt my own health not a little by sitting up with him when I was myself far from well: nor was it an easy matter to oblige him even by compliance, for he always maintained that no one forbore their own gratifications for the sake of pleasing another, and if one did sit up it was probably to amuse one's self. Some right however he certainly had to say so, as he made his company exceedingly entertaining when he had once forced one, by his vehement lamentations and piercing reproofs, not to quit the room, but to sit quietly and make tea for him, as I often did in London till four o'clock in the morning.[12]

Boswell underplays the importance of the Thrales in Johnson's life, not least because Mrs Thrale was a major rival to him as a biographer. Her *Anecdotes of Dr Johnson* came out early in 1786 and was a tremendous hit: the first edition of one thousand copies sold out in a day. Three more editions followed over the next two months. In capturing this ready market, she beat not only Boswell into the field but also Sir John Hawkins whose official *Life* did not appear until the following year. Arthur Murphy, whose *Essay on the Life and Genius of Dr Johnson* came out in 1792, after Thrale, Hawkins and Boswell, commented on how newsworthy Johnson was: 'the death of Dr Johnson kept the public mind in agitation beyond all former example. No literary character ever excited so much attention.' The press, 'teemed with anecdotes, apophthegms, essays, and publications of every kind'.13

So closely was Hester Thrale associated with Johnson that she became part of the Johnson legend; she is Dr Johnson's Mrs Thrale – not her own person nor anyone else's. But by 1784 and the dinner at Mrs Garrick's, Johnson was estranged from her. The death of Henry Thrale in 1781 had made his continued domestication in her home awkward; he took a formal final leave-taking of Streatham Park in October 1782, after reading the Bible in the much-loved library there. There were other tensions. Mrs Thrale's feelings were mixed: she lost the most important friendship of her life but she was also relieved of a burden. She was still only forty. Later she recalled the 'venerating solicitude which hung heavily over my whole soul whilst connected with Doctor Johnson', a solicitude that made her feel 'swallowed up and lost' in Johnson's mind. She was ready to break free, intellectually and emotionally. Her love for Gabriel Piozzi, the Italian music master who was shortly to become her second husband, was unacceptable to Johnson. In this he reflected public opinion which was savage about the connection. The press and most of her friends accused her of degrading herself by marrying a man socially beneath her, and a foreigner too. She admitted she was being 'selfish' and defended herself with sarcasm: 'I have always sacrificed my own choice to that of others, so I must sacrifice it again: – but why? Oh because I am a woman of superior understanding, and must not for the world degrade my self from my situation in life.' 14

Johnson felt abandoned and he reacted violently. When Hester Thrale wrote asking for his approval – 'I feel as if I was acting without a parent's consent' – she received a letter back in which the words still have power to shock. Johnson lashed out at her: 'you are ignominiously married … If you have abandoned your children and your religion, God forgive your wickedness; if you have forfeited your fame, and your country, may your folly do no further mischief.' Her dignified response demonstrated that she was, indeed, not one of the 'weak-nerved' people:

> Sir – I have this morning received from you so rough a letter, in reply to one which was both tenderly and respectfully written, that I am forced to desire the conclusion of a correspondence which I can bear to continue no longer. The birth of my second husband is not meaner than that of my first, his sentiments

are not meaner, his profession is not meaner, – and his superiority in what he professes – acknowledged by all mankind. – It is want of fortune then that is ignominious, the character of the man I have chosen has no other claim to such an epithet. The religion to which he has always been a zealous adherent, will I hope teach him to forgive insults he has not deserved – mine will I hope enable me to bear them at once with dignity and patience. To hear that I have forfeited my fame is indeed the greatest insult I ever yet received, my fame is as unsullied as snow, or I should think it unworthy of him who must henceforward protect it.[15]

She had not 'forfeited her fame' (honour), but if she had married for reasons other than social status or wealth, the conclusion was inescapable: she had married for passion. It was this which threw not only Johnson but also most of her women friends into a lather of rage. Fanny Burney exclaimed, 'How *can* she suffer herself, noble-minded as she is, to be thus duped by ungovernable passions'. Mrs Montagu, meanwhile, repudiated her on behalf of the larger community of intellectual women:

I respected Mrs Thrale, and was proud of the honour she did to the human and female character in fulfilling all the domestic duties and cultivating her mind with whatever might adorn it. I would give much to make every one think of her as mad ... If she is not considered in that light she must throw a disgrace at her sex.[16]

She was thus not bad as a woman of the old stereotype – weak-willed and lustful – but mad as an individual, an eccentric deviation from the new norm. Mrs Montagu was a politician and her response was political. As she saw it, there was something larger to defend: the gains women had made in her lifetime. Governing passion, or being seen to believe in the importance of governing passion, was an essential weapon in the armoury.

Mrs Montagu's own passions were characteristic of a wealthy woman: she had a passion to rule and a passion for power, as well as a passion for literature. Busy in the management of her husband's lucrative collieries, she was 'a critic, a coal owner, a land steward, a sociable creature'. Her interest in architecture, landscape design and interior decoration led to the fitting up of sumptuous houses and the patronage of artists and craft workers as well as writers. She looked back to her namesake, Queen Elizabeth I, a woman whose abilities she admired, whose state papers she had studied and about whom she wanted to write. She had in her possession six china plates which the queen had once owned; Johnson paid her a well-judged compliment in saying that the plates 'had no reason to be ashamed of their present possessor, who was so little inferior to the first'. Boswell's suggestion that Mrs Montagu might have made a fourth at Eva Garrick's dinner was misjudged: not only was there, by then, outright hostility between Johnson and Elizabeth

Montagu, but the idea of Mrs Montagu being anything but a commanding first in any assembly was provocative in itself. She was the 'Queen of the Blues' and acknowledged as the supreme hostess in literary London.

With Boswell as his courtier, Johnson clearly became a king in the realm of literature. Unlike Mrs Montagu, he was not dubbed king of anything and was therefore spared the specific mockery that attaches itself to what subsequent generations read as overweening self-love. Elizabeth Montagu was 'Queen of the Blues' because she was the richest, the most powerful and possibly the cleverest of the intellectuals who came to be known as the bluestockings in the mid eighteenth century – a term which at first applied to men and women alike but later came to be applied only to women and still later took on its pejorative meaning. She was also 'Queen' because she sought pre-eminence. She sought to rule. Her kingdom, as she and her supporters conceived of it, was the kingdom of arts and letters.

Johnson's respect for Elizabeth Montagu – a precondition, it might be argued, for his sense of rivalry – is evident in his response to Boswell. Mrs Montagu was 'extraordinary'. Though fully aware of the flattery and homage she was accustomed to receive, he did not question her assumption of queenship nor read it as the overinflation of a wealthy woman by servile courtiers. As a thinker and a talker, she was, in his opinion, a genuine force. So, too, was Charlotte Lennox. Johnson believed in kings and queens; he was not a democrat, nor a radical and certainly not a revolutionary. He believed in hierarchies of rank. His ideas about how the literary world should be ordered were modelled on the monarchical system, a system that balanced deference, homage and praise on the one side with privilege and responsibility on the other.

Some years before Mrs Montagu became 'Queen of the Blues', Johnson made a determined bid to have Charlotte Lennox crowned queen in the realm of literature. The occasion was the 1751 publication of her first novel, *The Life of Harriot Stuart.* Boswell does not tell us about it, but Sir John Hawkins, Johnson's official biographer, does. Sir John Hawkins, older than Boswell, was a member of the discussion club of that time, the (all male, of course) Ivy Lane club and it was at the club that Johnson made his proposal for what was, effectively, to be a coronation. Under the circumstances, the slight tone of protest one can hear in Sir John Hawkins's account is not to be wondered at. After explaining that Mrs Lennox's first novel was 'ready for publication', Sir John Hawkins tells us:

> One evening at the club, Johnson proposed to us the celebrating the birth of Mrs Lenox's first literary child, as he called her book, by a whole night spent in festivity. Upon his mentioning it to me, I told him I had never sat up a whole

night in my life; but he continuing to press me, and saying I should find great delight in it, I, as did all the rest of our company, consented. The place appointed was the Devil tavern, and there, about the hour of eight, Mrs Lenox and her husband, and a lady of her acquaintance, now living, as also the club, and friends to the number of twenty, assembled. Our supper was elegant, and Johnson had directed that a magnificent hot apple-pye should make a part of it, and this he would have stuck with bay-leaves, because, forsooth, Mrs Lenox was an authoress, and had written verses; and further, he had prepared for her a crown of laurel, with which, but not till he had invoked the muses by some ceremonies of his own invention, he encircled her brows.

The party with its 'pleasant conversation, and harmless mirth' went on till dawn. About five in the morning, 'Johnson's face shone with meridian splendour, though his drink had been only lemonade'. Most of the others were drunk and sleepy. Sir John Hawkins, slightly appalled at himself for such excess, groggily left the tavern at eight, a full twelve hours after Johnson had persuaded him to enter it.[17]

The crowning of Charlotte Lennox was a mock coronation but for writers like Johnson and Lennox it had a deadly serious point. Neither of them had other means to fall back on. They were neither aristocratic, nor gentry, they had neither place nor portion; they were the new breed and both were precariously dependent on literature for a living. Crowning kings and queens, inventing ceremonies and playfully insisting on homage due, was a form of institution-building. It acknowledged a status hierarchy alongside the hierarchy of social rank. The aristocratic Mrs Montagu, already high in social rank, could establish her place at the top of the hierarchy of merit by a combination of native ability, wealth, privilege and patronage. She could work productively alone or within institutions such as the Society of Arts and Manufactures. Though not uncomplicated, her route to power and position in literature made possible by her talent was cushioned by social advantage. Johnson wanted to rewrite the script for the working writer lacking those advantages. The bay-leaves and crown of laurels were the classical symbols of high achievement, the social sign of powers. They marked honorable entry into the elite. For Samuel Johnson, as for Elizabeth Montagu, that elite included women as well as men.

Johnson's enthusiastic determination to launch young Charlotte Lennox's novel, *Harriot Stuart*, with all due ceremony and to crown her as an authoress before a large gathering, presents him to us in a very amiable light. She was to go on looking to him for support for the rest of his life. In this she was not alone. In his early years, Johnson helped writers who were barely worse off than he was himself. It was not until the publication of his *Dictionary* in 1755, after nine years of unremitting labour, that he was elevated from Grub Street to the literary establishment; and it was another seven years after that before he had any kind of financial security with the granting of a crown pension. By then he was in his fifties. The pattern of his life was set and it included helping those who needed his help. Charlotte Lennox asked for money and well-turned words: she wanted Johnson to write dedications and prologues, and to smooth the relations between her and her booksellers. Others wanted advice about suitable topics, information, comments, help with raising subscriptions or just permission to deploy the power of his name. He did a good deal of note-writing, drawing on his profound understanding of the workings of the literary world and his many connections. He socialised with booksellers and printers, recognising the pressures they were under; and he took destitute people into his own house and supported them on a day-to-day basis.

The best-known 'unknown' woman who was helped in this way was Anna Williams, an intellectual with no source of income but a passion for science, whose 'universal curiosity and comprehensive knowledge' made her a valued companion to Johnson after Tetty's death. An operation to cure Anna Williams's blindness failed; she continued to live in Johnson's house and he provided for her. His habit of taking tea with her when he returned at night, no matter how late the hour, suggests the reciprocity of the relationship; as Mrs Thrale was to discover, Johnson feared the moment when everybody else went off to bed and he was left alone. Anna Williams looked to Johnson for help in raising subscriptions for a volume of her poems and he wrote the proposals – essentially, a printed advertisement to be distributed to those who might pay in advance and enable the author to publish at his or her own risk and take all the profits. The more persuasive the proposal, the longer the list of subscribers. The volume was announced in 1750, though her *Miscellanies in Prose and Verse* did not appear until 1766. We would be mistaken if we assumed Johnson thought of Anna Williams as a specially neglected genius whom he nurtured but the world spurned. Rather, she was representative not exceptional. She was one of many women with a love of knowledge and an ability to think whose entitlement to play a part in the world of printing, publishing, reading and writing Johnson took for granted, and whose need for protection happened to be great.

Boswell called Anna Williams 'peevish', which she may well have been, and he was irritated by Johnson's habit of considering her feelings and needs since they often competed with his own. (In this respect, his first encounter with Johnson set a pattern.) When she died in 1783, Johnson summed up his relationship with her in a letter to his stepdaughter Lucy Porter at Lichfield: 'Last month died Mrs Williams, who had been to me for thirty years in the place of a sister: her knowledge was great, and her

November 4, 1752.

PROPOSALS

For Printing by SUBSCRIPTION,

POEMS

ON

SEVERAL OCCASIONS.

By the
Author of the FEMALE QUIXOTE.

S U B S C R I P T I O N S are taken in by
Mr. MILLAR, in the Strand; and Mr. DODSLEY, in Pall-mall.

conversation pleasing. I now live in cheerless solitude.' Johnson needed a
constant flow of society. His fear of solitude meant he was often desperately
reliant on company. Boswell judged him to have seen a more varied range
of human characters than most men; certainly to have observed them with
more perspicuity than most:

> Volumes would be required to contain a list of his numerous and various acquain-
> tance, none of whom he ever forgot; and could describe and discriminate them
> all with precision and vivacity. He associated with persons the most widely
> different in manners, abilities, rank and accomplishments.

Boswell contrasts the lords and ladies who sought Johnson out with 'awkward and uncouth Robert Levett', the physician to the poor who became
part of Johnson's household along with Mrs Williams and others; and 'good
Mrs Gardiner, the tallow-chandler, on Snowhill' whose charitable efforts
on behalf of destitute girls and young women Johnson supported.

A firm believer in social hierarchy, Johnson made full use of his own
licence to move between society's extremes. He enjoyed the comforts of
wealth. He was not inclined to sneer at the opulence of Mrs Montagu's
receptions, nor the abundance of Mrs Thrale's table and the convenience
of her house and carriage. As he said, 'When I was running about this town
a very poor fellow, I was a great arguer for the advantages of poverty; but
I was, at the same time, very sorry to be poor.' Johnson had known failure
and poverty and absolute despair. Though an outstanding scholar, he had
been forced to leave Oxford after less than a year because his money ran
out. Without a degree, he could not enter a profession. He had to devise
all his own schemes for living. All his life he had traded on his wit. He
knew at first hand what it was like to be excluded from those clubs of men,
the professions, within which powers were tested and strengthened, abilities
acknowledged and rewarded.

In this respect, Johnson was comparably situated to the lively-minded
women whose company he so much enjoyed. For trading on wit in the
form of writing was one of the few available ways of trying to make money
open to men and women alike. (Only Mrs Montagu did not 'make a trade
of her wit' because her wealth was such as to make any payment booksellers
could give her an irrelevance.) The men eager for Johnson's conversation
at the Essex Head club were, by and large, like most men who interested
themselves in letters and scholarship, professionals in other fields: doctors,
lawyers, clergymen and the like. Such professions were not open to women
as women were not allowed to study at the universities or take degrees.
Women with some education (of whom there were plenty) who needed to
support themselves and their dependents drudged in lowly-paid occupations

like teaching. Those with exceptional talent and drive, however, looked to forms of work which held the potential of greater rewards, chief amongst which was writing, followed by performance arts such as singing, acting, dancing. What Boswell, speaking of Johnson, referred to as a 'noble ardour for literary fame' could translate, for the lucky few, into improved funds and an elevated social position. Johnson, acutely aware of the difficulties faced by individuals who had to make their own way in the world since his own had been despairingly, damagingly arduous, understood that the best help he could give anybody was the power to help themselves more effectively.

Much is symbolised by the juxtaposition of Johnson's dinner dates on May 14 and May 15 1784. The Essex Head club was a form of sociability he relished: a group of men drawn from varied walks of life meeting in an atmosphere of comfortable conviviality. The objective was good conversation, with an emphasis on information and knowledge; the purpose of good conversation being not just pleasure but improvement. Johnson liked to talk medicine with the doctors, law with the lawyers, divinity with the theologians, and literature – broadly defined – with all of them.

He was, however, equally at home amongst groups of women and in mixed groups. That Eva Garrick should have invited him to dine with her at her home in the Adelphi, a short stroll from his own house in Bolt Court, is no surprise. That she was considered one of the leaders of society *is* perhaps a little surprising. Still, the one-time opera dancer had, by this time, the necessary qualifications: to personal grace, elegance and charm she added a large income, a spacious house in the Adelphi, and connections of friendship with 'the best people' whom she entertained 'in the most handsome way'. Devoutly religious and famously devoted to her husband, she had been an active partner in David Garrick's theatrical schemes throughout the years of his dominance of British theatre, from the time he took over Drury Lane in 1747 until his death in 1779. Garrick had relied heavily on her professional judgement. She was shrewd, intelligent and well-read. Socially, she had gone about with Garrick everywhere and together they embodied the modern idea of theatre as a place of moral probity.[18]

It was no small part of the Garricks' achievement to have displaced older ideas of the stage as a sink of vice in favour of a new version: theatre as an instrument of refinement and elevation. Eva Garrick played a significant part in this transformation. She was also a hardened professional, accustomed to the endless warfare that was theatrical production. She had grown up in Vienna, a young dancer trained to the highest standards at one of the most cultivated and sophisticated Courts in Europe. She knew French and Italian and spoke English with a heavy German accent. In the 1740s, at the age of twenty-one or twenty-two, she travelled to England with introductions from the Viennese aristocracy to take up a contract as a ballet dancer in the Italian Opera Company in the Haymarket. Almost immediately she was invited by the Earl and Countess of Burlington to live with them at Burlington House in Piccadilly. Her debut performance was attended by the King and Queen and many of the English aristocracy, all of whom accepted her as an artist of rare distinction. 'La Violette', to give her her stage name, dancing at Drury Lane with Lady Burlington waiting in the wings with a *pelisse* to wrap around her when she came off to thunderous cheers, was the toast of the town.

As her patrons and protectors, the Burlingtons first refused to countenance David Garrick as a suitor; then, when the couple were married, they came to depend heavily on them for companionship and managerial assistance with their various properties. Lord Burlington died in 1753. Lady Burlington, increasingly ill, lonely and suspicious, unable to run her household, insisted on Eva Garrick's constant attendance. Whatever the difficulties posed by an unhappy Lady Burlington and her disaffected staff, the connection gave Eva and David Garrick entrée into some of the most magnificent houses in England: Burlington House, Chatsworth, Chiswick and Londesburgh. They were able to assimilate aristocratic culture at its best so far as their own aesthetic passions were concerned, for the values that prevailed were those of connoisseurship and collection, and support for artistic merit. Being known to be intimates of the Burlingtons opened many doors. David Garrick, an actor-manager of immense talent and charm but no other social capital, was able to put the wealth he gained from his theatrical success into acquiring the accoutrements of the landed classes. His wife's contribution to this, besides her connection with the Burlingtons, was her unblemished reputation and her social graces.

The first thing was an estate: 'I own I love a good situation prodigiously,' Garrick wrote, falling easily into the voice of a country squire, 'and I think the four great requisites to make one are, wood, water, extent, and inequality of ground.' Failing to find a desirable estate in the shires, he settled on the outskirts of London, buying a villa at Hampton and launching a huge restoration and expansion project. Like the house at the Adelphi, the villa was richly furnished, filled with fine paintings and books; and the Garricks set about establishing their reputation for elegant hospitality. This was the second requirement: it was not enough to have the estate, it was also necessary to act out the life. They were 'the aristocracy of accomplished hosts'.

The worlds of politics, art, religion and literature came together around the Garricks. Wit of every kind was admired: the wit of quick repartee, but also the wit to rehearse what one had read or experienced and to express informed judgement about it. Unlike Elizabeth Montagu and, later, Hester Thrale, Eva Garrick did not seek to be a saloniere in her own right: David was always the star attraction, the life and soul of the party. For the diffusion of knowledge, men could establish clubs like the Essex Head. For women, such formal organisation with membership dues and attendance require-ments were less likely to suit (though women did form clubs) and it is hard to imagine Eva Garrick or Elizabeth Montagu traipsing out to a tavern three times a week to display their conversational skills. Wealthy women issued invitations to assemblies at their own homes and gained reputations as hostesses: the Adelphi for Eva Garrick, Hill Street and later Portman Square for Mrs Montagu. Though not herself usually considered a blue-stocking, and not an aristocrat, Eva Garrick was part of the mid century movement which transformed the social status of men and women active in arts and letters by bringing them into contact with the quality.

The new gatherings were distinguished from the active sociability that had gone before by a revulsion against card-playing in favour of a self-conscious encouragement of conversation. Conversation – the means of diffusing knowledge and uniting the social circle – was rated highly; it was by fluent conversation that pre-eminence could be achieved in these newly emerging elites of literature and learning. Hannah More was a great talker, a wit who took wing when she was the centre of attention. Cards bored her. She praised the Garricks for the 'decorum, propriety, and regularity' to be found in their household, making a special point of adding 'where I never saw a card' and – an interesting detail which revealed how extremely cautious David Garrick felt he had to be about the separation of home and work – 'where I never ... even met (except in one instance) a person of his own profession at his table'. Evidently, the working actor who played host to other actors might compromise his performance as an aristocrat. Hannah More herself, as a writer for the stage, was in fact 'a person of his own profession'. Mrs Garrick (another person of his own profession) contributed 'elegance of taste ... correctness of manners, and [a] very original turn of humour' to a conversational circle that Hannah More applauded for being 'decidedly intellectual'.[19]

The ideal had been shaped in the 1740s. David Hume emphasised the importance of conversation in several essays describing the rise of civil society or what he called 'the conversable world'. The sociable disposition of women made them eminently suited to the task of civilising men: 'What better school for manners,' Hume asked, 'than the company of virtuous women ...?' In the 1750s Mrs Montagu began inviting literary people to breakfasts rather than suppers. It was easier to insist on the priority of talk in the mornings than it was in the more dissipated evenings. These breakfasts soon gave way to evening meetings fuelled by lemonade and tea and biscuits. Men of affairs and women of learning and fashion mixed and mingled, hunted up the literary lions and made 'each rising wit' the object of social competition. The new ways, it was agreed, were so much better than the old. Elizabeth Carter had disliked the fashion for parties that resembled 'a rout, a racquet, a hurricane, where every chance of conversation was driven away by that foe to human society, whist'. Lady Mary Wortley Montagu commented that the fashion for mixed assemblies of the 'enlightened' sort which her granddaughters were able to enjoy in the 1760s gave 'a kind of public education, which I have always considered as necessary for girls as for boys'. The assemblies fostered an 'enlarged way of thinking'.[20]

Hannah More celebrated her own acceptance into bluestocking circles in the 1770s with a poem advertising the new virtues. 'The Bas Bleu', subtitled 'or Conversation', is a spirited and self-confident piece of occasional verse in which Mrs Montagu, Mrs Boscawen and Mrs Vesey are the three hostesses credited with a social reformation, the revival of conversation:

> Long was Society o'er-run
> By Whist, that desolating Hun;
> Long did Quadrille despotic sit,
> That Vandal of colloquial wit;
> And Conversation's setting light
> Lay half-obscur'd in Gothic night.

Under the initiative and leadership of these women, helped by writers like Elizabeth Carter and sympathetic men, new improved values were established. A veritable cultural revolution took place – or so Hannah More triumphantly asserted – in which good taste was restored, and common sense prevailed. Hannah More's poem is a fine piece of promotional literature. Meanwhile, the 'Advertisement' which prefaced the poem when it was published in 1787 (it had circulated widely in manuscript amongst admiring bluestocking circles for years) acknowledged that 'these little societies have been sometimes misrepresented' and defended them as circles in which pleasant and instructive hours were passed. The bluestocking gatherings were, she wrote defensively, gatherings

> in which learning was as little disfigured by pedantry, good taste as little tinctured by affectation, and general conversation as little disgraced by calumny, levity, and the other censurable errors with which it is too commonly tainted, as has perhaps been known in any society.[21]

Pedantry, affectation and calumnious gossip were the sins women always stood accused of. The special needs the bluestocking circles met were female, even though the assemblies were mixed. The wealthy and well-read hostesses aspired to promote 'pleasing and rational society' in their own very opulent drawing rooms. Inevitably, since they sought out 'the votaries of the Muses' and were interested in encouraging intellectual and literary abilities wherever these qualities showed themselves, their guest lists included the indigent. Johnson himself was once seized by the collar and mistaken for a tramp as he mounted the stairs in the wake of better dressed companions. No less obscure and provincial in his origins than Johnson, such a fate would never befall David Garrick. His wealth enabled him to entertain as well as be entertained. Queenly Elizabeth Montagu stayed with the Garricks at Hampton, at the time of a visit by Lord Lyttelton, gentleman-amateur man of letters, who had been one of the first of the 'Greatest Persons in England' to congratulate Garrick on his acting. Lyttelton was a politician, author and patron of authors who lived in great splendour in his country mansion at Hagley. The condescending tone Johnson adopted towards him in *Lives of the Poets*, referring to 'poor Lyttelton' and laughing at his anxious vanity as an author, was the contempt of Grub Street for an aristocracy that no longer held possession of letters. The Garricks went to Hagley, staying for the summer of 1771 with Elizabeth Montagu and Elizabeth Carter. On visits such as these, the leaders consolidated their positions. In essays such as Johnson's, the 'dictator' of literature revenged himself, perhaps, for the drawing-room indignities he had endured in a lifetime dedicated to raising the status of the 'author by profession'.

2

Elizabeth Carter

Elizabeth Carter was the senior female author at Eva Garrick's dinner and by that time she was almost a national institution. Fanny Burney had described her in 1780 with the respectful praise appropriate to one so much above her in age and learning: Mrs Carter, she wrote, was 'really a noble-looking woman; I never saw age so graceful in the female sex yet; her whole face seems to beam with goodness, piety, and philanthropy'. A year after the dinner, in 1785, Elizabeth Sheridan (sister of the playwright) was at a gathering at Mrs Vesey's where she had her first sight of Elizabeth Carter. The account she left, while vividly capturing the distinguished scholar's appearance and demeanour when amongst company, also serves as a reminder that Elizabeth Carter was famous and that to see her for the first time was an event in a young person's life:

> After tea our circle was increased by the arrival of *Mrs Carter* – on her being announced you may suppose my whole attention was turn'd to the door … She seems about sixty [she was in fact sixty-seven]. She is rather fat and not very striking in her appearance, dressed in a scarlet gown and peticoat, a plain undress cap and perfectly flat head – a small work bag hanging on her arm, out of which she drew some knotting as soon as she was seated – but no fuss or airs about her. She entered into the conversation with that ease which a person has who has both their thoughts and words at command, but no *toss of the head* – no *sneer* – no emphatical look – in short no affected consequence of any kind.[1]

The expectation that a celebrated woman would display signs of 'affected consequence' was, of course, deeply embedded in the national culture, for however much the British might boast of their learned ladies they were never entirely comfortable with them. Praise of Elizabeth Carter was often designed to counter unspoken assumptions drawn from the stereotype of the learned lady as both arrogant and pedantic. When Betsy Sheridan noted her conversational ease it was a way of acknowledging that Elizabeth Carter, though a deep scholar, did not enter the social circle in order to draw attention to herself or score points by pedantry.

Hannah More at first found her 'poetical' in the sense of unbrushed and ill-dressed, but she also warmed to her 'affability, kindness, and goodness'. At large gatherings the 'poetical' scholar, being most at ease amongst her

books, could be uncomfortable, suffering from short-sight and social awk-
wardness. Johnson chided her for being too reserved in conversation on
subjects she was very well able to speak about, a reserve that he attributed
to 'her modesty and fear of giving offence', which is perhaps another way
of describing her habitual avoidance of conflict. She liked to knot or sew,
so as to keep her hands busy and perhaps to reinforce in unthinking people's
minds the idea of a harmless old maid. But she was shrewd and observant;
and, however self-conscious she might have been about her appearance,
she never hesitated to speak out on the side of virtue and integrity. Once
at least she publicly and very sternly reproved Laurence Sterne for his over
free conversation.

Friendship with Johnson (not one to indulge in over free conversation)
began in 1737 when the two first met as writers for the *Gentleman's Magazine.*
New to journalism, Johnson found himself in the world he was to make
his own for the rest of his life. Elizabeth Carter was already there. After a
few years' flirtation with Grub Street, however, she left and forged an
independent path. The life Johnson led of hand-to-mouth dependence on
projects and contracts, of real scholarship vying with deadlines and drudgery,
did not correspond with her notions of liberty. Professionally, they went
their separate ways. A classicist with a special interest in the teachings of
the ancient Stoics, Elizabeth Carter chose a life that was manageable, and
in which happiness could reasonably be produced and scholarly studies
pursued. In her case this meant living at home at Deal, a small fishing port
on the Kent coast, under the protection of her father.

London continued to have special importance as the centre of literary
society. Carter agreed with Johnson that London was the place for ideas,
and added that it was also 'the place for friendship' – for friendship was
the means by which the social role of author was lived out, in London and
elsewhere. It was her custom to leave Deal around the end of December
and take lodgings for the winter in Clarges Street off Picadilly. There,
her rooms were modest and not designed for receiving guests. She neither
cooked nor entertained. With a very extensive circle of friends, many – like
Elizabeth Montagu – wealthy and of high social rank, she dined out every
evening, returning to her rooms no later than 10 o'clock. This mode of life
suited her. It balanced the solitude she required for her extensive reading
and thinking with an inveterate sociability she both desired and believed
was a moral virtue.

Elizabeth Carter was the most highly regarded learned woman in England,
having held this position since the 1730s when, barely into her twenties, she
had achieved European celebrity for her scholarly acquisitions. She had
taught herself nine languages. She read everything and knew everybody.

Her pre-eminence was assured by her translation from the Greek of *All the Works of Epictetus* (1758), the Stoic philosopher. This handsome volume, printed for the author by Samuel Richardson and subscribed to by the great, the good, the erudite and would-be erudite, made a sound profit. She was able to buy a large house at the southernmost edge of Deal with an uninterrupted view of the sea. This was where she was generally to be found during the summer and autumn (though even then she made long visits to stay with friends). At any time of day or night she could step out of her house to walk long distances up or down the shore-line she loved so much or sit on the shingle to be 'soothed by the murmurs of the ebbing tide, and the glimmerings of moon-light on the waves.'[2]

Johnson's respect for Carter's scholarship was unequivocal; he rated her as possibly the best Greek scholar in the land, avowing that nobody he had ever known knew more Greek than she did. In her scholarship, she was his equal and it is tempting to think of her as in some ways a female version of him and to imagine how different her life would have been had she been male.

Knowing Greek, and being known to know Greek as comprehensively as she did, was in many ways the bedrock of Elizabeth Carter's independent life. No man could condescend to her. Her position as an authority was unassailable, and this in spite of being female and in the absence of formal institutional structures to confirm her status. Johnson recognised this, though one of his 'occasional sallies' which concerned Elizabeth Carter and her Greek has been frequently cited to 'prove' the opposite. He praised her for combining erudite scholarship with domestic competence, remarking that:

> A man is in general better pleased when he has a good dinner upon his table, than when his wife talks Greek. My old friend, Mrs Carter, could make a pudding, as well as translate Epictetus from the Greek, and work a handkerchief as well as compose a poem.[3]

Johnson liked nothing better than to praise his old friend and knew her well enough to know that a balanced existence, in which long hours of hard, serious study were broken up by gardening, cooking, care of friends and family and – above all – long walks across rough country or along the shore, represented her ideal. His comment, it is worth noticing, was actually about what men wanted not what women could or couldn't do.

In turning away from Grub Street, Elizabeth Carter turned towards an older, aristocratic or courtly style of conducting a writing life which valued scholarship for its own sake, and circulated ideas, books, and manuscripts amongst a carefully selected coterie. The most important literary friendships she cultivated, with Catherine Talbot and Elizabeth Montagu, were with women of considerably higher social class than herself. She looked to them and to their contacts with scholarly bishops (Talbot) or aristocratic men of letters (Montagu) rather than to Johnson for support in her writing and scholarship. In the 1760s and 1770s she and Johnson met regularly at bluestocking parties but there is no evidence that they sought each other out elsewhere, nor that they much corresponded, and Carter was not part of the Streatham circle where Mrs Thrale presided and where Johnson spent much of his time.

By 1784 Elizabeth Carter was likely to be held up as the pre-eminent example of a woman whose achievements went beyond what society expected of women. For one who sought to lead by example, it was an awkward position to occupy, implying as it did some criticism of 'what society expected of women'. A conservative with a deep adherence to the status quo, she was openly dissatisfied with the treatment of women in general and intellectual women in particular. Her much loved and dutiful nephew, Montagu Pennington, writing in 1808, admitted that she had been 'very much inclined to believe that women had not their proper station in society, and that their mental powers were not rated sufficiently high'. He added:

> Though she detested the principles displayed in Mrs Woolstonecraft's wild theory concerning the 'Rights of Women' and never wished them to interfere with the privileges and occupations of the other sex, yet she thought that men exercised too arbitrary a power over them, and considered them as too inferior to themselves. Hence she had a decided bias in favour of female writers, and always read their works with a mind prepared to be pleased.[4]

Mary Wollstonecraft's A Vindication of the Rights of Woman, sometimes described as the founding text of modern feminism, had appeared in 1792. It applied the new political language of rights to the position of women. For conservatives like Carter, it was a deeply troubling text. A passionate polemic, full of scorn for a defunct order, it polarised issues the older woman had spent her life negotiating and in some ways trying to avoid. We have no other evidence of what Carter made of Mary Wollstonecraft, but it is interesting that Montagu Pennington should mention her at all in this context. At the time he wrote the Memoir, Wollstonecraft had been dead for almost ten years and her reputation was such that most respectable people took care not to be associated with her. Pennington no doubt felt that his aunt was safe from contamination by association. He explains that she would never read any writing in which 'there seemed to be the least tendency towards levelling or democratic principles'.

Celebrated as an exception, Elizabeth Carter took care to present herself in every other respect as ordinary. As time went on, she played down her achievements and played up her 'eccentricities' in a way that seems to have been designed to deflect potential aggression. She wanted to preserve her place close to the centre of public life, engaging in debate about current issues, hearing the opinions of those – mostly men – who were close to the action of national affairs, and expressing her own opinions. Her philosophy and her religion both stressed the importance of responsible self-government and duties to society. These, in her view, were imperatives laid upon men and women alike. They were also pleasures and rights – the right of an intelligent woman to a social existence equal to her 'mental powers'. By the 1780s she had completed some five decades of social existence as a celebrity feted for her intellect. She brought a weight of experience and understanding to her role. From her emergence as a public figure in the 1730s to her death in 1806 she lived through many changes in society's view of women and their 'proper station'.

The first substantial tribute to Elizabeth Carter's genius appeared in 1739 as part of a long article in the *History of the Works of the Learned*. The article was a review of her second book, a translation from Italian, *Sir Isaac Newton's Philosophy Explain'd for the Use of the Ladies, in Six Dialogues on Light and Colours*, and in it she was hailed as a 'phenomenon':

> This lady is a very extraordinary phenomenon in the Republic of Letters, and justly to be ranked with the Cornelias, Sulpicias, and Hypatias of the Ancients, and the Schurmans and Daciers of the Moderns. For to an uncommon vivacity and delicacy of genius and an accuracy of judgement worthy of the maturest years, she has added the knowledge of the ancient and modern languages at an age, when an equal skill in any one of them would be a considerable distinction in a person of the other sex.[5]

She was twenty-one years old and the book demonstrated both her command of the Italian language and her appetite for Newtonian science. At the same time it indicated what she thought one particular niche for herself as a writer might be since the author, Francesco Algarotti, had specifically targeted a female readership. Algarotti's book had been published in Italy in 1737 and Algarotti himself – young, handsome, bisexual – was a charismatic figure at home in English aristocratic and literary circles. *Sir Isaac Newton's Philosophy Explain'd for the Use of the Ladies* was a topical book to choose for an English readership. In deciding on it for her second major project the young phenomenon had taken advice. She was at that time living in London and writing for the *Gentleman's Magazine*. Among her colleagues were Thomas Birch and Samuel Johnson, both ambitious, learned, hard-working employees of the magazine's founder and editor, Edward Cave.

By 1739 Carter had already published one translation, an essay in French by Pierre Crousaz, a professor of mathematics and philosophy. This was a critique of Pope's *Essay on Man*. No doubt she was attracted to Crousaz because of her own critical interest in Pope and by the issues raised in his *Essay on Man*, four verse epistles which seek to understand human nature and propose a system of ethics. The translation she produced included explanatory notes and some critical observations of her own on Crousaz's response to Pope. The philosophical questions that animated Pope's *Essay on Man* were also questions that preoccupied Carter: the nature of happiness, the relation of self-love to social, of reason and passion, and – above all – the place of God, or Providence, in the scheme of things. When it came to deciding on a second translation project, she was obviously concerned to choose something with an equivalent intellectual weight. There was no shortage of hack work she might have taken on. Novels, plays, memoirs, light reading of a semi-scandalous or frankly scandalous nature, much of it from France, were being rapidly translated and fed through the presses at a tremendous rate. But she had come to London to build a reputation on the strength of her learning. Johnson suggested she take up Boethius's *Consolations of Philosophy*, a good suggestion under the circumstances: as well as the intrinsic suitability of the sixth-century Latin text, Boethius, already one of the most translated works in history, had had the most distinguished translators. By choosing *De consolatione philosophiae*, Elizabeth Carter would have put herself in a tradition which had begun with King Alfred in the 890s, and had continued via Chaucer and Queen Elizabeth I. However, she chose not to follow Johnson's suggestion but opted for a more contemporary text. Algarotti's book on Newton had been suggested by Thomas Birch and it was Thomas Birch, possibly somewhat in love with her, who published the encomium on her genius which appeared in the *History of the Works of the Learned*.

The location for these discussions and decisions, friendships, rivalries, admirations, aspirations and promotional activities was the offices of the *Gentleman's Magazine*. The *Gentleman's Magazine* had been founded by Edward Cave in 1731 as a monthly digest, the first of its kind to describe itself as a 'magazine'. It was a periodical that was destined to survive into the twentieth century, finally ceasing publication in 1914. In spite of its title, it was to be enormously important to women readers and writers. By 1739 it had already shifted from mostly offering digests of news reports that had appeared elsewhere to featuring original contributions – a change that

The *Gentleman's Magazine:*

St JOHN's GATE.

For **A P R I L**, 1737.

probably had not a little to do with the extraordinary calibre of Cave's writers. Its emphasis was on serious criticism, essays, coverage of important publications (often with long extracts) and parliamentary reports. It was the prototype of the modern intellectual journal, seeking to inform and stimulate. The offices were in Clerkenwell, very close to Grub Street itself, that narrow road where printers, lodging houses and taverns were huddled together and where writers in varying degrees of desperation toiled to order. The *Gentleman's Magazine* was picturesquely housed in rooms above the old medieval arch of St John's Gate (it was once the entrance to a monastery, and still stands). Johnson 'beheld it with reverence' when he first arrived in London. Cave used its image as a striking front-page colophon for the magazine.

Edward Cave was an unusual bookseller, being like Robert Dodsley a man of business who was also a patron of literature. He rarely left the office and, according to Johnson, 'never looked out of his window, but with a view to the *Gentleman's Magazine*'.[6] By trade a printer, he had been a reporter and then an editor; a self-made man, son of a shoemaker, he was quiet, shrewd and determined, and engrossed in the affairs of the magazine which was to make him a fortune. Like other early periodicals, the *Gentleman's Magazine* solicited contributions from its readers, especially poetry, which appeared under pseudonyms – classical or pastoral mostly – or anonymously. Elizabeth Carter began her long career as a writer by sending in a poem, a riddle on fire, when she was just sixteen. Evidently she was not concerned to hide her identity since her riddle was signed 'Eliza' and a few months later, as was often the case, another writer answered her in a manner which made it clear that her name was known: 'To Miss Cart-r Author of the Riddle in Nov. 1734'. It was signed. 'Sylvius'. Miss Carter replied to 'Sylvius' with a poem in the next issue.

It is possible that she too, like Johnson, had sometimes been to gaze with reverence at St John's Gate, the symbol of who knows what dreams and aspirations that then beat in the young girl's breast, for from 1735 she had begun spending part of each winter in London at the Bishopsgate home of her uncle, a silk merchant. We do know she was the first woman poet to establish a reputation in the *Gentleman's Magazine* and that Edward Cave was a friend of her father. Coming to London in this way might well have been part of a conscious strategy to launch her poetic career which had begun so auspiciously. Certainly, the question of Miss Carter's 'launching into the world' was a matter that was being thought about and discussed by her father and his friends. The precocious girl who rattled off her brother's Latin and Greek for him, who from her infancy had longed to be a scholar, and who had been given by her father the same classical education he had given his sons, was well known in her neighbourhood of Kent. The local aristocracy had taken her up. The Hon. Mrs Rooke made it her business to introduce her to 'many persons of distinction in rank as well as letters' during the London season, an experience which, according to Carter's nephew-biographer, 'first gave her a taste for such society, as out of London can hardly be met with'. She in her turn was a welcome addition to these circles: 'her acquaintance,' we are told, 'was much courted, and esteemed as it deserved'.

Her father, the Rev. Nicholas Carter, was proud of her and an avid scholar himself. A farmer's son, he had come to classical learning relatively late in life – it wasn't until he was nineteen that he began studying the all-important learned languages, Latin, Greek and Hebrew – and he remained an enthusiast. A restless man (his daughter identified restlessness as a family characteristic) and volatile, he published tracts of controversial divinity as well as sermons. Elizabeth was the eldest child and first daughter among a number of sons. She was evidently gifted, though not particularly quick to pick up the rudiments of a classical education. But she had a determination to be a scholar, the will power to persevere and a maturity of judgement and seriousness of purpose that impressed all who knew her.

The relationship between father and daughter was close and remained so. They lived together after a fashion all their lives, amidst a changing, often numerous household – by his two marriages, Dr Carter had seven children, two of whom died whilst on active service in the navy. In the early days, money was a problem: he was 'really so pressed by want of money that I hardly know which way to turn'.[7] But turn he did, setting an example of energy and aspiration, seeking what life had to offer, not in terms of material wealth or display but to establish his children securely, giving them the best he could in education and connections. He was happy for Elizabeth to spend long periods with the family of the Dean of Canterbury, Dr Lynch, whose daughters were of an age; she lived for a year with a French Protestant family in Canterbury to polish up her French.

The closeness between Elizabeth and her father can be attributed in part to the early death of her mother, Nicholas Carter's first wife, who died when Elizabeth was ten, supposedly of 'a decline' that followed on the loss of her fortune in the South Sea Bubble. (We know very little about the effects of this on the family, but it was clearly a traumatic event. Elizabeth was two and a half at the time of the South Sea Bubble so throughout her early childhood her mother was an ailing, probably very troubled, presence.) The closeness also reflects similarities of temperament and interests. Above all, what Elizabeth was later to call her 'darling independence' was respected by her father. Within the family, she was looked to for responsible leadership, a role which incorporated shopping for household supplies, helping to make shirts and educating the younger children. Nothing was insisted on, everything followed from her choice. Her father's letters all emphasised that she was to judge and make appropriate decisions on matters large and small. For example, on the question of when and how she should return from a stay in London to Deal, he wrote:

> when you are determined to come down give me timely notice, and you may have my chaise, either to come wholly to London, where staying one day to refresh the cattle it may return with you – and so home. Or if you like it rather it should meet you at Tunstall, or at Rochester – whatever you choose, let me know in time ... Before you come down, when it suits you, you must buy sugar of all sorts, according to your judgement, except that of the very coarsest kind ... Powder blue and stone blue. Starch according to your will, and whole rice. Flower of mustard. Salad oil, nutmegs, cloves, anchovies, icing-glass. Pepper. Morells. Best almonds. Raisins. Coffee. And anything else, of whatever kind you think is wanting. Your brother will receive money from me, and you may have from him what you want.

He was resourceful and, though money may sometimes have been tight, they were not poor. Dr Carter's own patron and friend was the local MP., the aristocrat Sir George Oxenden, a man of affairs close to the Prime Minister, Sir Robert Walpole. Sir George was a gentleman-scholar, happy to find in his curate an intellectual who was also a keen hunter and congenial companion. Together with Lady Oxenden, Dr Carter accompanied Sir George on trips, once making an extended visit to Bath, leaving Elizabeth, then aged twelve, at home with the other children. Naturally she wrote to her father. She wrote in Latin. Dr Carter took care to show the letter to Sir George who – liking to write his own letters in Latin or Greek – was impressed. He commended her vocabulary and accuracy and was one of the many influential people who took an interest in her future.

Dr Carter's guiding principle in education was that no distinction was to be made between women and men; indeed, even concerns about propriety disappeared when an equal education had been given. In 1737 Elizabeth, having asked his advice about her friendship with an intellectual young man, was told, 'there is no reason why you should fear the friendship ... Is there any matter on which a young woman can not answer a young man? If both be educated what can be more appropriate?' He trusted her absolutely, a trust that was founded in his recognition of her good judgement as well as his experience of her good behaviour. Rather than keeping her immured safely at home, his impulse seems to have been to push her out into the world. When Sir George Oxenden suggested that perhaps Elizabeth should add German to the many languages she had acquired, in order, possibly, to find a place at Court (a path Fanny Burney trod with dire consequences later, but without learning German), Dr Carter took the idea further: he envisaged his daughter not only learning German but travelling about in Germany, consolidating her knowledge of the language and culture, making connections and deepening her under-standing of life. He was not afraid that she would be tempted from the path of virtue and assured her that virtue could be preserved anywhere 'at court as well as in the country'. Sir George, he explained to Elizabeth in 1738, 'promises to be a generous patron'. Sir George's patronage (and therefore protection) evidently extended to the ambitious, adventurous, twenty-year-old gifted female.

At home, the young prodigy kept separate quarters, her own library of books and ordered her time as she saw fit. As well as German, she taught herself Spanish, Portugese and Arabic (whilst keeping up her Latin, Greek, Hebrew, French and Italian). She studied ancient geography and mathe-matics, religion and history, and developed a passion for astronomy. She had a habit of keeping late hours, studying or writing through the night and taking stimulants to stay awake – snuff and green tea being the drugs of choice. Her father congratulated her when she resolved to give up this practice (and the wet towel wrapped round her head, and the wet pillow on her stomach). He approved of her aiming to be in bed by midnight but he raised no objection to her enthusiasm for walking on the beach by night and observing the stars. Nor did he object to her insistence on very early rising. To ensure this she had a bell fitted to the head of her bed, with a long rope hanging from it out of the window and down into the garden of the house next door where the sexton lived. It was his custom to get up at around four or five in the morning. Each day he obligingly pulled the bell-rope and woke her. She went straight to her books: 'I sit down to my several lessons as regular as a school-boy, and lay in a stock of learning to make a figure with at breakfast.' Before breakfast, however, she liked to take a long walk, sometimes alone, sometimes with her young half-sister, Mary, who was 'as strong as a little Welsh horse', sometimes with a friend who was generally only half awake. The friend was allowed

the extreme consolation of grumbling as much as she pleases without the least interruption, which she does with such a variety of comical phrases, that I generally laugh from the beginning to the end of our journey ... Many are the exercises of patience she meets with in our peregrination, sometimes half roasted with the full glare of sunshine upon an open common, then dragged through a thread-paper path in the middle of a corn field, and bathed up to the ears in dew, and at the end of it perhaps forced to scratch her way through the bushes of a close shady lane, never before frequented by any animal but birds. In short, towards the conclusion of our walk, we make such deplorable ragged figures, that I wonder some prudent country justice does not take us up for vagrants, and cramp our rambling genius in the stocks. An apprehension that does not half so much fright me, as when some civil swains pull off their hats, and I hear them signifying to one another, with a note of admiration, that *I am Parson Carter's daughter.* I had much rather be accosted with 'good morrow, sweet-heart,' or 'are you walking for a wager'.

The breakfast which followed these exertions was, like tea in the afternoon, 'extremely chatty ... the most sociable and delightful parts of the day'. On matters intellectual, Elizabeth and her father were a match for each other, full of appetite for books of all kinds, ranging across languages, cultures and subject-matter. The account of a typical day of her life at Deal, from which the above extracts are taken, was written in 1746, when she was in her late twenties, but it serves very well as a picture of both earlier and later years. At the time of writing, there were relatively few members of the family at home:

Our family is now reduced to my eldest sister, and a little boy, who is very diverting at other times; but over our tea everybody is so eager to talk, that all his share in the conversation is only to stare and eat prodigiously. We have a great variety of topics, in which every body bears a part, till we get insensibly upon books; and whenever we go beyond Latin and French, my sister and the rest walk off, and leave my father and me to finish the discourse, and the tea-kettle by ourselves, which we should infallibly do, if it held as much as Solomon's molten sea. I fancy I have a privilege for talking a vast deal over the tea-table, as I am tolerably silent the rest of the day.[8]

The 'privilege' of talking a vast deal around the domestic tea-table had its origins in a sense of entitlement to both speech and silence. When she chose to spend long hours alone in her room 'quietly and decently in the sober conversation of books' nobody protested. She could be (like her father) volatile and impatient, easily bored in company, finding cards intolerable and working off her 'restless dissipation of thought' in long, energetic walks. Nevertheless, she viewed proper social behaviour as a duty. As a devout Christian, she understood her life on earth as a preparation for eternal life after death and judgement. Nobody else could answer for her when she stood before God on Judgement Day. She would be judged on her works by an all-seeing, all-knowing God. Such a belief placed great emphasis on individual autonomy, for it was not just the comfort and convenience of the present day that was at stake but eternal reward or eternal punishment. A good Christian lived a responsible social life, helping others towards the same end. An important element in the help that one

Christian could give another in living a moral life included helping them to exercise their own best judgement.

Dr Carter acknowledged the strength of his daughter's judgement implicitly and explicitly, encouraging her at all times to do whatever she thought it was best to do. An early and striking instance of this relates to the question of her 'launching into the world'. This began to be a pressing question from the mid 1730s onward and it posed itself at first, not surprisingly, as a question about marriage. Would she marry at all? If so, whom? From Dr Carter's point of view, marriage was strategically desirable since he was not wealthy and, though he could support her while he lived, he did not have enough to leave her provided for if he should die. The prospect that she might lose her freedom of choice, the dignity of independence – which he took such pains to ensure was available to her – troubled him. He suggested she should seriously consider the offers of marriage that began to be made to her when she came of age. But he was prepared for the fact that she would probably think otherwise, her dislike of the idea of marriage being no secret. 'Very early in life', the official biography tells us, 'Mrs Carter seems to have formed a resolution, or at least an intention, which she was enabled to keep, of devoting herself to study, and living a single life.' Her father, not unreasonably, wanted to be clear about his own duties in this regard. If she was looking for a husband, she would need financial backing; if not, she could live more cheaply. The choice was hers, but the decision had implications for both of them:

> If you intend never to marry, as I think you plainly intimate in one of your letters, then you certainly ought to live retired, and not appear in the world with an expense which is reasonable upon the prospect of getting a husband, but not otherwise.[9]

Matrimony, she considered 'a very right scheme for everybody but herself', and after one long and demanding wedding in the house – her brother's – she consoled herself with the thought that 'though she was very much tired of a wedding, it was not her own'. Dr Carter pointed out the social and personal as well as probable economic consequences of her stance: marriage 'procured more consideration than single life, which is often errant, and seldom meets with much respect'. And, more directly: 'I cannot forbear saying that when I die, and you are single, you will certainly find a vast difference with regard to the respect of the world.'

As it happens she proved him wrong, but his 'sharp uneasiness' about the matter is understandable. He did not press his point of view. Her 'square cornered heart' which she roundly declared was 'uninvadable' showed no sign of melting towards any man. She often remarked on it: 'I can perfectly well remember that when I was about ten years old, I looked upon having a *sweetheart* with as much horror as if it had been one of the seven deadly sins.' There is no doubt that the loss of autonomy that marriage entailed at a time when a married woman became, as far as the law was concerned, incorporated into her husband, offended her. Though an advocate of self-regulation, she did not think she would be able to regulate herself into the disciplines of married life. With outward good-humour, she set her face emphatically against the possibility, joking and teasing her way out of offers which she seems to have regarded as traps sprung to catch her. Her father wrote with partiality about one suitor, but ended:

> I have said all this to discharge the duty of a parent, but not to influence you against your own judgement. You may have reasons which can justify a refusal in the eye of Providence, and these ought to make you easy. I have that dependence on your prudence, that I do by no means desire to know what they are; and then, I think, others have no right to that explication. I end, as I began, in leaving you to your own inclinations, and in assuring you of my indulgence and affection in whatever part you take.[10]

Her romantic and sexual inclinations were never towards men. This was so obviously a fact that throughout her life it was openly acknowledged by her friends and acquaintances. She did not seek to live with a woman, but scandal would not necessarily have followed had she done so no matter how intimate the connection was allowed to be. Elizabeth Montagu's sister, Sarah Scott, left her husband and settled happily in Bath with Babs Montagu where they lived and worked as a couple; and the Ladies of Llangollen, Eleanor Butler and Sarah Ponsonby, who eloped together from Ireland, were much feted as an adoring 'married' pair – both of them wearing men's clothes – by literary and other folk.[11]

Elizabeth Carter's father seems always to have adopted the position outlined in his letter. He trusted her 'prudence' and was satisfied that her own 'inclinations' would point her in the most appropriate direction. Her own judgement, in his opinion, was the judgement that should prevail on questions to do with her own life:

> I must do you the justice to say, that I think you are an exception. I am extremely unwilling to cross your inclination in anything, because your behaviour to me is more than unexceptionable. I leave you, therefore, to act agreeably to your own judgement. My exceeding fondness of you must necessarily make me anxious and fearful; but it does not prevent me from being convinced that I may safely leave a great deal to your own judgement.[12]

She was an exception, but perhaps we should acknowledge that her father was too. There is something very touching about the mutual respect outlined here (based on self-interest and 'fondness' combined), an image of fatherhood to throw into the balance on the other side.

If Elizabeth Carter's place in the world was not to be established by marriage, it seemed likely, given that she was an exception, to be determined by her intellectual and literary abilities. Instead of thinking of her in relation to a husband, her father, and other interested parties such as Sir George Oxenden, thought of her in relation to the world of letters. This was, of course, dominated by men.

Like other gentlemen-scholars, Sir George and Dr Carter were keen observers of the literary scene. They followed Elizabeth's early fortunes as a published writer very closely. Having chosen the pen-name 'Eliza', it transpired that another 'Eliza' was gracing the pages of a second periodical in 1734. Dr Carter felt confident that Elizabeth need not be concerned since most people knew she had written the riddle, but at the same time he saw an opportunity discreetly to further her fame. He advised: 'An advertisement in the magazine asserting only a matter of fact (that the Eliza in the *Magazine* is not the Eliza in that *Almanack*) I think would not savour of ostentation, but be very right and prudent.' Being 'prudent' was an elastic quality which stretched to being pushy. Later, her father responded to a letter of Elizabeth's describing her new London friends, that the name of Samuel Johnson was 'a name with which I am utterly unacquainted. Neither his scholastic, critical, or poetical character ever reached my ears.' This was not a sign that he was out of touch, except in so far as the countryside would always be one step behind the town. In 1738 Johnson had yet to make his mark. Pope's was the name to conjure with.

Dr Carter shared with Elizabeth his view that 'Mr Pope's reputation seems to be on the decline. It has had its run', and regularly discussed such matters with Sir George, taking care at all times to bring Elizabeth's literary researches forward. He wrote to his daughter: 'Sir George asked me whether I had seen the new *Dunciad*. This occasioned me to shew him your quotation. His opinion is, that nobody but Mr Pope could write it. He imagined that the line *Exile, Penalties, and Pains*, has an indirect look towards the late Bishop of Rochester.' The young Elizabeth's decision to translate Crousaz's critique of Pope's *Essay on Man* was a decision which the worldly Sir George understood as a calculated bid to gain Pope's attention. He issued a warning in one of his regular letters to Dr Carter:

I dare say Miss Carter knows what she does. I could write a volume upon the subject of her launching into the world. You may be assured nobody has more respect or concern for her, who is not related to her, than myself; and nobody loves you more. One thing, however, I may add, which is this; that there is hardly an instance of a woman of letters entering into an intimacy of acquaintance with men of wit and parts, particularly poets, who were not thoroughly abused and maltreated by them, in print, after some time; and Mr Pope has done it more than once.[13]

Sir George's observations and experience of the behaviour of 'men of wit and parts' towards women writers were not offered as arguments to dissuade Elizabeth from becoming a woman of letters; they were a recognition that such a role already existed, and that it had a history. If her 'launching into the world' were to be a launching into the world of literature, then she needed a strategic understanding of the dangers she might encounter. But neither she, nor Sir George, nor her father thought of her as a passive victim of a fixed system: her own drive, her own behaviour, and the decisions she made about how she conducted herself and the kind of writing she elected to pursue, would determine her fortunes. Her father, as always, emphasised the power she had in herself to produce from others – including men of letters, including poets – a respectful response. He advised dignified self-assertion: 'As you never abuse others, you may hope not to be abused. Hold your own, but without any appearance of ill-nature or contempt.'

It was Sir George Oxenden's considered opinion that Miss Carter probably knew what she was doing. His respect for her ability to make sound judgements about her own 'launching into the world', is worth attention for it emphasises a certain worldly-wise quality in her which might otherwise be underestimated. Carter was very far from being a timid recluse. She sought a 'proper' knowledge of people and things, one that was equal to her capacities, and she shared Johnson's view that 'nothing but conversing with the world can give the very best understandings proper notions of it'. She had an extremely good understanding and she was not willing to be sold short, especially since she believed that intelligent people had a responsibility to explain the world as they experienced it; they needed to do what was necessary to develop 'proper and affecting arguments'. In other words, having a good understanding brought social responsibilities to women as well as men. She, like any man who was similarly gifted, owed something to the wider society, something very much like leadership. She had to develop the arguments in order to communicate them, to 'give those notions to others'.

Her early fame as a gifted writer did not emerge by accident and it was not simply by chance that her name was known across Europe and as far away as Russia. Her 'launching into the world' was deliberate, determined, focused – and achieved by immense hard work. She had resolved from an early age on literary scholarship and celebrity. Going up to London to write for the *Gentleman's Magazine* was an obvious move, all the more so since she already had connections there: family, a reputation with the circles she had been introduced into by the Hon. Mrs Rooke, her father's friendship with Edward Cave, and Sir George Oxenden's patronage and his extensive network indirectly available to her through her father.

Throughout the year that Carter spent in London working full-time, between spring 1738 and early summer 1739, she, Samuel Johnson and Thomas Birch were a threesome. Of the three, she was very probably the most advantageously situated so far as getting on as a writer was concerned. As a woman, and especially as a young woman, it was easy to play the card of exceptionality, and in any case, having been publishing since 1734, she was already a veteran though only twenty. Neither Birch nor Johnson had so immediate a way of distinguishing themselves from the many literary men desperate to get known. Birch worked tirelessly, writing, networking and generally running about as Horace Walpole was later to observe 'like a young setting dog in quest of anything, new or old'. This good-natured and industrious self-made cleric was, like Samuel Johnson, a man making his way in the world without the benefit of a university education. An antiquary and scholar, he was an enthusiast, indiscriminate in his tastes, willing to turn his hand and head to whatever literary job might carry him forward; and caught, as Johnson was also to find himself, in the toils of dictionary drudgery. Birch wrote over six hundred articles for the English edition of Pierre Bayle's *General Dictionary* which was published between 1734 and 1741. Seemingly able to write unstoppably, he also talked unstoppably: he had, said Johnson rather sourly, 'more anecdotes than any man', which flowed from him 'like the river Thames'. His energy was not matched by brilliance. Johnson rated him 'a dull writer', or worse, barely a writer at all: 'Tom can talk; but he is no writer.'

Birch was a collector and a follower. He had a special enthusiasm for women writers. The collection of his manuscripts in the British Library includes many carefully transcribed copies of poems and other writings by women of the time. It is possible that he was planning to put together an anthology of his own, and he was certainly acquainted with the Anglo-Saxon scholar Elizabeth Elstob, whose notes provided the basis for George Ballard's *Memoirs of Several Ladies of Great Britain Who Have Been Celebrated for their Writings* which appeared in 1752. Thomas Birch was working in an editorial capacity for Edward Cave by 1738 when Elizabeth Carter arrived. He attached himself to her, not only making suggestions about new writing projects such as the Algarotti book on Newton, and involving himself in the day-to-day working out by reading drafts and discussing particulars, but also promoting her wherever he could. His fulsomeness might not have been entirely to her taste, but she did not stop him striving to get Lady

Hertford's agreement to have the Algarotti Newton dedicated to her (she refused); and his glowing review in *The History of the Works of the Learned* did her reputation no harm.

Undoubtedly, Birch was personally attracted to the brilliant new addition to the *Gentleman's Magazine*. In his early thirties, he was already a widower. He kept detailed records in Latin about his meetings with Elizabeth Carter during her time in London in 1738–39 and these records show that they were often together – though not necessarily alone. Johnson was often present, as perhaps were Richard Savage or James Thomson – the most famous poets of the time. There were meals, trips, working sessions at the offices at St John's Gate. An outing to Richmond included Savage, Thomson and Johnson as well as Birch and Carter. The entry for 29 August reports that the two of them dined alone. All through the winter there were letters from him to her, outings, lunches, dinners. They travelled to Hertfordshire and Oxford making visits; they went to the theatre and saw plays together, 'a clergyman and a sober young lady'. The friendship clearly incorporated romance elements on his part. But there is no indication that she recipro-cated (no letters from her to him) and quite a lot of evidence that romantic overtures from Birch or any other man were of no interest to Elizabeth Carter.[14]

His strategy, it appears, was 'to pose and effectually act as a kind of patron-impressario to the marvellous Eliza'. He praised her in letters to his friends, helping to circulate the sense of her prodigiousness, introduced her to influential people she might not otherwise have met, accompanied her to public functions, got on splendidly with her father who was frequently in town, and even went so far as to circulate her own letters. This she objected to. The boundary between private and public was not only blurred, it seemed to have disappeared altogether in the minds of people like Thomas Birch. He was an incorrigible publicist. He explained:

> whatever things you write are so elegant and graceful that they seem most worthy of preservation ... Several of my friends – leading judges in the republic of letters to whom I showed a copy of your note written three days ago to your brother – make this judgement.

Carter was not a novice and it may well be that the 'note' to her brother was a showpiece (rather like the letter in Latin written at the age of twelve to her father) intended to be circulated in exactly this way and by this means. But it was not necessarily comfortable to be passed around in this fashion, especially for a young woman of marriageable age. Niceties of judgement were endlessly called for and if she experienced some ambivalence or concern it is hardly surprising.

Johnson also attached himself to Elizabeth Carter. The truth of the matter is that she was of more use to these men at that time than they were to her. Johnson, new to London, had fewer literary connections than Thomas Birch who had been born in Clerkenwell, and less security than Carter whose extended family supported her and with whom she lodged in the City. He had also sustained in his life more difficulties and disappointments than either of them. His hopes of literary success with his play *Irene* had come to nothing. The school he had established and attempted to run at Edial had failed. He was married, but his wife – whose capital had been sunk and lost in the school – remained in the midlands. Johnson had in desperation come to storm London, the centre of cultural life, home of the printing industry, the only place in the early eighteenth century for a literary reputation to be launched.

That London had an imaginative hold on Johnson can be seen in the poem he set about writing soon after his arrival, an imitation of the Third Satire of Juvenal. This was itself modelled on the current literary success: Pope's imitations of Horace's satires. Johnson's *London* was his first successful publication. He was paid ten guineas for it, it came out under Dodsley's imprint – the leading poetry publisher – and it made his name well-known in the right circles. *London* appeared in early 1738 and, as with all authors with a new publication, it was important for Johnson to get his name about. One way of doing that was to engage in print with an author who was already known. That winter, Elizabeth Carter was particularly active on the pages of the *Gentleman's Magazine*: in November 1737 she published her translation of Horace's Ode 10 Book II and in February 1738 a poetical riddle on dreams, followed by an imitation of Horace's Ode 22 in March. It was the riddle on dreams which caught Johnson's attention. He wrote to Edward Cave, 'I have compos'd a Greek epigram to Eliza, and think she ought to be celebrated'. His epigram came out in Greek and Latin in the April issue. Without delay, 'Eliza' replied, also in Greek and Latin, in the May edition. Each thus benefited the other and together they served the *Gentleman's Magazine*.

Elizabeth Carter's publications in the *Gentleman's Magazine* during her year in London seem designed to display her range and keep her in the public eye. In April there was an imitation from the Spanish of Quevedo; in May a satire with an epigraph from Juvenal; and in June a poem about the universe with an epigraph from Virgil. In July that year she was excited by an outing to Richmond, where they walked through the meadows to Twickenham and to Pope's house (a veritable gathering of poets). The company were allowed to wander in the poet's garden. Sure enough, the visit was immediately put to use by both Johnson and Carter. In the *Gentleman's Magazine* for July appeared an epigram ascribed to Johnson which placed

'Eliza' in direct lineal descent from Pope: he depicted her as rightfully taking the laurels from Pope's garden – in other words, as the true inheritor of his genius. In the next edition, in August, no fewer than three translations of this epigram appeared, one of which was by Johnson himself:

> As learn'd *Eliza,* sister of the Muse,
> Surveys with new contemplative delight
> *Pope's* hallow'd glades, and never tiring views,
> Her conscious hand his laurel leaves invite.

Furthermore, printed immediately after this complimentary verse, was a response from Elizabeth Carter herself. It was published in both a Latin and an English version:

> In vain *Eliza's* daring hand
> Usurp'd the laurel bough;
> Remov'd from *Pope's,* the wreath must fade
> On ev'ry meaner brow.

Such a modest disclaimer was all very well, but the overall effect is to fix an image of 'Eliza's' absolute entitlement to reach up for the laurel bough. The occasion of the visit is self-consciously turned for purposes of literary myth-making and it is quite likely that the epigrams were composed in concert – perhaps whilst travelling back, perhaps at the *Gentleman's Magazine* – but certainly not in privacy and secrecy. Johnson and Carter together asserted the importance of their association with the highest levels of literary achievement: Pope represented the summit and both felt fit to aspire to it. Sharing in recognition, they deployed their access to a public platform to further their aim.

That same month, Edward Cave brought out a volume of 'Eliza's' poems, *Poems upon Particular Occasions.* Although it did not feature her name on the title page, it did carry the *Gentleman's Magazine's* trademark image of St John's Gate and included the poems she had first published there. The publication of this slim volume – only a twenty-four page quarto pamphlet, full of Latin and Greek inscriptions – was an important sign of 'Eliza's' value to a shrewd businessman like Edward Cave. Conversely, her intimacy with him made her sought after by aspiring writers, for, like Johnson and Birch, she had editorial influence. In later life, she downplayed her early reputation as a poet – as she also downplayed her journalism and early translations. In his memoir, her nephew offers the orthodox family line that those translations were 'unworthy of her powers' as the future translator of Epictetus; they were modern and familiar languages which could have been translated 'by any common Grub Street writer'. As to the volume of poetry, he observed that it was very scarce and that his aunt thought few of the poems worth preserving (although, as will be seen, many of them were reprinted by her in 1762). But he acknowledged that the writings made her very well known and 'highly esteemed, both in town and country'. These were the years in which she established a reputation that was to serve her for the rest of her life.

As well as striving to fix herself in the public mind as an appropriate inheritor of Pope's laurels, Elizabeth Carter also at this time laid claim to a place in a specifically female poetic tradition. In April 1737 she had published in the *Gentleman's Magazine* a poem, *On the Death Of Mrs Rowe*, which mourned the passing of the most celebrated female poet of her time, Elizabeth Rowe. Mrs Rowe's brother-in-law, Theophilus Rowe, was engaged in gathering materials for a commemorative Life and Works and he wrote to Carter asking if he might have permission to include her poem among the many other celebratory odes and poems he had received, all of which testified to Elizabeth Rowe's visibility and high status. She agreed, revising the poem in such a way as to stress more strongly the elements of a lineage and her own desire to be part of it. In the second version of *On the Death of Mrs Rowe*, 'Philomela', as Mrs Rowe was known, is figured as the poet who cleaned up 'the records of female wit' so that virtuous followers, like Elizabeth Carter, could announce the intention to model themselves on her without risk to their own reputations. The 1737 version had addressed the admired poet – 'our sex's ornament and pride' – from the position of an 'artless' admirer; by 1739, Carter was prepared to make her own ambitions explicit:

> Fix'd on my soul shall thy example grow
> And be my genius and my guide below ...
> And oh! forgive (tho faint the transcript be,
> That copies an original like thee)
> My highest pride, my best attempt for fame,
> That joins my own to PHILOMELA's name.[15]

She had in fact been joining her own to Philomela's name for a number of years. The profile of her early career imitates that of Elizabeth Rowe in every significant particular. She took from her predecessor important lessons about how to conduct her life as a writer. The example Elizabeth Rowe handed down was this: that a woman could put her thinking and writing self at the centre of her existence and be universally praised and admired for it. Mrs Rowe was deeply religious. But so was Elizabeth Carter. They both also liked to have a lot of time to read, write and think their solitary thoughts uninterruptedly at home or walking along country lanes. Like Elizabeth Carter, Elizabeth Rowe's home and favourite abode was far from the metropolis, in the Somerset countryside. Both lived amongst families who encouraged their dispositions. They made friends with others of intellectual and literary persuasion, developing relationships with men who had access to the world of print and public opinion. From the 'retirement' of Somerset (Rowe) and Kent (Carter) each was able to keep in very good touch with developments in literature: aristocratic and clergy friends supplied the latest books and ideas and circulated letters and manuscripts; editors were keen to receive copy posted to them from all corners of the land. That it could produce and nurture an individual of singular talents was a source of pride to a neighbourhood. Members of the Somerset aristocracy, the Thynne family at Longleat, took the brilliant young Elizabeth Singer (as Mrs Rowe then was) to their bosoms; and the aristocracy of Kent similarly interested themselves in promoting 'the famous Miss Carter'. There was, in another words, a cultural currency in talented young females from at least the 1690s onwards which Rowe did much to help cultivate and Carter was able to exploit.[16]

Theophilus Rowe was like Thomas Birch in being an ardent supporter of women. In his correspondence with Elizabeth Carter, he told her he had 'long been convinced of the injustice of custom, in restraining the ladies from the improvements of knowledge and learning' and congratulated her on setting an example that 'wisdom and philosophy can sit with grace and ease on a lady – even a young one'. He sent her his two-volume edition of the *Life and Works of Mrs Rowe* when it appeared in 1739. She sent him her Algarotti. He was in contact with Lady Hertford, who had been Elizabeth Rowe's patron. Although Lady Hertford had declined to have the Algarotti dedicated to her, her letter of refusal had been 'considered as so flattering both by Mrs Carter and her father' that she received a copy of the book in the post along with Elizabeth Carter's *Poems on Several Occasions* and, for her further edification, the recently published volume of Dr Carter's sermons. Meanwhile, Theophilus Rowe benefited from the connection: in her editorial capacity, Elizabeth Carter arranged for the *Life and Works of Mrs Rowe* to be serialised in the *Gentleman's Magazine*.

We have here in microcosm a sample of the overlapping, mutually obliging nature of the literary world. Gender, genre and class boundaries proved softly permeable; obligation and advantage were conferred and received at different levels in different ways. The patron, the poet, the periodical writer and editor, the translator, the curate with a volume of sermons to promote and the biographer were all invested in literary activity, all seeking to push their product, all making use of the elements that served their purposes. It is helpful to recognise this when we discuss women writers if only to be aware of the different ways and degrees in which women particularly served these purposes. The magazine editor who published Elizabeth Singer, 'Philomela', in the 1690s – John Dunton, founder of the first literary magazine the *Athenian Mercury* – made much of her to help on sales of his magazine in a way that offered a model for Edward Cave in the 1730s. This is demonstrable and factual. What is not demonstrable is how it felt to be such a woman and live such a life.[17]

The career path that opened out before Samuel Johnson and Thomas Birch as they began to achieve recognition was far more straightforward than it could ever be for Elizabeth Carter. For all the approbation and encouragement she received from the men in her life – father, friends, patrons, publishers, brothers, nephew – the model of the author currently being given strongest definition was a male model. Johnson gave it authoritative expression in the *Life of Richard Savage* in 1744. The only account of a female author to compare with this was the *Life* of Elizabeth Rowe, which, though celebrating her as a poet was offered as an exemplary Christian life. Elizabeth Carter repeatedly urged her friends to read this text which was reprinted throughout the century. It is not a book scholars turn to nowadays (and many of Elizabeth Carter's friends, such as Hester Chapone, were resistant to her commendation) but Carter's enthusiasm for it was deep and lasting. This is surely at least partly because it offers a compelling portrait of a female poet and writer who succeeded in forging an autonomous path.

The shortage of models for a respectable woman writer is significant here because of the change of direction in Elizabeth Carter's life. Though her time in London had been professionally productive and successful, and personally not unhappy (nothing she wrote or said later indicated any unhappiness), she nevertheless decided in the summer of 1739 to leave London and return to Deal. It is possible that she always viewed the time in London as short-term. The example of Elizabeth Rowe showed that a literary reputation could be built and sustained from the deepest rural solitudes. The official biography depicts the return to Deal as a 'retreat', a turning away from the hubbub of city streets and the bustle of metropolitan ambition. There is an assumption of defeat, though nothing is specified. No regret is expressed; rather, there is a tight-lipped approval which signified a later generation's embarrassment and ignorance. Montagu Pennington did not know much about his aunt's early years as a writer, nor about the literary world in which she moved. What he did know was that her times – the dim and distant 1730s – were far more *louche* than his own in the early nineteenth century when he was assembling her letters and composing his memoir. It must have been quite difficult for him to imagine his highly respected scholarly spinster aunt consorting with disreputable poets like Richard Savage, writing copy for the press and dreaming of fame. Later commentators have speculated that Thomas Birch's attentions became too pressing, or that some other man proved too persistent in his attentions. It is likely that she was the object of male sexual interest, and likely, too, that avoidance was her preferred strategy where possible.

We simply do not know if Elizabeth Carter ever seriously contemplated setting up as a writer in London. But the tendency to think about her return to Deal as a 'retreat' and as some sort of acknowledgement of defeat is surely mistaken. There had been no defeat; her story was one of continuing success. It makes more sense to view the return to Deal as a decision made from mixed motives. These included the recognition that she did not need to be based in London. She could do what she wanted to do without sacrificing elements in her life that were important: control of her time, family, local friends, the countryside, the sea. What 'she wanted to do', however, seems to have become less rather than more clear to her at this point in her life.

Crucially, leaving London did not imply abandoning her ambitions as a scholar and writer. But it did involve a rethinking of the nature of that role. In the months that followed her departure she was in correspondence with Edward Cave about a number of literary projects, none of which came to fruition. From the way she spoke about these years much later in her life, we can guess that she made a strategic decision not to associate herself with any more translation work from modern languages such as French and Italian, probably because such work was increasingly being done by the moderately educated, desperately poor hack writers, female and male, who filled Grub Street. As literary work, even if she translated philosophical and scientific writings about Newton or critiques of Pope, it was low class. Work of that sort was not going to maintain her reputation nor extend it.

The writer whose career offered the most likely model for her own was not Johnson, whose great talents had yet to distinguish themselves from any other Grub Street writer, and who laboured under his poverty and provincialism, but Alexander Pope. Pope's example was an important one in two respects. First, Pope achieved financial independence and literary prestige by following Dryden in translating a widely known classical Greek text: Homer's *Iliad* in 1720 and the *Odyssey* in 1725–26. Pope needed to make money from his writings; disabled, and a Catholic, he could not follow a career in the professions or politics. He was to become the first truly professional poet in England. Until the translations, he earned a little from his poetry and he had a small inherited income, but no more. That 'the life of a wit is a warfare upon earth' was no less true in material terms than any other. Pope decided to publish the translations from Homer by subscription, an arrangement which was to prove astonishingly profitable. It is estimated that he made some £10,000 on the two texts, which provided him with an ample income for the rest of his life. Even more important, perhaps, Pope's professionalism about his writing, his success in combining in himself the roles of patron and poet to improve his profits, did him no harm socially. His status was unimpaired. He stood apart from Grub Street. Elizabeth Carter, a scholar with a particular love of ancient Greek and a father with the aristocratic connections to drum up subscriptions, took due note. Secondly, Pope's satires on the literary world of the 1730s, especially his *Epistle to Dr Arbuthnot* (1735) and the *Dunciad*, the final version of which appeared in 1743, were instrumental in marking out the boundaries between high and low, between literary gentlemen, squirearchy and Grub Street. The self-promoting, self-deluded, amateur poet infesting the land and pestering the famous was given wide currency as a figure of fun. Writing and printing poetry, according to Pope's counterblast, was sadly all the rage. The real poet (Pope) had to bar his door to defend himself against besieging mobs – poetic parsons, the 'maudlin poetess', the 'rhyming peer' – they were all at it:

> Fire in each eye, and papers in each hand,
> They rave, recite, and madden round the land.

Instead of raging and reciting, printing and quarrelling, Pope's version of the literary life foregrounded gentlemanly choices: to write or not as he chose – 'Heavens! Was I born for nothing but to write?' – and to live in quiet domesticity taking care of his mother. His ambition, as he protested just a little too much in the *Epistle to Dr Arbuthnot*, was to:

> Maintain a poet's dignity and ease,
> And see what friends, and read what books I please.[18]

Holding one's own, as Dr Carter advised his daughter, extended to making decisions about the kind of writer one wanted to be, the kind of engagement one wanted to make in the literary world. If it was a challenge for a man like Pope to 'maintain a poet's dignity and ease', and at the same time woo an income out of the purses of booksellers and readers, it was even more of a challenge for a young woman. Elizabeth Carter, like Pope, had a vision of a balanced existence, one which included the satisfactions and pleasures of a private life whilst according some of the rewards of public achievement.

It is possible that in London the experience of working to tight deadlines for immediate periodical consumption both wearied and disenchanted her. Her appetite for publication diminished in the 1740s: no more volumes of poetry appeared, she undertook no topical translations. By 1746 Edward Cave was complaining to her father who passed the message on to her. Dr Carter wrote: 'I had a letter from Mr Cave last night, in which he says, I cannot persuade Miss to undertake anything, and the world wants to know what she is about.'

What she was about was a very great deal of reading, reflecting, walking and cultivating some significant friendships. With hindsight, one can see the 1740s as an important formative decade for Elizabeth Carter, more important perhaps than her early celebrity in the 1730s. In the 1740s she made herself into the kind of writer she wanted to be. Not the writer her father and Sir George Oxenden envisaged; not the writer Edward Cave and 'the world' wanted; not a writer like Samuel Johnson, Thomas Birch, Richard Savage or Alexander Pope. None of these men could offer her a model. She had to form her own, one suited to her particular tastes and temperament. She was a woman of deep piety, obedient to the precepts of her time in manners and morals, but she also valued 'the Freedom of unfetter'd Thought'. In a poem addressed to her father, Carter thanked him for granting her intellectual freedom:

> Ne'er did thy Voice assume a Master's pow'r;
> Nor force Assent to what thy Precepts taught;
> But bid my independent Spirit soar,
> In all the Freedom of unfetter'd Thought.

Her independent spirit gave her the confidence to make up an independent life, one which took courage from the example of Elizabeth Rowe. (Words like 'soar', 'freedom', 'unfetter'd', evoke Rowe's poetry.) When Carter's nephew wrote her biography he was anxious to stress the piety. He produced a picture of a quaint, harmless, much revered aunt who just happened to have been one of the leading intellectuals of her day. But even in Montagu Pennington's *Memoirs* another Elizabeth Carter constantly breaks through. This person is possessed of enormous restless energy: she is opinionated, self-assured, bold, determined, obstinate, ambitious and self-respecting. She knows what she likes and dislikes, approves and disapproves. She knows what she needs and feels entitled to organise life so that she can get it. She lives according to values she has weighed, sifted, tested and found worthy. She is proper and cautious but also excitable; has a huge appetite for learning but also for loitering along the sea-shore and clambering about the country. She is private and sociable, repressed and passionate. She is especially passionate about friendship, and especially about female friendship.

One way of maintaining a poet's dignity was to have friends of high social rank. In a hierarchical society, this was not a cynical ploy. People characteristically congratulated each other on being friends with the nobility or being brought into acquaintance with some local worthy. For a writer, to have friends who were both learned and socially eminent was a means of advancement. Thus in 1741, when Elizabeth Carter was introduced to Catherine Talbot, a young woman also celebrated for her learning, whose social position was higher than her own, it was an advantageous friendship to develop. They were brought together at Mrs Rooke's house by the astronomer Mr Wright, who had been instructing both young women in astronomy and mathematics. Elizabeth Carter's response was unequivocal. She told Wright, 'Miss Talbot is absolutely my passion; I think of her all day, dream of her all night, and one way or other introduce her into every subject I talk of'.[19] It was a passion which was to modulate into a deep, though not uncritical, friendship and which we might justifiably view as a frustrated love affair. Frustration is certainly an appropriate word to use in connection with Catherine Talbot.

Catherine Talbot lived with her mother in the household of Thomas Secker, in turn Dean of St Paul's, Bishop of Oxford and later Archbishop of Canterbury. She had extremely good connections with the aristocracy, especially those who were patrons of letters, like Lady Hertford. Catherine Talbot's own poetry and epistolary prose circulated in these circles and she had a reputation as a clever young woman, having been well educated in the classics, in English and French literature, and in history. The *Gentleman's Magazine* carried a poem in 1741, 'On Miss Talbot's Conversing with a Lawyer at Bath'. She was, however, a troubled young woman. Her father having died before she was born, Secker took on the role of foster father to her and gave life-long support to her widowed mother. For all his undoubted kindness, Secker's generosity seems to have produced a gratitude in the younger woman that was at times paralysing. He told her when she was thirteen:

> You are the only child of a very good woman, our dear friend, and in stead of a child to my wife and me. The affection we all have for one another is united in *you*: for ourselves, all we can expect is, some continuance of our present happiness; but *You are our growing hopes*. The only way our enjoyment of life can much increase, is by seeing your mind, and temper and behaviour coming near to what we wish it.[20]

With the burden of the happiness of three adults placed upon her frail shoulders, it is little wonder that Catherine Talbot grew up to be dissatisfied with herself. Her introspection and self-denigration often called forth quiet rebukes from Elizabeth Carter.

Intelligent, intellectually frustrated since there was nothing substantial to do with the education she had been given, inclined to depression and self-blame, Catherine Talbot looked to Elizabeth Carter for encouragement in her spiritual and mental life. Deeply religious, she strove to be content within a limited arena. She had none of Carter's robust independence of thought, nor the intellectual confidence that came with it. Nevertheless, she had ambitions to be a writer and devoted her life to self-improvement via schemes of study and programmes of reading, all of which, predictably, were sabotaged by the inroads of daily life. The letters between the two women, like so many instances of correspondence in the eighteenth century, were semi-formal, self-conscious writerly expressions pitched somewhere between private and public. By agreeing to engage in a correspondence with a known literary celebrity, Catherine Talbot laid claim to her identity as a writer. The systematic exchange of letters provided a forum for debate about literature, philosophy, life; and it formed the basis for more intimate personal contact, the tea drinkings, visits and late night conversations in which understandings were established. Though her visits were not frequent, Elizabeth Carter became a cherished member of Catherine Talbot's household, referred to as her 'daughter' by Mrs Talbot, a sort of ideal sister for Catherine. The emotional tie between them was strong, but their face to face meetings were not always successful. No matter how much they each expressed the longing to 'chat quietly and comfortably for an hour', in practice, Miss Talbot, doing the honours of the archbishop's household, was forever among crowds and Miss Carter was a martyr to headaches which would send her to her pillow.

Talbot served Carter in a mixed capacity, somewhere between a friend and love object; she was also a patron whose access to the scholarly resources of learned divines, notably Thomas Secker and his clerical friends, was a compelling part of her appeal. At Lambeth Palace Carter loved nothing better than a good scholarly debate. Hers was a critical mind. She might describe herself as too volatile and impatient to apply herself to any one thing long enough to become proficient (a self-description that was manifestly untrue); but she was impatient with false reasoning or poor scholarly interpretations, especially when they led to philosophies about life and universal principles which she felt were mistaken. None of the women Carter mixed with had anything like the command of ancient literatures that she had, though many, like Talbot, were eager readers of the moderns.

She could share opinion on contemporary novelists and essayists, discuss Mme de Châtelet's 'false philosophy' or Dante's obscurity, but for a sounding board for her opinions on Greek, Latin or Hebrew she was limited to a small number of men in her family and friendship circles.

Thomas Secker was a serious scholar in Greek, Latin and Hebrew, well versed in the early documents of church history. With him she could argue minute inflections of interpretation, biblical and other, upon some of which large systems had been constructed. For example, in her reading of the Bible she was accustomed to compare the translated version with the Hebrew or Greek originals. She found an anomaly in the rendering of one verb in Paul's First Epistle to the Corinthians in the Authorised Version. When it was applied to the husband, the translators rendered the verb in an active form; when applied to the woman they rendered it passive. For Carter, this was a sign of their support for the superiority of the husband; it demonstrated that translation was not neutral and nor was it gender blind. She carried the argument to Secker. Secker insisted, from memory, that the words in the original were not in fact the same words. She held her ground:

> 'Come with me, Madam Carter,' said he at length, 'to my study, and be confuted.' They went, and his Grace, on consulting the passage, instead of being angry that he was found to be in the wrong, said with the utmost good humour, 'No, Madam Carter, 'tis I that must be confuted, and you are in the right.'[21]

We can safely assume she would be in the right – a woman with the temerity to argue such a point with a leading theologian would have checked and double-checked her sources first.

Like Sir George Oxenden and Dr Carter, like Edward Cave, Catherine Talbot concerned herself with the question of what Elizabeth Carter intended to do with her manifest abilities. During the 1740s, the woman who had been so prodigiously hard-working as a child and teenager claimed to be making up for lost time in the department of life's pleasures: she had abandoned her books and was partying and rambling. She lived at home without any obvious purpose besides helping out with the usual demands of a large family. Sometimes she accused herself of indolence, or of being a 'trifler':

> When I was in the world, its employments, or perhaps amusements, always had their attractions for me, as well as the more quiet life I now lead in retirement. But I am a trifler, and trifles were admirably well adapted to me; the world and I were upon very good terms.

Being on good terms with the world, being contented, finding an appropriate form of living which would bring maximum contentment, was a philosophical challenge she was resolved to meet. Thinking through these issues during her late twenties and early thirties, she declared herself on the whole contented with her life, but 'other people do not seem to think it a life to be contented with'. There was a pressure to take up some larger project. Sufficient inducement, however, was lacking, for the love of independence and liberty always came first, or at least was always available as an explanation to herself for her reluctance to commit to schemes proposed by others, whether they were schemes for marrying her off or schemes of work. 'To give up one's ease and liberty, and be under perpetual restraint, for the sake of wearing a finer gown, eating a greater variety of dishes, or seeing more company and fewer friends, appears to me a very strange scheme', she wrote, defending herself as she often had to do in these years.[22]

Catherine Talbot worried about what she owed such a friend. Her thoughts were focussed by a book to which she had subscribed and which appeared in 1751. This was an edition of the works of Catherine Cockburn with a *Life* by Thomas Birch. The subscription scheme had been intended as a benevolent effort to provide Mrs Cockburn – another young prodigy who had written poems, plays and tracts in her youth which had been much admired but who later sank into poverty and neglect – with some money, but she had unfortunately died in 1749. Talbot saw a parallel between her own gifted friend and Cockburn:

> She was a remarkable genius, and yet how obscure her lot in life! It seems grievous at first, and such straitness of circumstances as perplexes and cramps the mind, is surely a grievance, but on consideration what signifies distinction and splendour in this very transitory state? ... But methinks those who knew such merit did not do their duty in letting it remain so obscure. E:C: is her superior – alas will not she live and die perhaps as obscurely, and what alas can I do to prevent it?[23]

Helping merit into the light was a duty. On the other hand, religion taught that worldly distinctions and splendours did not signify.

The question of how best to live one's life, especially with regard to what was owed to others, was an uncomfortable one for Catherine Talbot. Enmeshed in dependencies and obligations, she was liable to feel that her authentic self was being frittered away. To her Elizabeth Carter, with her unapologetic intellectual approach to life, represented the possibilities of greater seriousness. For example, her command of languages meant that Elizabeth Carter had direct access to the sources of knowledge and debate; she did not have to depend for her intellectual and imaginative sustenance on books read aloud, in company, in bad translations. Catherine Talbot did, and it reinforced her feelings of inferiority and frivolity. In 1743 she complained of being confined to

> dull imperfect translations of the noblest authors. The translation of Livy that we are reading together in a family way, is absolutely the most absurd thing I ever met with. The greatest sentiments clothed in the meanest words, raise in one such a mixture of admiration and laughter, that I cannot tell whether to be most pleased or angry.[24]

Giving a little sociable laugh and reconciling oneself to making do with what was available did not resolve the frustration. Feeling bad about herself, she looked to her friend to rescue her from those feelings by rescuing her from bad translations. Two years later, the same complaint was uttered but with more particular application to a certain clever person who knew many languages ancient and modern but who for the moment neither translated nor composed any original work:

> For our family book we are reading Dion Cassius translated from Xiphilin; it is surely a great pity we have no better translations of most of the Greek historians; we lately read one of Arrian's life of Alexander, which was full of faults, and yet with all that disadvantage an admirable book, but few clever people will deign to employ themselves in making translations, and if they would favour the world with making originals one would never complain of them.[25]

In 1747 she was reading Pliny's *Letters* in translation and this time commending the public spirit of good translators, though it was still the case that the 'common herd of translators are mere murderers'. How were those without the benefits of a classical education, women like herself and Mrs Talbot who formed part of the domestic group for family readings, to share in the knowledge and improvement diffused from such texts if those who were capable of rendering them accurately and guiding readers through them with appropriate critical commentaries would not 'deign' to do so?

Catherine Talbot suffered from a profound ambivalence about writing as an aspect of her own commitment to self-improvement. Sometimes she argued that her full days spent managing servants, attending to the poor, feeding chickens, being 'in cheerful company', taking 'airings' and admiring the landscape were both satisfying and worthy. At other times, she strove to order her time in a systematic way with literary ends in view, knowing, what her friend made no secret of, that it grieved others to see 'Miss Talbot with such talents, and such virtues, worn down by so many little teazing affections, to objects which seem so far below the powers of her mind'. In fact, as well as being a writer, she was a gifted artist, though this rarely featured in the correspondence with Elizabeth Carter.

As a friend of Lady Hertford, Catherine Talbot spent long weeks with her at her ancestral home of Percy Lodge. The Somersets had a tradition of literary patronage, the Countess having been from childhood the close friend and correspondent of Elizabeth Rowe. At Percy Lodge was the famous 'Green Book'. This contained manuscripts, letters, poems and other materials relating to Elizabeth Rowe. Elizabeth Carter was anxious for these writings to be properly edited and published. She urged Catherine Talbot to take up the project. Talbot wrote an essay on Matthew Prior, also a poet patronised by the Somersets, instead. Like many women who lamented their own unproductiveness, she in fact produced a respectable amount of publishable work as well as a huge number of letters. Her edifying *Reflections on the Seven Days of the Week*, which Carter saw into the press after her death, went into many editions and sold in vast numbers.[26]

By the late 1740s, Elizabeth Carter had resolved on a way of life that more or less met her varied desires. It incorporated writing and teaching, scholarship and criticism, and satisfied her sense of duty to family, friends and self. It was also sufficiently challenging. And it allowed her to remain in Deal for as much of the year as she chose. She undertook two projects: she became the home educator of her young half-brothers and sisters, and she launched into the major task of translating from the Greek all the works of Epictetus, the Stoic philosopher whose writings appealed so much to her and to Catherine Talbot, who had urged her on. Together, these projects structured her life for the best part of a decade.

They functioned as a pragmatic answer to the twofold pressures on her as an unmarried scholarly celebrity: the pressure to marry and the pressure to produce a work of literature. Though she was not a mother, she had, as she explained, 'four as fine children as need be desired'; and though they were not, indeed, 'fed with my own plumb pudding, because I have not any to give them ... as far as they have any appetite for the slender diet of learning, all I have in the world is much at their service'. Her responsibilities left her 'scarcely ever a minute's leisure' as she had now and then to remind Catherine Talbot. Fending off criticism that she ought to make herself more available to her friends, she represented herself as embedded in teaching and translating and sewing shirts. Even so, the pleasures of a self-directed, bohemian sort of existence were liable to burst through:

> My children keep me in pretty constant employ till three o'clock, and this fine weather we usually form some party for the afternoon. You cannot imagine what odd, good-humoured sociable kind of things these parties of ours are, which give us a very complete enjoyment of this charming country, as most of us are good walkers ... We generally drink tea in some village or at a lone farm-house, and

by this method of rambling discover a thousand beauties which would be unobserved in a more regular scheme.[27]

Furthermore, if 'want of time' was her excuse for not writing letters – 'between my pupils, my gossiping, and Epictetus, I have scarcely ever a minute's leisure ... I am just setting out on a walk of three miles to dinner, and Harry is bawling all manner of hard words in my ears' – it is noticeable that the beginning of Epictetus and the teaching of her young siblings coincided with her reappearance in print. Though living in Deal, she kept up with literary developments in the metropolis and, even if she didn't undertake work for Edward Cave, she maintained her connections. Talbot was a friend of Samuel Richardson, as was a new friend and correspondent of Carter's, Hester Mulso (later to be better known by her married name of Mrs Chapone). Meanwhile, Samuel Johnson had launched his periodical the *Rambler* in 1750. There was much interest amongst these women in this publication, Catherine Talbot, especially, identifying it as an opportunity for moral writings of her own. She wanted to see Johnson lighten it up by writing about manners as well as morals, and by accepting contributions from others; and she wanted Elizabeth Carter, as his old and respected friend, to tell him so:

> I wish most violently you was in town, for I have set my whole heart upon the success of the *Rambler* ... and you could talk more persuasively to the author than anybody. Mr Cave complains of him not admitting correspondents ... But why then does he not write now and then on the living manners of the times? – The stage, – the follies and fashions. I had a long battle with him t'other night.[28]

She must have had some success for she contributed *Rambler* 30, which was an allegorical account of Sunday as a charming young woman; Elizabeth Carter contributed *Rambler* 44 and *Rambler* 100. The only other 'correspondent' admitted was Hester Mulso.

Talbot urged Carter to contribute 'a cheerful paper' to the *Rambler*, knowing that cheerfulness was a part of her philosophy. In this, though loyal throughout her life to her old friend and colleague, Johnson, Carter was in fact very different to him. She did not share Johnson's pessimism. She did not conceive of human life as Johnson did in his 'Vanity of Human Wishes', where he asks,

> Must helpless man in ignorance sedate
> Roll darkling down the torrent of his fate?

She had none of his terror of solitude, his bleak failures to find human consolation, his desperation and panic whenever he was without the support of company. When Johnson read Epictetus he picked out a sadistic maxim to approve: 'a man should accustom himself often to think of what is most shocking and terrible, that by such reflections he may be preserved from too ardent wishes for seeming good, and from too much dejection in real evil'. But Elizabeth Carter took a much more detached and critical perspective, feeding her reading of Epictetus with observation and psychological understanding. She commented: 'I am inclined to think that real misfortunes when they do come to pass, are not rendered at all the lighter from people having tormented themselves beforehand, and damped every cheerful enjoyment of present blessings by looking forward to their loss.'

That a pious Christian woman, obedient to the injunction to enjoy God's blessings and rest content with whatever Providence decreed, should be drawn to a pagan thinker whose philosophy was, at the very least, objectionable to Christianity is interesting. His appeal evidently lay in his emphasis on reason and a pragmatic self-discipline. Epictetus taught that the route to happiness lay in self-government, not as self-denial but as a means of controlling one's response to circumstances, fitting desires to likely outcomes. By 'happiness' the Stoics meant something more like 'flourishing': how to be the best that one could possibly be. One way was to cultivate an indifference to the sorts of rewards which brought 'false' happiness – wealth, status, pleasures. The wise and the good placed their own 'governing faculty' at the centre of existence, and at the heart of that was the faculty of choice: 'elevated, free, unrestrained, unhindered'. The passions, defined as disappointment of desires and the incurring of aversions, were the problem: 'It is this which introduces perturbations, tumults, misfortunes and calamities: this is the spring of sorrow, lamentation and envy: this renders us ... incapable of hearing reason.' According to this philosophy, reason enabled and passion disabled. The point of Stoicism was not to put up with limitations or merely learn how best to bear the unbearable, but to extend the full range of possibilities through a balanced relationship of inner and outer founded in emotional detachment. Stoicism recognised the self and subjectivity as worthy of close attention. It placed self at the centre, as one of Carter's notes acknowledged:

> One cannot help observing ... the selfishness of the Stoic doctrine; which, as it all along forbids pity and compassion, will have even a king to look upon the welfare of his people ... as matters quite foreign and indifferent to him.[29]

There was no translation in English of the complete works of Epictetus, although there were Latin and French translations and English translations of some of the books. His philosophy had attracted earlier feminist thinkers: Mary Astell and Mary, Lady Chudleigh were drawn to Stoicism, and Lady

Mary Wortley Montagu had spent the summer of 1710 translating some of Epictetus. Elizabeth Carter, we should note, did not set out to make a small contribution: her ambition, which she fulfilled, was to produce an English version of *All the Works*, properly annotated and introduced, a complete, critical edition which would serve scholars for generations afterwards. (Hers was still the standard English version at the beginning of the twentieth century.) She was able to borrow books from Bishop Secker and James 'Hermes' Harris, a well-known classical scholar who could also answer queries. The task demanded all her tenacity and self-discipline. Often she felt she was doing it badly, producing 'a strange, wooden, blundering translation'. It occupied her from early in 1749 until 1758. As she completed sections, she sent them to Talbot and Secker for their comments. They discussed the style, debated awkward passages, disputed the doctrines. Bishop Secker passed on to other learned men any queries he could not himself answer, thus drawing in a wider intellectual community. Firm views developed about how the translation should be presented to the public and what kind of guidance readers needed to be given.

The crux of the matter is that Elizabeth Carter had chosen to translate an awkward text for Christians. Women were encouraged towards Stoicism in so far as its doctrines supported approved notions of female behaviour: self-government, resignation and submission to some kind of divine will. In that respect it resembled Christianity – but a Christianity without Jesus and the Gospels, 'a mere moral system'. Catherine Talbot worried about the impact Epictetus might have on Christian belief since,

> 'tis so much the way of the world to reduce Christianity to a mere moral system … discoverable by mere reason and natural light, that I could not help earnestly wishing to have persons continually reminded in reading his excellent morals, how insufficient and imperfect *mere* morality is.[30]

She wanted an introduction and notes which 'continually' engaged Christianity and Stoicism, a text conceived within a critical frame which incorporated a debate between translator and philosopher. The translation had ideological work to do: it had to argue against contemporary deists, the 'false Enlighteners' of the mid eighteenth century who would 'reduce Christianity to a mere moral system' such as that of the late Stoics. This very resemblance made an interventionist approach vital. Both Catherine Talbot and Bishop Secker had confidence that Elizabeth Carter could guide her readers safely through these waters to the conviction they all shared: that Epictetus was a wise and good man devoted to truth but that his system was full of 'errors and defects', founded on 'dangerous notions'. The Epictetus could not, then, be mindlessly consumed; it had to be thought about. It displayed the translator's rhetorical and critical skills and it required a critical response since it was a defence and critique of the culture which spawned it. A classical text, it carried social and political implications for the world of eighteenth-century England. Catherine Talbot and the bishops pointed out the awkward truth that her cultural production involved Elizabeth Carter in political responsibilities.

The publication of *All the Works of Epictetus* proved that Catherine Talbot's fears for her friend were groundless: Elizabeth Carter was not destined to live and die in obscure poverty like Catherine Cockburn. With her excellent connections and professional determination, she had no difficulty in building up a healthy list of subscribers. After paying all expenses, she was left with a clear profit of a thousand pounds. Epictetus confirmed her reputation as a scholar and spread her name into the highest reaches of the land: 'the famous Miss Carter' became a topic of conversation amongst lettered aristocracy and scholarly clergy, and in the universities.

One immediate effect of this fame was Carter's friendship with Elizabeth Montagu, a friendship which was to be at the heart of the bluestocking movement over the next decades. Montagu, the more senior in rank, made the first approach. She had none of Talbot's guilty uncertainty about how far she should exert herself as a patron; she knew she had much to offer. In the 1750s she was cultivating friendships with men of letters and becoming aware of areas of discontent in her own life. She had grown up amongst a large family of clever and happily disputatious brothers – with one sister, the novelist Sarah Scott – in which smart repartee and the ability to sustain an argument against opposition were valued. She excelled in both. Married to a man of retiring disposition much older than herself whose passion was mathematics, with no children after the death of her baby son, Punch, Elizabeth Montagu was restlessly aware that many of her faculties were unused. She was a hungry reader, especially of drama, Sophocles and Shakespeare being her favourites. Once, fully dressed to go out to a ball, she sat down and read through Sophocles's *Ajax* and *Philoctetes* and then wrote a long critical letter on the two dramas, with the result that she missed the ball and went to bed at dawn. Her writing table was set up under the shade of the elms at her country house, Sandleford, in Berkshire, and this was where she spent many happy hours. But she also liked the bustle and variety of town life. A day after arriving at Hill Street in 1754, she put on her 'great hoop' and, 'in my town character, I made fifteen visits last night'. Unlike Elizabeth Carter she was not a great walker but she was, she declared, a great *stander* in rooms full of talkers.

By 1757, the woman who had been nicknamed Fidget was in her late thirties and sadly bemused by what seemed a mysteriously pointless existence. She wrote to her eccentric but learned friend Dr Monsey,

> Having spent the first part of my life in female vanities, the rest in domestic employments, I seem as if I had been measuring ribbons in a milliner's or counting pennyworths of figs and weighing sugar candy in a grocer's shop all my life ... If you envy me, or know anyone who does, pray tell them this sad truth. Nothing can be more sad. Nothing can be more true.[31]

Elizabeth Carter's Epictetus gave hope that a female life could be spent on weightier matters than ribbons, figs and candy. At the time Montagu made her approach to Carter, she was in fact involved in discussions with Lord Lyttelton about his book, *Dialogues of the Dead* (a title drawn from Lucian but which also paid homage to Elizabeth Rowe's popular *Friendship in Death: or Letters from the Dead to the Living*) and was on the verge of contributing to it and thus going into print for the first time. Carter's identity as a professional writer and her immersion in the classics made her a valuable resource. She had, Montagu told her, 'all the keys that unlock the treasures of antiquity'. Montagu knew Latin but not Greek. To Carter she could admit to being 'an ignorant animal talking continually of Sophocles and Euripides, who never spoke to me but by an interpreter' while at the same time telling her, 'You give me ardour for my work when you encourage me'. A thoughtful and reflective reader, Montagu was very far from being 'an ignorant animal' in general. But Carter, having been in the public realm of print, was 'an author in form'. She was a powerful ally to be enlisted against Montagu's ambivalence about taking on such a role for herself. As for Carter, the completion of Epictetus established her in such a way that she probably felt equal to the delicate negotiation of friendship with a woman of Montagu's wealth and power, although a struggle between the obligations of a patronage relationship and the charms of 'darling independence' loomed large.

Awareness and anxiety about this issue can first be heard in the exchange of letters between the two women concerning Elizabeth Carter's trip to London in the winter of 1759. There was a question to be settled about where she should be accommodated. Montagu wanted her as a guest at her sumptuous house in Hill Street. Carter, apologising for being 'delicate' and 'whimsical', explained it as one of her 'follies' that she was unable to enjoy London 'unless I am in a lodging'. A lodging of her own was necessary to her comfort, for it provided the one comfort she needed to be assured of above all others: the comfort of freedom. She explained: 'my spirit of liberty is strangely untractable and wild; I must have something like a home; somewhere to rest an aching head without giving anybody any trouble; and some hours more absolutely at my own disposal than can be had in any other situation'.[32]

Elizabeth Montagu knew better than to counter such strong insistence. Eager to show herself worthy of the attentions of a scholar, and aware that differences of rank could be awkward (but not in the least inclined towards any democratic dismissal of rank), she was all agreement. She insisted that what Carter called faults in herself were really virtues, 'particularly when you accuse your self of a wild and untractable love of liberty, because you want a place where you can enjoy some hours every day uninterrupted. This is my own turn, and I thought it an excellence, a perfection and almost a virtue ...' Furthermore, aware that her own life was lived at a pace unlike that of her rural correspondent, she added dutifully that 'repose and reflection' were necessary to health and virtue, and she would be unhappy to think 'a mind like Miss Carter's, which must reckon meditation and reflection among its duties, was continually whirled about in the silly busy world'. (Montagu's 'silly busy world' was the world of commerce and high politics.) She offered to find her some rooms, 'a neat lodging on reasonable terms', near enough to Hill Street for them to dine together. And she would also provide for the other requirement, Miss Carter's desire for solitude:

> When you choose to dine at home which must often be more convenient to you, I send you a boiled chicken in the heated element in which it was dressed, or a roast rabbit with a cover on the dish and an envelope of napkins on that and thus we get rid of the trouble of a kitchen, hiring a stranger for the time or having the trouble of bringing one up. I never use a coach in the afternoon, in the morning I could carry you wherever you please, in the evening you carry the coach wherever you please ... I shall not allow you to use the vulgar phrase 'trouble you for a coach' take 'such a favour' words which unkind reserve may use to a suspected or unmeaning offer. You and I will know very well where the obligation will lie, if you know in how superior a light I see you, you will be assured that I should not have asked you to receive a favour – tho I ask you to do one.[33]

Such generous hospitality verged on the overcontrolling. Carter declined the arrangement outlined here, not comfortable with the idea of kitchen staff running back and forth along the streets of Mayfair carrying platters of cooked meat. She thanked her friend but assured her:

> When I am once settled, I shall shift extremely well; the thought of your being perplexed every day to think of a dinner for me, frightens me out of my wits. Besides, whenever I dine by myself, I revel in cake and tea, a kind of independent luxury in which one needs very little apparatus, and no attendants; and is mightily consistent with loitering over a book.[34]

Inequality of wealth and social position was to be balanced by mutual intellectual respect and need. Nevertheless, the relationship between the two did take the form – in the first few years – of patron and client, manifested in Elizabeth Montagu's encouragement of her new friend's published poetry. Carter had published no poetry since the volume brought out by Edward Cave in 1737 but she had gone on writing. Mrs Montagu now urged her to revise the original volume, add new material, and bring it out under her own protection and patronage. These were new ventures for Montagu whose career as a patron of literature (a sizeable library could be assembled simply from the books that Mrs Montagu subscribed to) and friendships with Johnson, Garrick, Laurence Sterne and others date from this period. Carter evidently welcomed this degree of patronage for she was soon busily revising and transcribing. The autumn of 1761 was entirely taken up by the activity. In correspondence between the two, it was represented as something done under the guidance of the more wordly Montagu. Carter deferred to her, though of the two she was the experienced and published writer. She wrote:

> Do you think what I have enclosed will do for the dedication? Do you rather choose I should put my name to it? Pray tell me about this, and everything else that you think necessary; and be so good, not to forget to furnish me with a title, about which I am utterly at a loss.[35]

Whatever modest disclaimers might accompany this performance of amateurism (which possibly had its origins in the desire to conform to some notion of the aristocratic style of being literary), the work was not unwillingly undertaken. In these years, Elizabeth Carter's poetic self was revived by Montagu. She wrote to her of her 'odd disposition' which she explained arose 'from the struggle of a philosophical head, against the fooleries and idle refinements of too sensible a heart'. Head and heart were warring entities, depicted in one of her poems as a cantankerous married couple. The separation of head and heart, those 'opposite principles', when brought together in one person was seen as producing 'fermentation'. Was this bad or good? Carter didn't know, but she allowed herself to feel it and enjoyed writing about it, knowing that Montagu could understand and share in the mixed feelings. Lost in 'idle reveries', she depicted herself as a 'peevish, fretful child ... crying to the moon' wanting what was out of her reach. She was either unable or unwilling to voice what those desires might be. Insisting she was not in love, she acknowledged that her feelings and behaviour could be interpreted as if she was. But hers was a poetical mood: 'My disposition requires some poetical shade, some soft twilight sky, the faint whisper of dying breezes, and the murmur of a sleepy stream.' Knowing what it required, the 'fooleries' of the 'too sensible heart' were allowed some play. She wrote to Montagu from Newbury, on her way to Bristol in the spring of 1759:

> I longed for you extremely the other night at Reading, to ramble by moonlight amongst the ruins of an old abbey ... consider how few people one would choose for companions in such a scene ... There are many very good sort of folks whom one may tolerate, and even be mighty well pleased with in broad sunshine, who would be quite insufferable by moonlight.[36]

Being insufferable by moonlight was to be unpoetical. Elizabeth Carter found in Elizabeth Montagu a poetical heart that few others seem to have been aware of. Or perhaps she was simply able to expose her own 'poetical' heart more freely than she had done before. Their friendship, for her, was filled with 'the gentle emotions of poetical and intellectual pleasure'. To some extent she played the poet – rural, natural – against Montagu's woman of society, forever in crowds. She felt that her place in Montagu's life belonged more to country than town, believing the other was more disposed to think of her 'while you are sitting among the flowers of the field, than when you are shining in a circle'. Partly this was because of her own shyness and preference for intimacies – the exchange of 'delicate sensibilities of the heart'. What she most enjoyed were their times together *à deux*, without ceremony, either at Sandleford or in the dressing-room at Hill Street where Montagu would give her her whole attention, 'talking from your heart, talking only to me, and talking that language of partial affection, which you have taught me to expect to hear'.[37]

Elizabeth Carter was captivated by Elizabeth Montagu. She used the language of the heart with some insistence, almost as a deliberate counter to Montagu's valuing of her as a fellow intellectual. It is not that Carter resisted this definition so much as that she seemed to want something else, something more from Montagu. It is likely that Carter had become familiar with her own responses in this regard, for her friendships with women were deep and lasting. As with Montagu, they invariably combined head and heart, or, as she tended to characterise these divisions, philosophy and feeling. Philosophy was meant to control feeling, as head was meant to rule heart. But increasingly she noted that it failed: 'I certainly cannot pretend to much philosophy, in cases where I happen to feel.' One such case was the planned removal from Deal to Wingham of one of her 'most intimate friends', Bethia Palmer, in 1761. Bethia's house, three miles from Deal, frequently formed the termination of Carter's long country walks,

> where, after the quiet exercise of many a solitary mile, I was always sure to find my thoughts enlivened by a peculiar spirit of joy ... with her, I have past some of my gayest and most pleasing hours. She kindly admitted me to a share in all

her social entertainments, as well as her more quiet amusements. With her I used to gather the first violets of spring, and the roses of summer, and we together enjoyed all the various beauties of the varying year. And now, perhaps this sweet abode, which makes a point of view to most of my walks, and which I have so long known perfumed by the fragrance of every flower, enlivened by music, and endeared by many a tender remembrance, will soon probably be overgrown with nettles, silent, solitary, and a mere picture of ruin, or perhaps fall into the possession of some roaring squire, or notable fat gentlewoman, insensible to all its beauties, who will tear up the roses and myrtles, that she may the more plentifully stuff her servants with potatoes, and increase her stock of dried marigolds and sage.[38]

Potatoes and marigolds and sage signalled the demise of poetry and love, of the 'peculiar spirit of joy' which this intimate friendship gave rise to. The image of the bustling, heterosexual, fat gentlewoman feeding her servants is less welcome to Carter than the vision of romantic ruin; it represents a more fearsome ravage of the 'sweet abode' and all its tender associations. Carter defended her feelings about Bethia's move: 'my head is not like the head of wise folks, or fine folks, nor their heart like mine. My quiet unimportant life, is so little engaged in the passions and interests, the business or the pleasures which employ the bustling people of this world, that I am left at full leisure to feel every affectionate weakness, and every tender regret.' The self-negating description allows no insight into what those feelings might actually be. This was perhaps not a conscious strategy but it was deliberate.

Montagu claimed to be relieved to discover on closer acquaintance with the translator of the Stoics that 'your heart does not talk the Greek of Epictetus'. Instead of preaching Stoicism, Elizabeth Carter took it upon herself to teach her aristocratic friend how to conduct an intimate and feeling friendship of the sort she herself had with the daughters of lawyers and clergymen in and around Deal. At the same time, the element of courtier and patron, the tension inherent in different class mores and assumptions, is present in the combination of worshipful distance and intimacy. In 1764, after they had spent the summer together, Carter wrote that she wanted Montagu to miss her, to wish she were not absent. Montagu protested that such a wish was cruel, for it was a wish for the other to feel the pain of absence. Carter insisted: regret and the pleasure of anticipation were two sides of the same coin. Without regret there would be no succeeding pleasure. And furthermore an intimate relationship had to include all the deepest feelings, those that were painful as well as those that were pleasurable. She wrote back:

I was quite scandalized ... at your saying, in your letter, that you would not 'communicate your gloom to me'; this seems a kind of denying my right and title to share in all the genuine feelings of your heart; a right which you have given me, and which I will never quietly resign. Your powers of entertainment, and your counterfeit spirits, are extremely at the service of the rest of the world.[39]

The 'rest of the world' featured extensively in Elizabeth Montagu's life. Carter's attempt to ground their intimacy in the personal and private was always in competition with Montagu's public activity, be it her munificent hospitality, her management of her collieries, the improvements to her several properties, or her glittering social life. Taken to Europe for the waters at Spa in 1762, in a party which included Lord Bath and Edward Montagu (there were twenty-seven people altogether, plus 'horses innumerable' for the three coaches-and-six and 'a regiment of servants on horseback'), Elizabeth Carter had difficulty keeping up with the pace. The trip left a residue of guilty feelings. Physically, she was not up to it. The amount of socialising the others took for granted, their enjoyment of crowds and public affairs, did not suit her. The familiar pattern of headaches and withdrawal asserted itself, probably reflecting a loss of control over her own time and movements. Possibly, also, it reflected the strains of too much of the wrong kind of intimacy: wishing for it in a letter was one thing, long coach journeys another. In apologising for her sense of failure, Carter explained that those closest to her, such as her step-mother and all her close women friends, understood and made allowances for her 'ways'. What she meant remains opaque. Perhaps desire and self-denial were in conflict. It is likely, in any case, that the trip exposed some of the uncomfortable ambiguities about autonomy and subordination in a relationship which combined patronage and friendship; and made it harder to ignore the way intimacy was also a construct inside the frame of patronage, part of the service given in return for favours granted.

This, as will be seen, was a dynamic that other women writers found themselves negotiating with greater or lesser success. Submission was marketable; and self-denial could be intrinsic to the selling of the self. The favours Mrs Montagu had it in her power to grant were considerable. Elizabeth Carter's management of the relationship, viewed in the light of other examples, stands out as strikingly successful.

3

Charlotte Lennox

Johnson told Boswell that he considered Charlotte Lennox 'superior' to the women writers he had dined with at Eva Garrick's on 14 May 1784. When he made the remark, which he apparently repeated on a visit to William Bowles – 'Of Miss Hannah More, Miss Burney and Mrs Lennox he spoke with great regard but seemed to prefer Mrs Lennox' – the verdict of his own times was against him.

At the height of her career, during the 1750s when she was most closely involved professionally with Johnson, Charlotte Lennox was a popular, successful writer, gaining critical applause as well as a wide readership. *The Female Quixote* was 'much in fashion' in the year or so after its publication in 1752. It went into a second edition within three months and was translated into German in 1754 and French in 1773. Many readers, including Catherine Talbot, were diverted by the amusing adventures of its heroine, the quixotic Arabella, who insists on living and understanding life according to the laws of the old romances in which she has been steeped – in other words, according to what she has read and imagined in the solitude of her engagement with books, not according to modern social experience. Miss Talbot wrote to Miss Carter from St Paul's Deanery:

> I have begun reading a book which promises some laughing amusement, *The Female Quixote*; the few chapters I read to my mother last night while we were undressing were whimsical enough and not at all low.[1]

The preoccupation with 'low' or 'high' is typical of these early days in the history of the novel when novel-reading was still a novelty. Catherine Talbot's uneasiness is evident; she was not quite sure what sort of book she was reading nor what sort of writer she was keeping company with. The allusion to Cervantes in the title was probably reassuring since everybody knew what kind of book *The Adventures of Don Quixote* was. Henry Fielding published a review of *The Female Quixote* in his *Covent Garden Journal* recommending it as:

> a most extraordinary and most excellent Performance. It is indeed a Work of true Humour, and cannot fail of giving a rational, as well as very pleasing Amusement to a sensible Reader, who will at once be instructed and very highly diverted.

Samuel Richardson, rather missing the point of the satire in finding the heroine 'amiable and innocent', nevertheless told his correspondent, Lady Bradshaigh, 'the writer has genius'.[2]

A couple of generations later, another writer of genius, Jane Austen, enjoyed *The Female Quixote* so much that she read it several times and was inspired to base her early novel, *Northanger Abbey*, on a similar idea. *Northanger Abbey* ridicules the Gothic horror that was in vogue in the 1790s in such novels as Ann Radcliffe's *Mysteries of Udolpho*, just as Charlotte Lennox ridiculed the popular fiction of *her* time in the 1740s. Returning to Jane Austen after reading *The Female Quixote* is to become aware of a pervasive similarity in sensibility and tone between the two authors. It is easy to imagine Jane Austen laughing as she read Charlotte Lennox, and taking courage for her own ruthless vision from the intelligence and wit of her predecessor.

Not much is known about Charlotte Lennox's early life except that she grew up in America, in New York and Albany, and came to England sometime in the 1740s. Her father was an army officer who she claimed was Governor, or Lieutenant-Governor, of New York. He was in fact a lowly captain of a foot regiment, but the inflation of her background is characteristic. It appears that Charlotte Ramsay, as she then was, was sent to England at about the age of fifteen, although her date of birth is uncertain, being variously put at 1720, 1727 or 1729. (The later dates seem more plausible.) She evidently was not without powerful connections. She was sent to live with a wealthy aunt in Essex who was either insane or who died or both; for whatever reason, she was unable to provide for her young relation. Through an introduction of some sort, the unprotected girl was taken up by several women of rank attached to the Court, especially Lady Isabella Finch who was first lady of the bedchamber to the royal princesses and a woman of literary interests, well known for being the only lady at Court with her own private library.

Charlotte Ramsay was already a keen and ambitious writer. Her poetry was encouraged by these 'great ladies' who perhaps were excited at having discovered a genius. Under their protection, in the structural relationship of patronage, Charlotte Ramsay had a home and a social position that afforded access to the highest social circles in the land. Lady Isabella Finch's closeness to the King and Queen made her a figure of some importance. In Bath in 1746, Caroline Fox dutifully visited Lady Isabella and left her card 'according to the form here', not because she wanted to but because she was told it was necessary 'for those who went to court'. Charlotte Ramsay may well have been among the entourage in Bath at that time, mingling in the assemblies, observing high life with relish, and sharpening her wit on some of the 'curious collection' of men Lady Isabella had at her card table, which included, according to Caroline Fox, 'a highwayman and a tape merchant'.

If among these exotics there was a genius from the New World, young, beautiful and inspired, Caroline Fox does not say. But to be taken up by Lady Isabella was by any reckoning an auspicious start to a literary career. The girl from nowhere had the run of a decent library – the evidence suggests she read French romances by the yard. She had access to high-class gossip and opportunities to observe aristocratic circles that were the contemporary equivalents of those dramatised in such scandalous popular novels as *The New Atalantis* by Delariviere Manley. Court circles were hot-houses of intrigue. There was endless vying for position. Secrecy and subterfuge, along with pomp and circumstance (and sex, wealth and power), produced a richly layered tapestry; and where much could be performed, much could be observed and imagined. The translation from provincial 1730s North America, where as an imaginative child Charlotte Ramsay had fed her fantasies on romances of high life, to the actual glittering world of England's royal circles was itself the stuff of romance – especially when we include abandonment by a wealthy lunatic aunt. Charlotte Ramsay pitched herself high and aristocratic circles welcomed her in. Far from being 'low', her literary beginnings were a great deal higher than any of the writing women to whom Johnson was later to compare her.

Her first publication, a volume of poems which appeared in 1747, *Poems on Several Occasions: Written by a Young Lady*, was dedicated to Lady Isabella in acknowledgement of 'the obligations you have conferr'd on me ... Your Ladyship's early favour and indulgence, as it was sufficient to satisfy the most boundless vanity, gives you the strongest claim to my perpetual gratitude'. The dedication was signed Charlotte Ramsay, although by the time the book appeared she had married Alexander Lennox.

This marriage at first sight seems to have been a 'low' connection: Lennox was employed in some capacity by William Strahan, the printer. He, however, claimed descent from the Scottish aristocratic family of Lennox. It is more likely that he had a romantic tale about himself exactly suited to catch Charlotte Ramsay's imagination. (We might compare this with Richard Savage's tale about *his* aristocratic birth which worked on Johnson's sympathies to powerful effect; his claim to be the illegitimate son of Lady Macclesfield and Earl Rivers was endorsed in Johnson's *Life of Savage*.) The following year, still using the name Ramsay for professional purposes, she cropped up amongst a group of new actresses performing a play at Richmond. Horace Walpole was in the audience and saw her there: 'a Miss Charlotte Ramsay, a poetess, and a deplorable actress'.

It is not known if she had left the protection and patronage of Lady Isabella Finch. Possibly she was struggling to survive and earn a living as an actress. She was certainly writing and had probably met Johnson, mixing as she did in theatrical circles and in the company of writers and printers. Whatever claims to 'perpetual gratitude' Lady Isabella's favour and indulgence might have deserved, one thing was soon clear: perpetual gratitude was not Charlotte Lennox's forte. Throughout her life she either bit the hand that fed her or contemptuously disdained to eat the crumbs. A satirical bent and a sharp tongue, combined with an aggressive energy and spirited sense of personal entitlement, made it almost inevitable that she would use her writing to revenge personal slights; and in a relationship of patronage, opportunities for feeling slighted were not few. In *Harriot Stuart*, her first novel, published three years after *Poems on Several Occasions*, the eponymous heroine is taken up by a female patron and duped into thinking that her fortune is to be made. Charlotte Lennox tells a story of disillusion from the point of view of the young writer and at the same time puts patronage under scrutiny. With an apparent disregard for caution or future support, her critical analysis focuses on the patron, whose motives are identified as self-interest and self-aggrandisement. There is little attempt at fictional disguise. Lady Mary Wortley Montagu, 'indolently perusing' the novel without any great enthusiasm for it, declared herself, 'roused into great surprise and indignation by the monstrous abuse of one of the very few women I have a real value for'. The character of Lady Cecilia was 'clearly meant', in her opinion, for Lady Isabella Finch. Lady Cecilia is represented as despicably making promises to her gifted protégée which she does not fulfil. Lady Cecilia, we are told, had a 'peculiar talent, in procuring dependents, by her affected benevolence, whom she never designed to serve, and raising hopes she never intended to gratify'.

Mary Wortley Montagu was a seasoned observer of the literary scene (albeit, by then, from her chosen exile in Italy. *Harriot Stuart* had been sent in a box of books selected for her by her daughter). Spites and betrayals did not shock her, but this portrayal did. She saw Lady Isabella Finch as the latest aristocratic victim of the patronage system. Authors were flexing their muscles and hitting back:

> I did not think she had an enemy upon earth; I now see 'tis impossible to avoid them, especially in her situation. It is one of the misfortunes of a supposed court interest ... even the people you have obliged hate you, if they do not think you have served to the utmost of a power that they fancy you are possessed of; which it may be is only imaginary.[3]

We can guess at the powers the young colonial poet, actress and novelist imagined Lady Isabella Finch might be possessed of and the life she dreamt of for herself. Mary Wortley Montagu's response is also interesting in another way, for she generalised from this particular to a universal truth: 'people you have obliged hate you'. Conferring benefits produced uncomfortable social relations. This dimension of the patronage relationship was not one that many moralists, patrons or writers wished to acknowledge. To admit the hate – and publish it in a form the world could read – was liable to be considered 'low'. (Love was a problem, too, of course: the range of emotional expressivity available to those in the middle range narrowed and tightened over the course of the eighteenth century.)

There is much in *Harriot Stuart* which corresponds with other sources to help build a picture of the young author. The novel was received by its contemporaries as being largely autobiographical, perhaps because it was an early fictional portrait of a woman by a woman novelist, perhaps because Harriot is presented as a literary prodigy, brilliant and beautiful, which is certainly the role Charlotte Lennox elected to play in these early years of her career. Mary Wortley Montagu was not impressed by a heroine who 'being intended for an example of wit and virtue, is a jilt and a fool in every page'. But Harriot is a compelling personality: fierce, sprightly, self-willed and clever, she displays a passionate obstinacy and a stubborn pride and self-assertiveness. Like Fielding's Tom Jones and Sophia Western in *Tom Jones*, she is offered to the reader as a character whose appeal lies in her sincerity and enthusiasm. An innocent who is at the same time a natural coquette – 'I was born a coquette, and what would have been art in others, in me was pure nature' – full of simple beliefs in self, individuality and love, she has to learn about the world. She has to go through misfortunes; but, unlike the heroine of Richardson's *Clarissa*, Harriot Stuart's author does not force her to internalise lessons of submission to men. Instead, Harriot is allowed to be what she thinks herself, both rebellious and sexily equal: 'I had confidence enough in my wit, to believe it would defend me against all the impertinence of gallantry, without being obliged to suppress the natural sprightliness of my disposition.' She is, after all 'a miracle. So much wit, such a depth of thought, in one so young!' as the rakish lover, Belmein, tells her.

The story of Harriot's life, related to her friend, Amanda, takes the reader on a breathless chase across land and sea, by coach and carriage and ship, in high society and low, in danger and in peace, through kidnaps and escapes, near-ravishments and passionate defences of honour. Amatory interest in Harriot Stuart is the driving force of the narrative throughout. On ship to England, enjoying the attention of so many men, displaying her social confidence and irresistible charms, Harriot is trapped in a cabin by the captain who attempts to rape her. In self-defence, she stabs him. The crew are outraged: 'What, our captain murdered by a girl, for such a paltry trifle as a rape ...! Hang law, and a court of justice, as she talks of; deliver her up to us ... let us punish her our own way.' Faced with the prospect of gang rape and death, Harriot gives up faith in her powers of persuasion and climbs to a window to jump into the sea. In a narrative full of 'surprising escape from so many dangers', it is no surprise that she escapes; nor, considering the nature of the genre, that she is unsubdued. She is a romance heroine with much to say for herself, not only about law and courts of justice, but also about the world of men and women, life and love, reality and fantasy. If she is full of 'wild and romantic notions and behaviour' both she and her author know this, for Harriot is endowed with considerable psychological penetration.

Like the heroines in the amatory fictions of Delariviere Manley and Eliza Haywood, Harriot's 'coquetry', her sex talk and behaviour, is the most fully realised aspect of her character. It is aligned with her 'vanity', a quality often referred to but rarely criticised; indeed, it appears to be part of her strength. Self-love and a recognition of her own merits are the basis of a self-confidence which allows her, when she is made anxious or feels neglected, to be 'fully determined to express some resentment'. Mistress of those 'little perplexing arts' which give women power over men, she is further aware of the pleasures of sadism: 'were power in my hands, I should take an infinite delight in the abuse of it; and, knowing my own temper so well, I am very glad I have never found an object to exercise my severity upon'. The idea of cruelty in a mistress towards her lover appeals: 'How I could like to sport with the honest sincerity of his heart! Make him feel fear and hope, joy and grief, in such a swift vicissitude ...' She admits to being 'full of that ill-natur'd pleasure which the consciousness of being able to give pain inspired.' And when her companion, Mrs Blandon, protests at these 'ill-natur'd principles', she justifies them with a standard feminist defence:

> But sure, madam, returned I, you cannot blame me, if, filled with resentment for the injuries many of my sex have received from men, I embrace any opportunity that is offered me, to revenge their wrongs, and retaliate the pain they have given!

Meanwhile, Harriot's opinion of women as a sex is no less 'ill-natur'd'. She invites her friend Amanda to agree: 'Is there anything more frail than female friendships? A conformity of temper, an equal attachment to some darling foible first cements them; a trifle, as invaluable, dissolves the brittle tie.' Some of the most vivid dialogue in the novel is between Harriot and her mother, a relationship from which Harriot can derive no comfort since her mother views her with a contemptuous scorn: 'These horrid romances, interrupted my mother, has turned the girl's brain. The heroines of these books are always disobedient and I suppose she intends to copy their example.' Relentlessly criticised at home, Harriot looks to other women, especially those who have power and high status, for her progress in the world. But she takes with her a scornfulness learned from her mother and the expectation (justifying the scorn) that she will be let down by them.

Harriot writes poems which she is careful to leave lying about where they will be discovered and admired. Having an 'exalted understanding' she welcomes admiration for her writing, though she also accepts it for her person: 'it was never a part of my character to be offended with any homage that was paid to my charms'. She drily recognises that 'homage' from men is wrested from their more habitual self-love and she enjoys the triumph: 'I contemplated with pleasure the effects of my power on a heart, which before had been only filled with the inchanting emotions of self-admiration.' Such willingness to reveal both psychological acumen and combativeness is a foretaste of the more sustained satire Charlotte Lennox achieves in *The Female Quixote*, where the 'inchanting emotions of self admiration' – in a woman – are taken (in burlesque mode) to their logical illogical extreme; and dramatised to hilarious effect with all the pleasurable self-knowledge and imaginative commitment of a woman who had been there.

Charlotte Lennox thought highly of herself. In projecting an ambitious and self-admiring identity as a writer, she had a number of strong traditions to draw from. On the one hand, there were the French romances of such writers as Mme de Scudery; and on the other, there was the racy, sexy English example set by post-Restoration women like Aphra Behn and Delariviere Manley. There were fictional voices of adventuring women like Moll Flanders, and the self-told lives of fiction writers like Madame d'Aulnoy and, again, Delariviere Manley. The popular 'little biographies of the bedchamber', histories of 'desire and voluptuousness', and scandalous memoirs full of love, romance and swashbuckling 'defence of dubious virtue' tended to be written by women. Eliza Haywood was the leading exponent of the genre in England by the time Charlotte Lennox began writing and *Harriot Stuart* owes a good deal to her example.[4]

Charlotte Lennox's *Poems on Several Occasions*, and a later poem, 'The Art of Coquetry', published in the *Gentleman's Magazine*, made the connections with the school of Aphra Behn abundantly clear, especially in the linking of wit with beauty in a sex-war rhetoric.[5] But it is also clear in the mocking, ironic treatment of the idea of woman-as-writer. Writing, like wit and beauty, is another way of getting on in the world, bringing together what

Pope maintained were the two ruling passions in the female breast, 'The love of pleasure, and the love of sway'. The woman who is acknowledged as a poet combines these powers. Harriot Stuart's 'little poetical productions' brought her applause, while 'my youth and sex stamped a kind of unquestionable merit on my writings, and procured me the addresses of all the wits; an incident that did not fail to increase my vanity'. Similarly, there is a poem in *Poems on Several Occasions*, 'To Aurelia, on her Attempting to Write Verses', which ends with an image that presages the mock-coronation at the Devil Tavern, and suggests that the idea for that celebration may not have originated from Johnson so much as from Lennox herself. The poem describes Aurelia, 'Ambitious of a Poet's name' who 'wept' 'sighed' and 'long'd for Fame' and finally asks Apollo to give her the 'sacred Fire'. Apollo indulgently passes the message on to Clio who

> obeys the God's commands
> With Joy, and swift as Thought descends,
> And at Aurelia's side attends.

Aided by the joyful Clio, Aurelia writes marvellous verses, which please Apollo so much that Aurelia becomes his favourite, displacing Daphne:

> Daphne, his once-lov'd charming Care
> Appear'd to him not half so fair:
> For the lost Nymph he mourns no more;
> Nor in his Songs her Loss deplore;
> But from the slighted Tree he tears
> Its Leaves, to deck Aurelia's Hairs.
> A Poet now by all she's own'd,
> And with immortal Honour crown'd.

The wish-fulfilment here – she gets the laurel crown, she gets the man and she upstages Daphne – is of a very knowing, sprightly kind, using the available conventions to display an unapologetic triumphalism. As another poem, 'In Answer to Consolatory Verses Wrote by a Friend', puts it, success is the objective because success is the only thing that is rated in this world:

> With Ease Advice to virtuous Woe we give,
> But ah! How few by Stoick Rules can live?
> Virtue distrest in melting Verse appears;
> Beauteous in Misery, and adorn'd in Tears.
> But in the World 'tis view'd with other Eyes ...
> Whatever Gifts we may to Nature owe,
> Success is all our Merit here below.
> By Fortune favour'd Fools may rise to Fame;
> Without it Virtue is an empty Name.

There is literature and there is life; there are books and there is the world. To be 'distrest' in literature – 'in melting Verse' – is one thing, but in life it is quite another, especially when by 'distrest' we understand not sorrow or sadness but starvation and cold. 'Stoick rules' are hard for most people to live by for many reasons; but the cultivation of indifference towards rewards like wealth and material comfort, for those who are already comfortably placed, with a reasonable confidence that food, warmth and shelter will always be provided, can be a luxury. Power and 'merit' come with wealth; the sentimental idea of virtue in rags has no purchase. As Charlotte Lennox was to put it more bluntly ten years later in her novel *Henrietta*: 'the world seldom espouses the part of the oppressed, because they who oppress have that on their side which is sure to exculpate them, and that is riches'.

Elizabeth Carter, one of the few making some attempt to live by Stoic rules, read 'The Art of Coquetry', which appeared in the November issue of the *Gentleman's Magazine* in 1750, in company with some of her young friends, all of whom were apparently 'much scandalized'. She told Catherine Talbot, 'The poetry is uncommonly correct, but the doctrine indeed by no means to be admired. It is intolerably provoking to see people who really appear to have a genius, apply it to such idle unprofitable purposes.'[6] The idle and unprofitable purpose of 'The Art of Coquetry' being, as the title indicates, to teach the skills of catching and keeping a man, it was hardly a poem designed to please Elizabeth Carter. The poem depicts a world inhabited by men and women locked in a struggle for pre-eminence. Men are tyrants to be subdued; women are divided between those who know their sexual powers – who 'justly set a value' on their charms – and those who don't and who, by implication, therefore deserve their servitude. The poem addresses itself to the first category of women, to those who

> o'er mankind would fain exert your sway,
> And teach the lordly tyrant to obey.

Love is the woman's way to power, and sexuality is her chief weapon. Love is a contest between tyrants and beauties; it is about resisting attack or subduing an attacker; it is about having and using weapons. 'The Art of Coquetry' undertakes to instruct women in the proper use of the weapon of beauty to achieve power, teaching them artfulness, and how to suit strategy to the nature of their individual charms. In the war of love different strategies suit different types: behaviour that would work well for a 'haughty nymph' would not work so well for one who was by nature 'languid'. At the same time, 'studious care' must be taken in judging how to treat particular men. Towards a jealous lover it is best to appear natural:

> To these an open free behaviour wear
> Avoid disguise, and seem at least sincere.

Not all women will manage to be successful coquettes. The 'tender', 'yielding' sort, those who show their feelings and display their willingness to be subdued, will not succeed; and there is a suggestion that they hardly deserve to. The crown of coquetry goes to:

> the nymph who liberty can prize,
> And vindicate the triumph of her eyes:
> Who o'er mankind a haughty rule maintains,
> Whose wit can manage what her beauty gains;
> Such by these arts their empire may improve,
> And unsubdu'd control the world by love.

One can almost see Elizabeth Carter's lip curling. There is a long tradition behind these lines, but the philosophy it serves is in direct contradiction to the philosophy of female manners adopted by the early bluestockings. 'Liberty' in the minds of these women did not consist in catching a man. Power was not defined by sexual conquest. Such poems, by an intelligent woman, were seen as regressive, a return to the bad old days of sexual manipulation. The coquette's performance of femininity, the playing of the masquerade, reinforced a sexual difference — and sexuality — they were anxious to underplay.

It was a bold move for a serious woman in 1750 to pronounce as Charlotte Lennox did on the arts of coquetry, and probably not a wise one. Minds, not bodies, were in the ascendant, and to view mind and body as separate entities — the one to be nourished and cultivated, the other to be managed as best as possible — was a commonplace of rational thinking. In Elizabeth Carter's comic poem, 'A Dialogue', she sets up a conversation between Mind and Body. Body and Mind can never agree on a comfortable way of living together and instead lead

> a most wrangling strange sort of a life
> As great plagues to each other as husband and wife.

Like husbands and wives, Mind and Body exist inside a hierarchical system: Body grumbles about being at once ignored and overrun, while Mind, turned to the outer world of 'weighty affairs', is cool and superior. Body blames Mind for bringing in,

> a disorderly Crew
> Of vagabond Rogues, who have nothing to do

> But to run in and out, hurry scurry, and keep
> Such a horrible Uproar, I can't get to sleep.

Sleepless, hungry, cold and neglected, Body has had enough. But the poem is not on the side of Body, whose sufferings get no sympathy:

> Poor *Mind*, who heard all with extreme Moderation,
> Thought it now Time to speak, and make her Allegation.
> 'Tis I, that, methinks, have most Cause to complain,
> Who am crampt and confin'd like a Slave in a Chain,
> I did but step out, on some weighty Affairs,
> To visit, last Night, my good Friends in the Stars,
> When, before I was got half as high as the Moon,
> You dispatch'd *Pain* and *Languor* to hurry me down ...

Body has no respect for the flight of the mind. Body is the source of all earthly troubles which 'Poor *Mind*' seeks to escape. There is a vengeful glee in the assertion at the end of the poem that Body will die and decompose into dust but Mind will live forever, free at last of its enslavement:

> I've a Friend, answers Mind, who, tho' slow, is yet sure,
> And will rid me, at last, of your insolent Power:
> Will knock down your Mud Walls, the whole Fabric demolish,
> And at once your strong Holds and my Slav'ry abolish:
> And while in the Dust your dull Ruins decay,
> I shall snap off my Chains, and fly freely away.[7]

A myth of spiritualised intellectuality, in which increases in knowledge were synonymous with advances in virtue, underpinned the new fashion for female learning. Such a myth offered new freedoms to men as well as women. Sociability between men and women could be conducted as an elevated mingling of minds not bodies. Johnson, in an early *Rambler* essay, expressed the view that 'virtue is the highest proof of understanding'. This also worked with the terms reversed: understanding was the highest proof of virtue; vice 'the natural consequence of narrow thoughts'. Men might share with women their greater understanding, women might add polish to men's uncouth ways.

In this myth, body had no place except as an encumbrance. Elizabeth Carter beat her body into submission by means of 'violent' long walks and cold wet towels. (Body repaid her with vicious headaches.) Elizabeth Montagu starved her body, lived in a 'constant hurry', was highly strung and inclined to accidents such as spilling 'a great quantity of *eau de luce*' into her eyes and mouth during a fainting fit. Montagu also had nervous panics such as that which seized her whilst walking in the woods near Spa with Elizabeth Carter – they had to walk themselves out of breath, to get within view of the town; and she suffered from chronic stomach ailments for which she drank the waters at Tunbridge Wells and Spa. That other bluestocking hostess, Mrs Vesey, meanwhile, was nicknamed 'the Sylph' in celebration of the fact that 'there seemed no particle of *matter* to have entered into her composition'.

Stout and hearty Elizabeth Carter was undeniably made of matter. But her presentation of self was elaborated around strict denial of 'female' concerns with bodily appearance. She wrote, 'I cannot indeed give any positive testimony how I look; for, though I very narrowly inspect my face every day, it is just as I should a saucer, which I was wiping, merely to see if it was clean, without any animadversion on the colours or the pattern'. Nor would she ever consider ornamenting her person at the expense of her mind. Sent a fan by Catherine Talbot, she proudly displayed it for her aunt who was duly astonished that her niece should have 'such a creditable thing belonging to me, for she knows I should sooner fan myself with a cabbage leaf than lay out any sum of money, in ornaments, that would buy a book'.[8]

The dread of female 'vanity' lay behind some of this, and coquetry was considered as a species of vanity. That it was also a means to power was a source of anxiety, an ever-present knowledge to be kept at bay. Elizabeth Carter's insistent representation of her body as an object as void of desirous intention as a blank flat saucer speaks volumes. She took an extreme position through these perplexities. Blanking out her body and refusing its 'insolent Power' was a way of denying female difference located in sex. Since it was commonly agreed that mind had no sex, mind's flight from body was a flight to equal terms with men. This was a perilous desire in itself, but equal terms with men might take women further: to power *over* men, a power that had been traditionally defined in terms of coquetry and which therefore returned women to the logic of sexual difference.

Fear of the underlying structure, with its unholy circularity of coquetry-vanity-power, runs like a stifled conversation in some of the texts available to us. Amongst the bluestockings, it peeps out in indirect ways. It was not addressed directly. We find it nudged and nibbled at, accidentally bumped into, or encountered in appalled recognition and hastily run from. The sparkling talkers and letter-writers of mid eighteenth-century sociable circles felt its pressure, however, and in ways that we can sometimes locate. Fiction, and discussion about fiction, is an obvious source. In 1750 Johnson identified a change that had taken place in fiction. What he called 'familiar histories' had become popular. These were stories which represented 'life in its true state, diversified only by accidents that daily happen in the world, and influenced by passions and qualities which are really to be found in con-versing with mankind'. Unlike earlier fictions, which were contrived by invention and imagination and could be written in solitude, these fictions depended on 'acquaintance with life', their authors were 'copiers of human manners', fed by the thoughts and experiences of living people:

> The task of our present writers ... requires, together with that learning which is to be gained from books, that experience which can never be attained by solitary diligence, but must arise from general converse and accurate observation of the living world ... They are engaged in portraits of which everyone knows the original, and can detect any deviation from exactness of resemblance.[9]

Without a doubt, the most important writer of 'familiar histories' was Samuel Richardson. As can be seen in the titles of his first two novels, the portraits he was engaged in writing were portraits of women: *Pamela: or Virtue Rewarded*, which appeared in 1740–41, followed by *Clarissa: or The History of a Young Lady* in 1748–49. It is impossible to overestimate the importance of these novels in the thinking and imaginative lives of readers in the mid eighteenth century. Richardson cared passionately about 'exactness of resemblance', to ensure which he drew round him a circle of reading and writing women whose opinions he solicited. His house at Fulham, North End, was a meeting place for literary discussion. It had a grotto and other appurtenances of literary living, and the many admiring young ladies who flocked there were known as 'honorary daughters' or 'songbirds'. Meanwhile, he maintained a huge correspondence, much of it directly related to his writings.

In *Pamela* and *Clarissa* Samuel Richardson took as his heroines well-behaved young women, women of virtue, and he put the sexual dimension of their lives centre stage. Bodice-ripping popular romances, such as Eliza Haywood's *Love in Excess*, which were the inspiration for Charlotte Lennox's *Harriot Stuart*, had always put sex and the female body at the centre. But their characters were not characters in whom virtuous female readers openly sought to find themselves. Whatever pleasures respectable readers found in such texts could not be explained as the pleasures of virtuous learning; the books could not overtly serve, in Johnson's words, as 'lectures of conduct, and introductions into life', however much they might actually serve that purpose. The books were read, guiltily or brazenly, for sexual excitement. Samuel Richardson, on the other hand, offered characters with whom thoughtful respectable women *could* identify (and find each other in: Elizabeth Montagu believed Samuel Richardson must have known Elizabeth Carter as a girl, since 'there is such a resemblance of character between you and Clarissa'). More than that, he invited those very women in actual life to help him make his characters up. Drawn into a discussion with the male novelist, feeding him information and ideas, writing letters, commenting on the texts he produced and modelling their own conversational and behavioural practices on the examples within the novels, the women in Samuel Richardson's friendship circle endorsed his rewriting of amatory fiction. That the virtues rewarded in *Pamela: or Virtue Rewarded* and *Clarissa: or The History of a Young Lady* tended to be suffering and resignation rather than energy and resourcefulness was perhaps the unspoken price paid for privileges granted. Richardson's *Clarissa,* as Johnson put it, 'taught the passions to move at the command of virtue'.

As a friend and welcome visitor at his home at North End, Catherine Talbot was one of a number of women who involved themselves in the debates about *Clarissa* and the issues raised about ideal men and ideal women in the later *Sir Charles Grandison.* For Richardson, Talbot was 'the Queen of all the Ladies I venerate'. She performed the heroic task of correcting the manuscript of *Sir Charles Grandison.* This involved many meetings with Richardson and much reading and criticising of the manu-script as it progressed. It was labour she enjoyed: 'Never did I spend in town so agreeable a winter as this has been.' Richardson's interactive working methods were not unique to him; in some ways they were characteristic of the period (something we should bear in mind when considering Charlotte Lennox's collaborative projects). From his women friends especially, he invited an engagement with his characters and their moral dilemmas as he staged them. The development of Richardson's novels involved a move-ment back and forth from fiction to real life, between speech and writing, between living selves and imagined selves. It produced eddies of talk and an ocean of epistolary exchanges. This method of production is replicated in the epistolary form of all his novels; the finished text in each case is an orchestration of voices. Serving as a mirror in which women could view themselves and their society, these books affirmed the seriousness *to* society of girls and women. They also affirmed the seriousness of the decisions women made about their lives.

In this capacity, the novels became a convenient channel for the exchange of thoughts that could feel dangerous. Heroines, especially, functioned as alter egos. Harriet Byron, for example, in *Sir Charles Grandison,* became for many intellectual women an emblematic individual. Catherine Talbot found herself in disagreement with her friends over Harriet Byron since everybody, she told Elizabeth Carter,

> that has read but a little way in the book, accuses Harriet of vanity. Is it vanity to repeat out of frank-heartedness, praises that she despises? Is it vanity for a woman of sense and principles to think herself superior to men foolish and profligate, and not to accept with a low curtesy the first that does her the honour to offer himself? And why such an outcry at the number of her lovers? Is there

a housemaid, be she ever so homely, that might not, if she would, talk to her Lucy of half a dozen sweethearts?

So far so good, few would quarrel with these orthodox observations. But they led Catherine Talbot to express what for her were rather wicked thoughts:

> Yet, between you and me, is there not a spice of this sort of vanity in every female heart of us all? And why? Because it is instilled into us from the very nursery, where we are told to *hold up our heads for there is money bid for us;* and partly, to own a mortifying truth, few girls can become of any consideration in the world, but from the proper regard paid to them by some one *of the conde-scending Lords of the creation* ... But do now write me an essay upon this sort of vanity, and its too frequent consequence coquetry. Not the art of coquetry like Mrs Lenox, but an edifying essay proper to be put into the hands of Misses.[10]

Differences of opinion about a fictional character had dangerously factual implications: 'few girls can become of any consideration in the world' except by gaining the attention of a man. It is the marriage market she means, and wealth and power that she is thinking about. But the 'proper regard' of an appropriately placed male who was *not* a potential husband and who did not therefore raise the spectre of coquetry-vanity-power – for example, Samuel Richardson and Samuel Johnson – could also lead a girl to some 'consideration in the world'.

Elizabeth Carter was appealed to as a philosophical friend who could 'settle' a conundrum by the power of her thought. She was also asked to sweep away Miss Talbot's reluctant recognition that both the psychic and the social are partly constructs: vanity was 'instilled' in little girls because there was a price on their heads and they had to cultivate behaviour that would help to sell them. Coquetry was one of those behaviours, a product of the circumstance women found themselves in. To practise it as an 'art' was wrong. Even to speculate on its relation to vanity was not quite right – there is a hesitation in that 'Yet, between you and me ...' However, to bring the matter out into the public arena in the form of an 'edifying essay' with a target audience of 'Misses' *was* acceptable. The shift is from literature (Harriet Byron) to life ('It is instilled into us from the very nursery') and back to literature (the didactic essay). It is also a shift from reading to writing. On a larger scale, this is a shift we can trace in the careers of many eighteenth-century women writers, often helped along by gaining the 'proper regard' of a well-placed man.

Catherine Talbot's earnest and slightly nervous reflections represent one end of the spectrum and Charlotte Lennox's 'The Art of Coquetry', the other in these strangely mixed, publicly private matters. The pressure of the fear of being accused of vanity is so pervasive that its presence is often best understood by absence of reference to it, as for example in the wide-spread agreement that the ideal woman was 'sensible and unaffected' – key words which carried a heavy ideological weight. Elizabeth Carter, for example, valued her sensible, unaffected women friends in and around Deal, none of whom were celebrated, and whose acquaintanceship was therefore nothing to boast about. Her choice of 'sensible' 'unaffected' friends played against her own known celebrity. It was analogous to, as well as part of, the choice for country obscurity against town glare. As a woman whose experience of celebrity had begun in her teens, she had had unusual opportunities to learn its complexities and she knew it for troublesome ground. Projecting a self through the printed word was an activity which brought consequences, just as holding one's head up because there was money bid brought consequences. Social practices concerning women aligned these activities – selling themselves in print, and selling themselves at a public assembly – in ways that social practices concerning men did not. Catherine Talbot's fear was a complicated one. A good woman should seek to be what good people in society wanted her to be: obedient and submissive. But what if, as a direct consequence of seeking to please, she became what society said it didn't want her to be: vain and coquettish? And what if she discovered in the process pleasures and excitements she was not supposed to enjoy? Coquetry could take place between men and women in forms not designed for sexual ends. The excitements of self-expression and self-discovery broke through Catherine Talbot's writing when she was involved with Richardson. Being invited by him to help revise *Sir Charles Grandison* was an honour and a thrill which aroused desire; not sexual desire for Richardson or to be sexually desired by him, but desire to speak truths about women's lives – her own in particular.

Catherine Talbot declared it a 'mortifying truth' that 'few girls can become of any consideration in the world, but from the proper regard paid to them by some one of the condescending lords of creation'. One mortification was the recognition of competition, and its consequence: the development of the arts of coquetry by those who were determined to get on. Another is the truth implied rather than stated: the desire to become of some consideration in the world. This was the unspeakable knowledge shared between thoughtful women for whom the problem of how to live their own lives, where to find satisfaction, was not resolved. Like Elizabeth Carter, Catherine Talbot knew very well that there existed more than a few girls who wanted to become of some consideration in the world. How should these girls go about it? How could they do it without vain display? What kind of consideration might the world pay them once they ceased looking to some chosen man for 'proper regard'? What would a 'proper regard' be if it was not founded in a sexual choice? Men, the 'lords of creation', might be condescending in person or otherwise, but the power they had to make or break women's lives was a matter of huge significance – significant in each individual woman's life, but also philosophically significant. Behind Catherine Talbot's apparently casual, 'Do now write me an edifying essay …' lay a deeply pondered wish: that women like Elizabeth Carter who *had* achieved 'consideration in the world' through other arts than coquetry and from other impulses than vanity should open the matter up and offer guidance.

Externalising and projecting the problem onto others was an obvious resource. It goes some way to explaining the attraction of didactic writing for clever women. The 'Misses' Miss Talbot evoked for Miss Carter's edifying essay were the same 'Misses' to whom Charlotte Lennox's poem, 'The Art Of Coquetry', was addressed. As a theme, coquetry served the purposes of female agency in both 'proper' and 'improper' form. So, in a similar way, could other questions about female behaviour that were given prominence in Samuel Richardson's novels. One young woman very keen to be of some consideration in the world was Hester Mulso. Under her married name of Mrs Chapone (and with the support of Elizabeth Montagu), she was to become the celebrated author of the sort of 'edifying essay' Catherine Talbot asked Elizabeth Carter to write, directed at exactly those same 'Misses' – represented in her case by a real-life niece who was the addressee of the text. *Letters on the Improvement of the Mind* did not appear until 1773, when it was much admired as a work of education and went into many editions. In 1750 the unmarried Hester Mulso was just twenty-three and, like Catherine Talbot, a favourite of Samuel Richardson. She was his 'little spitfire'. In other words, she argued with him, holding her own in an exchange of dialogue in exactly the way that Richardson's characters are shown to do in his novels.

Born into a family of lawyers and clerics lacking money, Hester Mulso had her way to make. Intellectually confident, encouraged by admiring brothers, her ambition to live a writer's life formed early. The friendship with Richardson was an event worthy of record; her brother John told a friend, 'My sister and the family are got into the acquaintance of Richardson the author of *Pamela* and *Clarissa*, in which they take great delight.' (John also reported on Hester's new friendship with Elizabeth Carter.) She did all the things a bright young woman wanting to draw attention to her talents would do: she wrote impressive letters to people capable of appreciating them; she circulated striking poems; she talked brilliantly in the social circle, displaying both knowledge and critical acumen; and she engaged in the debates about *Clarissa* in a way that served her own purposes.

Hester Mulso placed her own experience, her own thinking and knowledge, firmly on the agenda. In 1750 she wrote Samuel Richardson three long letters that took the form of critical essays on issues arising from *Clarissa*, particularly the question of Clarissa's obedience to her parents. Challenging essays, they pulled rank on Richardson by requiring him to respond to arguments that derived from a source of knowledge not available to him except by imagination and hearsay: a young girl's knowledge. These essays were framed as letters in much the same way that the letters in *Clarissa* or *Sir Charles Grandison* were letters: they evoked a recipient for dramatic purposes, but the true audience was the unlimited audience of the reading public. They were public statements not private communications. They were strategic interventions into an ongoing debate that she was well-equipped to participate in, and which allowed her to display her abilities. In her *Letters on Filial Obedience* (the title they were given when published) Richardson was brought into the writing as a character; while *his* characters – Clarissa, her parents, Anna Howe – took their places alongside half-anonymous but nevertheless real people Hester Mulso had known in her life. The real people Mulso introduced had faced problems which mirrored those that Richardson dramatised in his fictions. They were the Miss B——s, Miss W., Miss ——. Their lived experiences, known to Hester Mulso, served in her letters as counter images and counter arguments to the fictions of Richardson. But since Richardson's fictions incorporated exactly such living examples, provided for him by friends like Mulso, and themselves took shape in epistolary form, the letters of Hester Mulso both challenged and at the same time paid *Clarissa* the homage of imitation. They aligned themselves with the novel and the novelist. They functioned as an extension or elaboration. They sought to share the ground.

Hester Mulso made use of a number of fictions of her own in the *Letters on Filial Obedience*. This is most apparent in her self-presentation. Her determination to speak her mind she represented, coyly, as a desire to learn what Richardson had to teach her. Her desire to write letters of 'immoderate length' was represented as his desire to hear what she had to say. She was careful to explain that he had requested she should put down in writing her 'sentiments on the subject we touched on at North-End, of filial duty and parental authority'. These were very important themes in his novels and therefore her views were useful material to him, part of the research base by which his work was sustained. She declared herself grateful to him for 'taking the trouble to read what I scribble' when she knew very well that the one thing Richardson demanded of his friendship circle was continuous talk about his novels. And her thoughtful, carefully polished pieces, which displayed critical and rhetorical abilities of an exceptionally high order, deploying authorities like John Locke and attacking figures like Bishop Hall, 'who would reduce me to the condition of an Indian skreen, and allow my father to item me amongst his goods and chattels, and put me up for sale for the highest bidder', were described as 'the rude essays of an ignorant girl'.

Hester Mulso's girlishness was a kind of flattery which worked as the reward Richardson earned by having put the gift of so many girls into circulation for the reading community. The voice she adopted was an echo of Pamela's voice, full of well-articulated emotions, self-consciously understood and laid bare for public consumption. Combined with her reiterated 'regard' for him and his writings (which will bring her *his* 'proper regard' for *her* writings), the *Letters on Filial Obedience* can be seen as a form of intellectual coquetry. Elizabeth Carter, who understood the laws of these exchanges, did not choose her words carelessly when, abandoning her own fledgling correspondence with Richardson, she accused him of being a coquette.

In taking up the question of Clarissa's obedience to parental authority, which Richardson presented in his novel as an absolute, Hester Mulso argued that in giving Clarissa no moral agency in her own life Richardson made her guilty as well as miserable – guilty before God. This appeal to a higher authority was linked to rational thinking. Clarissa was supposed to be a woman of good understanding who could reason well, but on the subject of parental authority she was 'so fettered by prejudice that she does not allow her reason to examine how far her conduct is to be justified or blamed; but implicitly joins with her father to condemn herself, when neither reason nor religion condemn her'. Reason and religion were lined up against parental – meaning paternal – authority. Quoting Locke on natural rights and freedom, Hester Mulso related his arguments to women, having herself read and thought as a woman. Locke, she wrote, said reason and discretion made a man free, and 'the same shall make his son free too'. She then added in parentheses:

> (And if his son, I presume his daughter too; since the duty of a child is equally imposed on both, and since the natural liberty Mr Locke speaks of arising from reason, it can never be proved that women have not a right to it, unless it can be proved that they are not capable of knowing the law they are under.) [11]

The epistolary mode of Richardson's own novels – in this case, three dated letters incorporating some of his responses – and the conversational practices and pieties of his circle, out of which he built his novels, were the grounds from which Hester Mulso insisted on the real effects of the moral position his fiction adopted. In her text she brought forward a community of young women, real women living real lives. If, she asked, women must be in a state of subjection and must stay under the authority of parents whilst unmarried, what did Richardson have to say about particular young women whose lives she knew about at first-hand who were ill-treated by their parents? She instanced: the 'Miss B—s, whose mother used frequently to strike them down on the floor, and then trample on them'. In the household of the Miss B—s the 'maid servants have fainted away at the sight of the cruelties [the mother] exercised on her grown-up daughters'. What would Richardson's advice be to another friend, 'Miss W', whose father would not feed or clothe her? Or 'Miss —', Hester Mulso's intimate friend, who 'never knew one happy hour from the unheard-of cruelties of her father and mother'? She had been left some money by a friend who died; would not any reasonable person agree that she should be allowed to go and live in lodgings apart from her parents and independent of them? These were not rare occurrences, Mulso insisted, and nobody could be ignorant that such things went on: 'Instances of the like nature come within everyone's particular knowledge; and if I knew as much of the world as you, perhaps I should be able to produce as long and as black a catalogue of parents as you have done of children.' Her own 'particular knowledge' had taught her enough to list these casualties of the system against which the fictions of femininity (and its fiction-writers) could be arraigned.

For 'superior' women, like Clarissa, marriage itself might make her a casualty, since the doctrine of the natural superiority of men – carefully deferred to here – produced anomalies in particular cases. The husband, Hester Mulso pointed out, might be a 'mean wretch' strutting about,

> full of the sense of his new prerogatives, and puffed up almost to bursting, with the pride of having a creature every way his superior in his *power*, and bound to *obey* him. Oh Sir, you who could paint so well the *man of wisdom* tugging at the leading strings of his pretty fool, to restrain her from embracing a serpent; paint, I beseech you, the lovely, the wise, the noble, the good Clarissa, not in *leading-strings* but in *chains* ...[12]

A real Clarissa's chances of ending up in chains were not slim, especially where parents put money before happiness, making their daughters into 'Smithfield bargains, so much ready money for so much land, and my daughter flung in into the bargain!' Daughterly obedience under such circumstances could only mean entering 'very willingly into the dirty scheme of selling themselves' and being applauded for sacrificing themselves to 'a fool or a knave with a good estate'. Women, and especially superior women capable of observing the world and making reasonable deductions about it, who had wit and learning, an understanding of their moral obligations and a God who demanded they give an account of themselves, were worth more than this.

Hester Mulso complained at the way that,

> fathers and mothers, nowadays, frequently dressed out their daughters, and sent them into public places, with an appearance of five times the fortune they could give them, in hopes that they might catch – what? – Not a man of sense and worth, who should make them happier and better, but a fool, a rich fool.[13]

Perhaps it was this practice which Nicholas Carter had in mind when he advised his daughter that, if she had set her mind against marriage and was certain she did not wish to encourage suitors, she should live a more retired and less costly life. A show of expense by an unwed daughter signified a willingness to be courted. Understanding the codes has always been important; of these, rituals of courtship are perhaps the most talked about and best understood. But the complex interactions of women in public places were not confined to courtship rituals, nor were display and coquetry reserved for relations with men. The signals could sometimes be confusing. In the summer of 1757 Elizabeth Carter was busily accumulating subscriptions for *Epictetus*, and very pleased to have gained a dozen or so during her stay in Canterbury. She told Catherine Talbot that among the subscribers was:

> a very fine lady, who, after curtseying to me for several years past, with more civility than I had any title to, and with much more than fine ladies usually show to such awkward-looking folks as me, did me the honour this year to take to me mightily by way of conversation, which she introduced by subscribing in a very handsome manner to *me*, and railing very heartily at the *Stoics*. She is a very sensible and agreeable woman, and much more deeply learned than beseems a fine lady; but between the Spartan laws, the Roman politics, the philosophy of Epicurus, and the wit of St Evremond, she seems to have formed a most extraordinary system. In walking about the rooms, we were joined by one of the most celebrated beauties in the assembly, the study of whose life, as far as can be judged by appearances, has been Mrs Lenox's sort of coquetry, and there was something extremely diverting to see her listen for a considerable time with the most profound attention to a discourse which must have been for the most part as unintelligible to her as if it had been delivered in Arabic.[14]

The beauty, the fine lady and the scholar walk around the rooms engrossed in matters historical: three women, two of whom have nothing intellectual in their appearance, one of whom is judged to have nothing but vacancy in her brain. In this setting, the scholar was 'awkward-looking', while the fine lady possessed an unseemly degree of knowledge. But, by a curious twist, it is the very perfection of the fine lady's appearance, its entire suitability to the occasion, which allowed the scholar to give full vent to her appetite in such a place for such a conversation:

> To be sure I should have been mighty cautious of holding any such conversation in such a place with a professed philosopher or a scholar, but as it was with a fine fashionable well-dressed lady, whose train was longer than anybody's train, I had no manner of scruple.

As it happens, however, the 'fine fashionable well-dressed lady' seems to have been Catherine Sawbridge, later Macaulay, whose brilliant eight-volume *History of England* began appearing in 1763. She was, in other words, a scholar, though her appearance professed otherwise. Evidently *she* had no qualms about mixing the genres: speaking on intellectual matters while looking every inch the 'fine lady' whose time, it is assumed, was spent in dressing and attending to the effect (and power) of her appearance rather than the furnishing of her mind.

If the beauty at the Canterbury assembly who courted the attention of two of the leading scholars of her day read anything – and few genteel folk did not – the assumption is that she read romances. The reference to Mrs Lennox is the clue: high beauty meant low understanding, as a finely fashionable and well-dressed lady meant superficial learning. Low understanding meant intrigue and love. The 'study' of the beauty was the art of coquetry, not Spartan law or Roman politics; not the rigours of connected thought but the indulgence of sexual fantasy. Negotiating these matters was never straightforward, as Elizabeth Carter good-humouredly observed. Life threw up many contradictions. Meanings changed, or could not always be read off from appearances; values altered. Clothes were no more reliable a guide to the 'real' self than were books. As a young woman Elizabeth Carter had been 'vastly inclined to ascetic notions'. As she grew older, this philosophical asceticism gave way to a mixed view in which everyday comforts had their place, including the comforts of a drily humorous low expectation of human kind. In this respect, the novelist whose moral vision was closest to hers was Henry Fielding. His humour and broad humanity in *Tom Jones*, for example, seemed to her to offer 'the most natural representation of what passes in the world'. (Not a view Johnson shared: he was shocked to discover that Hannah More also admired Fielding.)

The young Elizabeth Carter might well have written 'edifying' essays, but the mature writer found didactic literature with its simplistic figuring of ideal types unappealing. In any case, observation of life had taught her that to do it well was not as easy as it looked: 'the fine folks of this world,' she wrote, 'are as sagacious in finding out the formidable genius of instruction, however beautifully disguised, and run away from it with as much horror as good people do from a cloven foot'.[15] Perfectly respectful of Samuel Richardson and, like everybody else, a reader of *Clarissa*, its inordinate length tested her patience. Richardson's 'prolixity' bored her and she made fun of it to a shocked Hester Mulso whose need to take Richardson at his own solemn valuation was greater than the older woman's. What she called Carter's 'unmerciful raillery' ('You say you honour Mr R. but you cannot honour his prolixity') was not the only thing that shocked Miss Mulso:

I am a little surprised that you ... should ever descend to the most tedious, as well as unedifying kind of reading in the world, I mean a romance. I make no scruple to call romances the worst of all the species of writing: unnatural representations of the passions, false sentiments, false precepts, false wit, false honour, and false modesty, with a strange heap of improbable, unnatural incidents mixed up with true history, and fastened upon some of the great names of antiquity, make up the composition of a romance; at least of such as I have read, which have been mostly French ones. Then the prolixity and poverty of the style is insupportable. I have (and yet I am still alive) drudged through *Le Grand Cyrus*, in twelve huge volumes, *Cleopatre*, in eight or ten, *Polexander*, *Ibrahim*, *Clelie*, and some others, whose names, as well as all the rest of them, I have forgotten.[16]

Romance was low because 'unnatural' and 'false'. The task of intellectual women was to lead other women out into the bracing world of truth. Romances, like clothes, were part of the system of signs. In this system, men like Richardson, aided by the women he encouraged to collaborate with him, were seen as helping to bring about something higher. *Clarissa* was fiction but it was not fiction as *Le Grand Cyrus* was fiction. It was prolix, but not so prolix as *Cléopâtre*. With her sharp critical intelligence, Hester Mulso knew which side of the argument she was on.

Catherine Talbot read romances when she felt feeble, doing so in the defensive spirit of one whose better self was capable of more. The life she shared with her mother, amongst aristocrats, bishops and other senior clergy, was socially elevated but constrained by formal demands. Elizabeth Carter saw it at close quarters when she stayed at Lambeth Palace. She observed an 'entirely uniform unvaried life, which they do not allow themselves to think unpleasant, though they feel it at every hour'. The result was languid spirits. Elizabeth Carter often scolded her friend into a less self-blaming view of herself by arguing that she owed something to the world – 'it is really intolerable of you not to let the world be somewhat better for you'. Writing was almost the only thing a genteel woman could put out into the world to make it benefit from her presence in it; but not many people would propose writing as an antidote to the unpleasant effects

of an entirely uniform, unvaried life. Such a notion was quixotic. In this
as in other generally unacknowledged ways, Elizabeth Carter and her circle
were more in tune with Charlotte Lennox than they or anybody else cared
to admit.[17]

Charlotte Lennox, the 'favourite of the author of the *Rambler*', on visiting
terms with Richardson and a great admirer of Henry Fielding, had obtained
the 'proper regard' of all these men, and in different ways their influence
can be seen in her work. The obligation did not travel only one way however.
When 'the author of the *Rambler*', not hitherto noted as a writer of fiction,
made his excursion into the genre with *Rasselas* in 1759, he took up themes
and ideas from Charlotte Lennox, particularly from *The Female Quixote*,
the novel she went on to write after the modest success of *Harriot Stuart*.

The Female Quixote (1752) could have taken its motto from quite other
sources than the writings of the distinguished male writers of the time. In
1748 Laetitia Pilkington published her *Memoirs*: racy, scandalous, full of
invective. Jonathan Swift called her 'the most profligate whore in either
Kingdom' but he also acknowledged the power of her wit. Outspoken and
disturbingly intelligent, she did not attempt to offer a version of female life
that conformed to stereotypical ideals. Hers was an extraordinary history;
that was its selling point. Wit in a woman, as Elizabeth Montagu pointed
out after reading Pilkington's *Memoirs*, was 'apt to have bad consequences;
like a sword without a scabbard it wounds the wearer and provokes assail-
ants'. Wit, in this sense, also meant anger. Pilkington claimed not to care,
declaring, 'Truly, I mean to give both pleasure and offence: Lemon and
Sugar is very pretty'. Extraordinary histories could not be easily assimilated
to ordinary life; they would inevitably offend readers since they dealt in
offence. But offence could also be pleasurable. This worldly understanding
lent a defiant aggression to the tone. Like the actress-courtesan Constantia
Phillips whose memoirs, *An Apology* (which made no apology) were also
published in 1748, Laetitia Pilkington drew on the literary examples of Aphra
Behn, Eliza Haywood and Delariviere Manley. The lives lived by these
women were both celebrated and lamented, full of adventure and injury –
or to use Constantia Phillips's phrase, 'Sorrow, Misery, and Infamy' – all
vigorously described, in locations that ranged from bedrooms to libraries
to prisons.[18]

The key word is 'adventure'. Charlotte Lennox, whose way of life placed
her with the adventuresses, possessing a wit and rage that was always liable
to harm her, took due note. Laetitia Pilkington's self-description, 'I have
been a lady of adventure, and almost every day of my life produces some
new one,' could be the motto for *The Female Quixote*. It could also serve

to describe what Prince Rasselas and the Princess Nekayah seek in quitting the 'tasteless tranquillity' and entirely uniform and unvaried life of the happy valley in Johnson's *The History of Rasselas, Prince of Abbysinia*. *Rasselas* pays homage to *The Female Quixote* and develops some of its central preoccupations.

To be 'a lady of adventure' was to be a prostitute but *The Female Quixote* is very far from being an account of such a life. It is a novel written in full awareness of the literature of the times, however, and of the difficulties Elizabeth Montagu recognised in her comments on Laetitia Pilkington. After observing that wit in women was like a sword without a scabbard, Montagu went on to express regret that:

> the generality of women who have excelled in wit have failed in chastity; perhaps it inspires too much confidence in the possessor, and raises an inclination in the men towards them without inspiring an esteem so that they are more attacked and less guarded than other women.[19]

(These reflections help account for some of Elizabeth Montagu's own caution in coming forward as a named and known author.) Less temperately, Samuel Richardson fulminated against the 'set of wretches', amongst whom he included Pilkington, Phillips, Manley, Haywood and Behn, whose writings existed to 'perpetuate their infamy'. He called on women to write books which would be 'an antidote to these women's poison!'

Charlotte Lennox, in *The Female Quixote*, did something far more interesting and very much in tune with what Elizabeth Montagu later set herself to do: to excel in wit without failing in chastity. Identifying as a novelist with Henry Fielding rather than Samuel Richardson, sharing Fielding's love of the quixotic and the absurd, Lennox rewrote Richardson's *Pamela* in ironic mode against the background of these scandalous memoirs. Her heroine is a lady of adventure who has adventures in the way that Cervantes's Don Quixote has adventures. Far from being an antidote to 'these women's poisons', her comic novel did what none of the moralising novelists of the time dared do: instead of repudiating such 'follies' as vanity and coquetry, so integral to representations of femininity, it confronted them and thought through them. It explored what it was like to inhabit such a state – which all moralists claimed was the quintessential female state – without apology and without moralising it away.

In *The Female Quixote: or The Adventures of Arabella*, Charlotte Lennox put into play a debate about the subjective foundations of knowledge. The novel explores the workings of imagination and fantasy in a female self. It asks such questions as: What knowledge goes to make up a self? What knowledge is useful in the world? What is the relation between the social world of others and the inner world of self, and how are each of these constructed? The heroine, Arabella, whose life is a series of adventures, appears not to know that her understanding of the modern social world is faulty. It is a product of her imagination, fed on a diet of those 'horrid romances' Harriot Stuart's mother disapproved of and Hester Mulso repudiated. But Arabella is no more silly or stupid than Harriot. Like her (and like Charlotte Lennox, Hester Mulso and those other readers of romances, Elizabeth Carter and Catherine Talbot) she is extraordinarily intelligent. She combines a vivid imagination with a powerful intellect. When she brings all her faculties to bear on a situation, she shapes it according to her vision. With absolute self-belief and a habit of command, hers is the dominant personality in every encounter. This force in Arabella is the key to a coherent understanding of *The Female Quixote*, for what Charlotte Lennox dramatised in this major work of fiction was the creative process itself. The dramatisation drew on female psychic and social experience and a female literary tradition to produce a text of such originality that its strengths have been largely overlooked. There is no doubt that this novel belongs with *Clarissa* and *Tom Jones* and *Roderick Random* as one of the defining texts in the development of the novel in the eighteenth century.

Arabella moves through a sequence of events resolutely determined to understand them only according to the terms of fantasy. She will not open her eyes to the realities around her; she will only believe in the truths she has learned from books, understandings fixed in her through the pleasures and excitements of reading. She will only be what she became when reading. The self she insists on putting into the world is the fantastical self formed through imaginative identifications. Arabella's inability to hear or see alternative versions, her insistence on fulfilling her imaginative needs, her resolution that life will be what she makes it, that her truth is not an arbitrary subjective truth but *the* truth, is rendered with controlled comic artistry. We laugh at Arabella but she never loses her dignity. She is funny and a source of humour, but she is not a figure of fun. This distinction is important. From some accounts of the novel it might be supposed that Arabella is presented as a foolish woman who cannot distinguish between real life and romance. But Arabella, like Don Quixote before her, is on a quest. Her mission is to reconcile inner with outer, to find a way of living and being as a woman in the world. The 'common sense' that she refuses to hear for most of the novel is not good sense. The social world was not shaped for this female self. The question Charlotte Lennox poses through Arabella's adventures in *The Female Quixote* is what kind of sense, and what kind of world, can a woman of supreme intelligence and imaginative power live comfortably in or bring into being.

As a character, Arabella is a type of the authorial self, full of inner direction and determination, committed to the truths of the imagination. *The Female Quixote* can be seen as an exploration of some of the more absurd elements of the female writer's life. Cool, ironic, humorous and self-knowing, it puts the fundamental extravagence of the role on display. The author conducts a dialogue with herself, looking to the past and the future, seeking to understand her own intellectual and imaginative formation and to establish a way forward. The result is a complex, many-layered text which lends itself to different interpretations. But it is grounded in a particular cultural moment: the beginnings of the novel and the early decades of authorship as a profession. It was written at a time when few women had adopted the mantle of authorial assurance and fewer still had presented heroines who insisted on their entitlement to shape the world according to their own notions of it. One can only observe that the combination of ridiculous seriousness and heroic grandeur in Arabella is wonderfully appropriate to the task Charlotte Lennox had set herself.

Like the standard heroines of amatory fiction, and like Johnson's hero and heroine in the later *Rasselas*, Arabella is an innocent, reared in seclusion. A blank page, she knows nothing of the world except what she has read in books of romance. The texts she refers to and according to which she forms her understandings of life are seventeenth-century French romances, such as those by Mme de Scudery, especially the ten volume *Le Grand Cyrus*, and La Calprenède's *Cléopâtre*, in twenty-three volumes. Arabella is obsessed with the stories in these books. In treating them as guides to life she reads them as if they are prescriptive literature. That is to say, she reads as mid eighteenth-century women readers were being exhorted to read, taking instruction and ordering their lives thereby; but she *mis*reads because she has applied the didactic model of reading to the 'wrong' texts. By this simple transposition, Charlotte Lennox opens up a range of comic possibilities which subvert idealising views about female knowledge and understanding in the social world. The woman reader of romances seeking to know herself discovers one overriding 'fact' about being a woman, which is: that every man is in love with her, that the transaction between men and women is exclusively about love and adoration. A woman's duty is to learn how to manage the correct forms for dealing with male adoration. Systems and protocols must be observed. Honour and dishonour are distributed according to correct performance. The language of gallantry and the language of courtesy must be properly employed. In romance codes, the rules of life for a woman are the rules of coquetry.

As a self-confessed adept in the arts of coquetry, Charlotte Lennox was well placed to pursue this logic to its extremes. She asks: what happens if you take this arrangement seriously? The logic of coquetry tells women they are at the centre of the social world, that through their sexuality women have power over men. A very small experience is enough to tell most women that this is a fiction, yet it is a fiction which endures; and with which women are fed and feed themselves. The desire for the fiction overwhelms recognition of social fact. Women's selves are formed according to it partly through desire but also because it has social sanction. What purposes, then, does it serve? Whose purposes? What is the real meaning of the fictions – social fictions, textual fictions – consumed so avidly by women and what is Charlotte Lennox, both avid consumer and writer seeking readers, to make of its significance for her?

The Female Quixote is a comic didactic novel, a satire which dramatises the collision of fantasy with newly available versions of the real. Through burlesque, Lennox is able to raise questions that draw attention to the social construction of femininity. Like Henry Fielding, she adopts an authorial voice which addresses the reader directly, thus keeping in play a self-consciousness about writer, reader and characters which demands an intellectual response. In this three way engagement, the author's collusion with the reader produces a fiction about fiction at the heart of which is the fiction of the female self. Arabella has to unlearn her dependency on romance – or artifice – in order to free her best self: the part that seeks and recognises truth. The reader, meanwhile, though offered in the subtitle, 'The Adventures of Arabella', is refused the anticipated pleasures: no voyeuristic sex, no titillation. Arabella's bodice remains unripped. In the terms of French romance, or of popular fictions like *Love in Excess,* Arabella's 'adventures' are false. In a scene where the gardener steals a carp, the reader knows that the gardener is a gardener stealing carp, not a young man of noble birth disguised as a gardener in order to be near Arabella whom he adores (which is how Arabella construes what she sees). Similarly, the reader knows that the escapes, kidnaps, mishaps and catastrophes that occur are ordained by Arabella's extravagant expectations. Should we miss any clues in the playful tone of the main text, there are helpful headnotes and footnotes to guide us.

The story Arabella is determined to enact is not the story we are allowed to consume. The very word, 'adventures', serves these comic didactic purposes. Like other words such as 'servant' or, in a different sense, 'questionless' and 'doubtless', its gendered and changed modern meanings are put under scrutiny in the text, just as the conceptual structures which the words evoke are scrutinised. To ask a modern genteel woman of the 1750s to relate her 'adventures', as Arabella is shown innocently to do, is an insult: it is a sexual slur. But the adventures of women in fiction *had* been sexual (and not only in scandalous memoirs) since the textual woman, like the social woman, was largely defined in terms of her sexuality. Meanwhile, the denial of sexuality in the real life performance of gentility was also a fiction.

As the heroine of her own imaginings, we might expect Arabella to have no patience with the petty decorums of gentility. But the analysis is deeper than that, and is directed towards the hypocrisy and intellectual vacuity imposed upon genteel women in the 'real' world – that social arena in which Arabella appears so ridiculous – through sexual codes which are also class codes. The heroic mode with its aristocratic associations acknowledged both intellectuality and sexuality, and it invested women with power. Gentility denied sexuality whilst requiring endless attention to its concealment, and it applauded women who deferred to men. In this sense the novel was not an attack on romance in favour of reality; it was an attempt to salvage strengths from older conventions, most importantly the strength of reason and the reasoning faculty for women. The character of Charlotte Glanville combines the new gentility with the old coquetry and offers a sour vision of both.

Arabella works her way towards insight and understanding. She sees where she has judged wrongly but her capacity for judgement is not at fault: the fault is false information, false premises. What she deduces on the basis of what she knows is sound. That she needs to put her judgement to work on better information about the world is one of the themes of the book, which is another way of saying that her mind matters. Original and powerful, however, hers is not a mind that is easily taught, for not many minds are the equal of hers.

Though Arabella has to learn new knowledge about the world, it is she who is in the position of instructor for most of the book. When she defers to wiser knowledge, when, like the reader, she acquires 'information absolutely necessary for the right understanding of this history', it is through the agency of a 'divine'. This figure is introduced at the end of the novel. He stands apart from the characters who have been caught up in the comic incidents and absurd misreadings that have led to the final climax in which Arabella, thinking (as usual) that she is about to be kidnapped and raped, has jumped into the Thames. The fever that ensues takes her to the edge of the grave. Recovery is both physical and mental: there is the disorder in her body to be cured and there are 'the disorders romances had occasioned in her imagination'. The divine is also a doctor, able to undertake both tasks at once, recognising the connection between mind and body. His separateness lends him an authority and his 'divinity' a godlike quality. This might justify Arabella's deference towards him, but in fact it is the doctor who defers to Arabella. They conduct a debate, during the opening stages of which the doctor has difficulty settling on the appropriate register. His respect and sympathy for Arabella lead him to fudge the issues. She has to bring him to order:

> Disingenuity, sir, said Arabella, does not become a clergyman. I think too well of your understanding, to imagine your fallacy deceives yourself: why, then, should you hope that it will deceive me? The laws of conference require, that the terms of the question and answer be the same. I ask, if I had not cause to be frighted? Why, then, am I answered, that no injury was intended? Human beings cannot penetrate intentions, nor regulate their conduct but by exterior appearances. And surely there was sufficient appearance of intended injury, and that the greatest which my sex can suffer. – Why, madam, said the doctor, should you still persist in so wild an assertion? – A coarse epithet, said Arabella, is no confutation. It rests upon you to shew, that, in giving way to my fears, even supposing them groundless, I departed from the character of a reasonable person.[20]

Far from lecturing Arabella, the 'good man' has to justify every philosophical point and every 'common sense' appeal he makes. The debate is conducted by the participants at a level of intense seriousness which occasionally serves for comic effect, as when the doctor attempts to prove that Arabella was never in danger of being immured by a ravisher in a castle, driven into the pathless desert, hidden in a cavern or abducted to an island in the middle of a lake. 'What then should have hindered him?' asks Arabella, receiving the answer: 'From all this, madam ... he is hindered by impossibility. He cannot carry you to any of these dreadful places, because there is no such castle, desert, cavern, or lake.' This is manifestly absurd since there are many castles, deserts, caverns and lakes in the world:

> You will pardon me, sir, said Arabella, if I recur to your own principles. You allow that experience may be gained by books, and certainly there is no part of knowledge in which we are obliged to trust them more than in descriptive geography. The most restless activity in the longest life can survey but a small part of the inhabitable globe: and the rest can only be known from the report of others. Universal negatives are seldom safe, and are least to be allowed when the disputes are about objects of sense; where one position cannot be inferred from another. That there is a castle, any man who has seen it may safely affirm. But you cannot, with equal reason, maintain that there is no castle, because you have not seen it.

The dispute is about 'objects of sense'. The dialogue is a parody of philosophical investigations of the time such as that of Bishop Berkeley about how far sense impressions were trustworthy sources for our understanding of the world. From philosophy the disputants pass on to history.

Arabella, having forgiven the doctor his hot-tempered dismissal of romance writers (he admits himself at fault in referring contemptuously to them as 'scribblers, not only of fictions but of senseless fictions'), challenges him to prove three things. First, that the romances from which she has drawn her information are not true histories; secondly, that they are absurd; and thirdly, that they are 'criminal'. The first proof is easy enough on the grounds of evidence: the events are supposed to have happened two thousand years ago, but none of the records on which they are based survive. Accepting that these writings are essentially fictions, Arabella willingly enters the second stage of the debate. She takes her stand on the proposition that there is 'a love of truth in the human mind, if not naturally implanted, so easily obtained from reason and experience, that I should expect it universally to prevail' and asks the question:

> what pleasure or advantage can arise from facts that never happened? What examples can be afforded by the patience of those who were never solicited? The great end of history is to shew how much human nature can endure or perform. When we hear a story in common life that raises our wonder or compassion, the first confutation stills our emotions; and however we were touched before, we then chase it from the memory with contempt as a trifle, or with indignation as an imposture. Prove therefore, that the books which I have hitherto read, as copies of life, and models of conduct, are empty fictions, and from this hour I deliver them to moths and mould; from this time forward consider their authors as wretches who cheated me of those hours I ought to have dedicated to application and improvement.

She wants him to tell her what can be said in defence of 'those tales which are told with the solemn air of historical truth', a characterisation which serves at once for the most far-fetched romances of the seventeenth century and the realistic fiction of the eighteenth.

It is no difficult task to demonstrate, by reference to ancient history and geography, that the world depicted in romances is an invented world. Nor that 'nothing is more different from a human being, than heroes or heroines'. Arabella's third question produces the severest response: romances are judged to be 'criminal' because of their tendency to inflame the passions, in particular the passions of love and revenge. At this point, when Arabella has already with great dignity conceded the argument on the two first points, each time thanking the doctor for sharing his thoughts with her (and thus enabling her own thoughts to develop), he hesitates to go on: 'I am afraid your ladyship will think me too serious.' Arabella's response to this is in her grandly elevated style: 'I have already learned too much from you, said Arabella, to presume to instruct you; yet suffer me to caution you never to dishonour your sacred office by the lowliness of apologies.'

From these heights, this is what Arabella hears about the 'criminal' nature of romances:

> These books soften the heart to love, and harden it to murder ... they teach women to exact vengeance, and men to execute it; teach women to expect not only worship, but the dreadful worship of human sacrifices. Every page of these volumes is filled with such extravagance of praise, and expressions of obedience, as one human being ought not to hear from another; or with accounts of battles, in which thousands are slaughtered, for no other purpose than to gain a smile from the haughty beauty, who sits a calm spectatress of the ruin and desolation, bloodshed and misery, incited by herself. It is impossible to read these tales without lessening part of that humility, which, by preserving in us a sense of our alliance with all human nature, keeps us awake to tenderness and sympathy, or without impairing that compassion which is implanted in us as an incentive of acts of kindness. If there be any preserved by natural softness, or early education, from learning pride and cruelty, they are yet in danger of being betrayed to the vanity of beauty, and taught the arts of intrigue. Love, madam, is, you know, the business, the sole business of ladies in romances.

It is the final stage of the debate. The argument is over. No more need be said. Arabella, blushing and suddenly tearful, abandons her former convictions. In the climactic moment she gives herself, not as a body to a man but as heart and mind to an idea. She grandly declares: 'My heart yields to the force of truth.'

In his *Rambler* essay of 1750, Johnson discussed 'The New Realistic Novel' and its relation to heroic romance in much the same terms that Charlotte Lennox depicts Arabella and the clergyman using in their debate. The present generation, Johnson argued, wanted to read about 'life in its true state'; they wanted representations of natural events, they did not want giants, ladies and knights, hermits in woods, castles or shipwrecks. Why romances – 'this wild strain of imagination' – remained popular so long in 'polite and learned ages' is, he says, a mystery. What is not a mystery is that while readers were eager to read them, writers would produce them; for compared to the demands of the new 'familiar histories' there was very little difficulty involved. With some fluency of language, and a mind heated with 'incredibilities', a book could be produced 'without fear of criticism, without the toil of study, without knowledge of nature, or acquaintance with life'.

Johnson's observations in this *Rambler* essay could be imported wholesale into the penultimate chapter of *The Female Quixote*, the chapter to which Charlotte Lennox gave the title, 'Being, in the Author's Opinion, the Best Chapter in this History', and in which she introduced a character who is unmistakable as an idealised portrait of Johnson. It has been said that Johnson wrote this chapter. There is no evidence for this.[21] The chapter stages in print and through the *dramatis personae* a conversation it is easy to imagine Charlotte Lennox and Samuel Johnson having. Just as she valued his wisdom and knowledge in life, so she took the liberty of bringing him, the wise and erudite man in her life, into her text, where his thinking could be put to work on concerns that exercised them both. Johnson was, like Lennox, an avid reader of romances. Thomas Percy, whose collection of seventeenth-century ballads and romances, the *Reliques of Ancient Poetry*, Johnson helped edit, gave the following account of his distinguished friend:

> When a boy he was immoderately fond of reading romances of chivalry, and he retained his fondness for them through life; so that ... spending part of a summer at my parsonage-house in the country, he chose for his regular reading the old Spanish romance of *Felixmarte of Hircania*, in folio, which he read quite through. Yet I have heard him attribute to these extravagant fictions that unsettled turn of mind which prevented his ever fixing in any profession.[22]

The psychic structure described here combines addiction with self-reproach. Other observers have left accounts of Johnson's intense absorption in such books, suggesting that the act of reading escapist fiction served emotional needs whilst producing a guilty backlash. Thomas Percy was very pleased to have Johnson's help with his project since it was 'a work for which he is peculiarly fitted by his great acquaintance with all our English Romances etc of which kind of reading he is uncommonly fond'.

The romances Johnson was fond of were chivalric romances, wild improbable tales of war and love, fanciful, full of wild scenery (to use the terms Johnson uses to define 'romance' in his *Dictionary*). These romances featured beauties and questing knights – and castles, deserts, lakes, caves, caverns and so on. There were woods and forests, sex and slaughter, witchcraft and magic. The quest formula in these tales was an elastic metaphor for the struggles of youth finding its way through life, overcoming perils, slaying giants, encountering seductions and obstacles, wishing, despairing and growing. It is an image of the human condition, the journey we all adventure out on. That Johnson saw it this way is clear from his writings about romance. But his imaginative identification – the 'unsettled turn of mind' he accuses romances of producing in himself – extended further. Johnson saw himself as an adventurer, or knight errant of literature, going out, in his own words, as all writers do as 'a kind of general challenger, whom every one has a right to attack; since he quits the common rank of life, steps forward beyond the lists, and offers his merit to the public judgement'.

In Johnson's writings quixotic metaphors abound. They are especially prevalent in his writings about writers, as for example William Collins who, like Johnson, like Charlotte Lennox (and, as we shall see, very much like Shakespeare as Johnson represented him in his *Preface* to the 1765 edition of *Shakespeare*) 'came to London a literary adventurer, with many projects in his head, and very little money in his pocket'. It is there in the *Life of Savage*. The writer is the quixotic archetype, his sense of self formed by reading romances and other deluding fictions. (All mental activity, all books, because mediated by imagination, could approximate to the condition of 'deluding fictions' and therefore quixotry in their relation to the social.) Johnson the biographer sought and found himself in the biographies of writers whose lives he told. The writer of the *Rambler* and the *Adventurer*, who also wrote the *Idler*, was stimulated by the tensions implicit in these terms: his unfixed life a rambling knight-errantry seeking adventure wherever it might be found, in thrall to imagination and chance, worrying himself sick that the whole affair was no more than idleness and delusion. Sharing a passion for romances, adventuring on the world as writers, Samuel Johnson and Charlotte Lennox met as equals, except that women were not supposed to have adventures. The wise countess in *The Female Quixote* has been 'adventureless'. (A good girl should have no story.) In *The Female Quixote*, chivalric conventions serve the feminine will to power. Charlotte Lennox brings the doctor and Arabella together as equals. Arabella's effortless self-assurance, even (or especially) when she is acknowledging her errors, is significant. She is not a suppliant. And when she gives up her belief in romances, it is to enter upon a larger and better life; she recovers 'the free use of all her noble powers of reason'. She represents an achieved ideal, and in so far as we can read Johnson into the doctor-figure – Mr Rambler elevated to doctoral divinity – she becomes what he aspires to. He moralises in a wishful way, unable to break the grip of pleasures that shame him; she acts and changes. She lets go of what has limited her. Whether we agree that reason is superior to romance, or the workings of the mind more commendable than those of the body, is a separate question.

Arabella's successful quest is depicted as a journey of enlightenment. She travels from a low place to a high and the reader's sympathies are enlisted on her side, that is to say, on the side of a fuller understanding of the complexities of growing up female in the eighteenth century. Charlotte Lennox knew that the 'high' place was as much a fantasy as the castles and deserts of romance. The mock heroic vision of *The Female Quixote*, the sustained satiric art evidenced throughout, does not disappear at the end. Fiction is piled upon fiction, romance story upon romance until we find ourselves reading about an actress disguised as a princess reciting the romance of her life in which she meets a prince who recites the romance of his life. The final chapters are a *tour de force,* comic and serious at once. They encapsulate the earnest and the absurd.

Some might argue that Arabella is rescued from gendered imprisonment in a lowly form of writing and lowly forms of thinking. Bound to old and outmoded ideas of women's limited capacities, she learns that more elevated opportunities exist in the modern world. It is true, as some critics have objected, that Arabella is shown as being 'cured' of her 'nonsense' so that she can become the proper bourgeois wife of her cousin Glanville, who loves her. In this view, the ending of *The Female Quixote* is a capitulation to patriarchal norms: the splendidly free Arabella is tamed and becomes subservient. The doctor is an agent of patriarchy, with no connection to the story or its themes. He comes complete. He is the representative of the system within which women are always subordinated. He speaks its authoritative language. But this was not the 'doctor' that Charlotte Lennox knew and brought into her text. That doctor, Samuel Johnson, was more troubled and bound by his enchantment to romance than Charlotte Lennox ever was. Like Jane Austen, who appreciated her so much and who also enjoyed escapist fictions, Charlotte Lennox was an intellectually ruthless artist. Observing life, she arranged her compositions.

We should consider also the treatment of the hero, Glanville. Throughout the novel, it is Glanville who is the subservient one in the sense that his role is to watch and wait, to obey Arabella's imperious orders, and to swallow copious amounts of bile and frustration in his inability to act or change her by his arguments and disagreements. He continues to love and – more importantly – admire and respect her. Finally, when she majestically changes her views after talking to someone smarter than Glanville but equal to her, she allows him to marry her. It is noticeable that no love scene between Arabella and Glanville is dramatised. This is because Arabella's marriage to Glanville is not the climax of the story and not the point of the novel. Glanville is not an intellectual. The issues that concern Arabella are matters of the intellect and judgement, not issues of love and marriage; what she thinks not what she feels. She is being rescued from 'love' as the 'sole business of ladies in romances'. Her debate with the clergyman or Johnson at the end of *The Female Quixote* is an entry into permission not a silencing.

When Johnson wrote *Rasselas* in 1759, he revisited some of the questions debated in *The Female Quixote.* Like Charlotte Lennox, he used romance conventions to elaborate a moral message for his own times. His tale is a fantasy told 'with the solemn air of historical truth' as the full title indicates: *The History of Rasselas, Prince of Abyssinia.* It is addressed to readers who have a false view of life:

Ye who listen with credulity to the whispers of fancy, and pursue with eagerness the phantoms of hope; who expect that age will perform the promises of youth, and that the deficiencies of the present day will be supplied by the morrow; attend to the history of Rasselas prince of Abyssinia.

But as history it is very false. It is a philosophical fable, making no pretence to any factual basis: 'Rasselas was the fourth son of the mighty emperor in whose dominions the Father of Waters begins his course ...' It is a satire on the folly of humankind in preferring illusion to the evidence of experience. Fancy and imagination, the love of story – 'Ye who listen with credulity to the whispers of fancy' – are represented not as sources of satisfaction but as the root causes of discontent. Miseries and misapprehensions arise from the 'hunger of imagination which preys incessantly upon life'.

Hester Mulso considered it an 'ill-contrived, unfinished, unnatural, and uninstructive tale' and she sought Elizabeth Carter's agreement with her view:

And what moral is to be drawn from the fiction upon the whole? I think the only maxim one can deduce from the story is, that human life is a scene of unmixt wretchedness, and that all states and conditions of it are equally miserable; a maxim which, if adopted, would extinguish hope, and consequently industry, make prudence ridiculous, and, in short, dispose men to lie down in sloth and despondency ... There is something too so strangely unnatural in drawing a young man and woman without any one passion or predominant inclination ...

Worse than 'unnatural', there were 'poisonous inferences' to be drawn from the 'frightful picture' Johnson offered of family life. These strong critical views, powerfully expressed, were balanced by deference strategies. In describing her letters to Richardson, she had coyly interjected, 'Does it not sound strange, my dear Miss Carter, that a girl like me should have dared to engage in a dispute with such a man? Don't you begin to despise me as an arrogant, self-conceited creature?' So now, in criticising Johnson to his loyal friend, she ostentatiously pulled herself up short: 'By this time I begin to fear you are angry with me, and consider me as a strangely presumptuous animal, thus to lift up my nothingness against the giant Johnson.' Both constructions served to highlight the strength of mind she displayed in contrast to the 'nothingness' of her girl's body. Presumptuous, she was also virtuous by virtue of the use to which she put her mind. Mulso repeatedly demonstrated Johnson's adage about *Clarissa*, ensuring that the passions – presumptuousness, grandiosity, conceit – should 'move at the command of virtue'.[23]

Johnson's pessimism was not to Hester Mulso's taste. The driving force behind her comments about *Rasselas*, however, lay in the shared ground between them. However much she objected to Johnson's depiction of 'the dismal history of private life' and the impossibility of finding happiness, she could hardly deny that his picture of the failings of parents with regard to their children was more like her own than it was like Samuel Richardson's. Whose view was correct? Whose story about life was to be trusted? Families, according to Johnson in *Rasselas*, were places of 'discord', each home 'haunted by some fury that destroys its quiet':

> An unpracticed observer expects the love of parents and children to be constant and equal; but this kindness seldom continues beyond the years of infancy: in a short time the children become rivals to their parents. Benefits are allayed by reproaches and gratitude debased by envy.
>
> Parents and children seldom act in concert; each child endeavours to appropriate the esteem or fondness of the parents, and the parents, with yet less temptation, betray each other to their children. Thus, some place their confidence in the father, and some in the mother, and by degrees the house is filled with artifices and feuds.[24]

The speaker here is the female searcher after truth in *Rasselas*, the Princess Nekayah, who has been pursuing her subject amongst ordinary folk, rather like Hester Mulso gathering up the evidence about wretched parenting for her arguments with Samuel Richardson.

Rasselas asks the question: what choice of life will bring happiness? (*The Choice of Life* was Johnson's original working title.) Prince Rasselas, having been born and grown up in 'the happy valley', shut off from the world, has never known misery and therefore never known desire. He escapes from the happy valley into the world of wider horizons, but he does not go alone, his sister goes with him: 'I am equally weary of confinement with yourself,' she tells him, 'and not less desirous of knowing what is done or suffered in the world. Permit me to fly with you from this tasteless tranquillity.' Rasselas does more than permit her; he apologises for not having taken her into his confidence earlier. There is no argument within the tale about Nekayah's equal entitlement to adventure into the world. Nekayah is a superior woman. She is accustomed to the intellectual conversation of the poet Imlac and her brother. In the houses she visits, she finds the daughters good natured but trivial, 'their thoughts narrow, their wishes low, and their merriment often artificial:

> Their pleasures ... were embittered by petty competitions and worthless emulation. They were always jealous of the beauty of each other; of a quality to which solicitude can add nothing, and from which detraction can take nothing away. Many were in love with triflers like themselves, and many fancied that they were in love when in truth they were only idle. Their affection was seldom fixed on

sense or virtue, and therefore seldom ended but in vexation. Their grief, however, like their joy, was transient; everything floated in their mind unconnected with the past or future, so that one desire easily gave way to another, as a second stone cast into the water effaces and confounds the circles of the first.
With these girls she played as with inoffensive animals ...[25]

It is a disparaging view of the generality of young women, rendered from the perspective of an exceptional woman – a woman rather like Arabella in some ways, serious and superior – who desires something better. Thus it becomes a critique. If we imagine Hester Mulso, or Elizabeth Carter, or Catherine Talbot reading these passages (as we know they did) it is not unreasonable to suppose that they identified with Nekayah rather than with the trivial good-natured daughters. Perhaps they felt, in different degrees, some hostile rivalry towards a male writer occupying their turf. This was their market. These unguided girls were the 'Misses' to whom edifying essays might be addressed. The 'giant' Johnson was poaching the territory Hester Mulso knew was her own, though she had not yet written *Letters on the Improvement of the Mind*. The anger in 'by this time I fear you are angry at me and consider me as a strangely presumptuous animal, thus to lift up my nothingness against the giant Johnson' is her own disavowed anger. As she demonstrated in her epistolary exchanges with Samuel Richardson, the complex feelings aroused by reading texts which spoke so directly to the experience of intelligent and desiring women could partly be soothed by entering into legitimate discussion about them. This drew welcome attention to the gifted writers, but it was only half an answer. Hester Mulso's energetic engagement with these men's texts seethed with impatience – not so much with them as with her confinement inside their agenda. She chafed, just as she argued that daughters chafed under tyrannic paternal authority. Unlike Charlotte Lennox, she did not imagine herself in equal debate and certainly not in control of the agenda.

Rasselas raised the question of the choice of life as an issue for women as well as men. It depicted an exceptional woman as a curious enquirer, a scientific observer going out to question, take notes and draw conclusions. Nekayah was active not passive in the business and she did not have to charm a man with any coquettish airs. Like Rasselas, she was subject to the 'hunger of imagination which preys on life'. This vision of the human condition had a particular meaning for women, given that the choice of life was more circumscribed for them than it was for men and that their opportunities to know were more limited. But were women like Mulso and Lennox merely listening with credulity to the whispers of fancy? Or could they, like Arabella, engage the questions that concerned them with dignity and passion and enter on a larger world suited to their capacities?

The Female Quixote was well received, but it was to be six years before Charlotte Lennox published another work of original fiction. Bringing Samuel Johnson into the final pages of her novel signified a larger shift, a turning towards the mixed community of writers, scholars and booksellers; and a change in what she chose to write and how she presented herself as an author. Charlotte Lennox's career, properly assessed, is typical rather than unusual for the mid eighteenth century but it is not typical of women writers. For this reason (among others) it has been misunderstood: strengths represented as weakness, success as failure, and sensible professional choices misleadingly construed.

She opted for the path her mentor, Johnson, was following. This did not mean becoming a Grub Street hack; it meant becoming a respected professional in the mode of her times, scholarly, serious about literature, and working closely with the booksellers. For all their popularity, novels were a tiny part of the expanding print trade. And for all Samuel Richardson's achievement, novels were by no means a secure genre in which to establish a reputation. Catherine Talbot, relieved to find *The Female Quixote* 'not at all low', living amongst bishops and mixing with literature-loving members of the aristocracy, represented the heights of Lennox's possible readership. From such readers as Catherine Talbot could flow sales, reputation, comforts, pleasure. It was in the power of the circles Talbot frequented to bestow the sort of queenly superiority that Johnson invoked when he crowned the young genius at the Devil tavern.

The success of *The Female Quixote* raised its author's market value in the eyes of publishers; building on her previous publications, it established her professional credibility. As a working professional, Charlotte Lennox was never without projects in the 1750s, some of them daunting in scale. It has been customary to represent her unflagging industry as a sign of servitude. By the end of the decade, she herself represented it as 'slavery', complaining to her patron, the Duchess of Newcastle, about the 'scanty and precarious subsistence' produced by her 'present slavery to the Booksellers'. But in the early 1750s the amount and quality of the work she was able to claim for herself in a competitive literary market was a sign not of servitude but of status. So, too, was her understanding that the trade of literature was beginning to coalesce into something resembling an institution. The popularity of the *Rambler*, which ran from March 1750 to March 1752 and appeared twice weekly, had hugely boosted Johnson's reputation. His presence was pervasive. His voice was the voice of dignity. He projected an authorial self that was serious and philosophical, offering a counter to what was otherwise characterised as 'the low and trifling taste of the age in general'.

The ending of *The Female Quixote* dramatised in fictional form the entry into Johnson's world. It was an announcement, an advertisement of mutual support and collaborative intent. The persona of the female author was redrawn. No longer a coquette, no longer a foolish reader forming her ideas about the world from the wrong sort of books (books designed to construct a female subjectivity defined by female sexuality and male desire), she was now a wise writer, a woman of mind fit to engage on equal terms with Mr Rambler, the most learned man of the day. Romance, that female form serving 'the low and trifling taste of the age in general', having been thoroughly investigated in the pages of *The Female Quixote*, lovingly but critically revisited and rewritten, was cast aside. The future was with the community of men and women (but mostly men) who recognised Johnson's leadership.

In 1752 Alexander Lennox went to the Orange coffee-house off the Haymarket, Piccadilly, on a mission. He was looking for a foreigner who, in exchange for conversational English, would teach Mrs Lennox his native tongue. The 'authoress of *The Female Quixote*', as she was now generally known after the success of that work, had a new project on hand and her husband was making himself useful. She was gathering together, reading and translating the original tales from which Shakespeare had taken some of his plays. As early as 1745, Johnson had published his proposals for an edition of Shakespeare in which he made reference to the importance of these sources. Charlotte Lennox's new work, which was to become the *Shakespear Illustrated*, a critical study of the sources and Shakespeare's use of them, may well have begun as a research contribution to Johnson's ambitious plans, the product of repeated conversations between them. It was collaborative from its very inception, part of the wider project of building a national literature from home grown products. Nevertheless, the resemblance between *Shakespear Illustrated* and *The Female Quixote* makes it clear that this was no casual undertaking, neither cynical nor merely commercial, but a deeply felt working out of matters that were significant to Charlotte Lennox's intellectual and imaginative development at this stage in her career.

In the coffee-house was Giuseppe Baretti, a struggling Italian scholar and poet. He already had sufficient command of English to be writing in the language; nevertheless, as an experienced tutor, he seized the opportunity of a useful connection which was to lead him from the Lennoxes to friendship with Samuel Johnson and, later, entry into the literary circles at Streatham. Thus it was that he became tutor to the Thrales' eldest daughter, organised tours of Italy for the Thrales, and was honoured by having his portrait painted alongside those of Johnson and Garrick in the new library at Streatham. (He grew to hate Hester Thrale and she him.) As a friend of Charlotte Lennox, Baretti became a typical member of the Johnsonian circle in the early 1750s: poor, hot-tempered, impassioned about his own national literature, not particularly likeable perhaps, unstable, unprotected. In 1769, after a fracas in Soho, he killed a man – apparently in self-defence, but there are other episodes of violence in his life – and was imprisoned in Newgate. Whilst awaiting trial, he was visited by a rival Italian teacher who explained that he planned to take over Baretti's pupils after his execution and would Baretti please write him a letter of recommendation. The combined testimonies of Johnson, Burke, Reynolds, Goldsmith and Garrick proved powerful enough to secure him a discharge, but the episode offers a glimpse of the edge along which the marginal – foreign, female, friendless – often trod. In an affecting scene inside prison, Baretti took the hands of Johnson and Burke in each of his and said, 'What can he fear that holds two such hands as I do' – a stark reminder of the importance of 'interest'. Most of the time, for individuals like Baretti and Charlotte Lennox (especially if they were incomers), there was a great deal to fear.[26]

Shakespear Illustrated, which was published early in 1753, contained translations from Italian, French, Latin and Danish, but by far the most were from Italian. Baretti worked very closely on these translations with Lennox; and, as will be seen, he became passionately concerned about the direction her writing was taking her, especially in regard to Johnson's influence. Collaboration also occurred at the other end of the social scale: a useful connection was made through this project with John Boyle, Earl of Cork and Orrery. Orrery was a well-known enthusiast for literature, and friend of Pope and Swift, sympathetic towards women writers (Swift had helped Mary Barber dedicate a collection of her poems to Orrery by writing a prefatory letter to the volume) and with ambitions of his own which had recently been displayed in his *Remarks on the Life and Writings of Dr Jonathan Swift*. Johnson reported that Orrery had expressed a favourable opinion of 'our Charlotte's book' (meaning *Harriot Stuart*). Orrery's style of gallantry suggests he knew what would go down well with her. In a note to Johnson shortly before the publication of *The Female Quixote*, he enquired: 'How is the enchantress, whose appearance I dare say will draw many to her castle? I shall be glad to be thought a knight errant in her train ...'

Bishop Berkeley said of Orrery, 'He would have been a man of genius, had he known how to set about it'; and Johnson, that 'He would have been a liberal patron if he had been rich'. An air of the ineffectual rises from these remarks, but Orrery was not a fool; nor, by comparison with his writer friends, was he poor. For Charlotte Lennox he became an excellent

'knight errant', eager to serve and respectful – thrilling, probably, to the
more commanding elements in her personality. Orrery had himself been
planning a book on Shakespeare and had been amassing materials. These
he obligingly sent to Johnson to hand over to Charlotte Lennox, admitting
that one reason for his failure to turn his own researches to account was
that he had been intimidated by the atmosphere of scholarship already
developing around Shakespeare's name. The enclosed papers, he explained
to Johnson, had

> long laid by me; were thrown aside because I would not walk into Mr P[ope]
> and W[arburton]'s province, who seemed to think that Shakespear was the Sanc-
> tum Sanctorum where they only were sufficiently holy to enter ... If even some
> words in them may be of service to her I am happy.[27]

Where a male aristocrat with well-established literary credentials dared
not tread, the young female novelist entered. Orrery served as her assistant
and co-author, an arrangement that survived for a good ten years. He had
classical learning and his library was a useful source of books. As well as
sharing in the collection of materials for *Shakespeare Illustrated*, he later
translated a substantial portion *of The Greek Theatre of Father Brumoy*,
another collaborative venture which included Johnson and some younger
male scholars, all under Charlotte Lennox's direction. Collaborative working
on large scholarly projects, of which Johnson's *Dictionary* is the best-known
and best-documented example, was a feature of mid eighteenth-century
publishing. It was not unusual for an author to delegate tasks or draw on
help from others, or incorporate a contribution from 'a different hand',
named or otherwise, into the finished product.

As we have seen, Elizabeth Montagu first went into print in this way,
contributing to George Lyttelton's *Dialogues of the Dead* which appeared
in 1760. She was not named as the 'different Hand' but was effusively praised
as such by Lyttelton in his preface. Wary of the 'low' associations of print,
Lyttelton's book enabled Montagu to show off her talents in a thoroughly
conventional venture which had a sound aristocratic tradition behind it.
Even the publicity-shy Catherine Talbot had contributed to something
similar twenty years earlier when she wrote four essays for the privately
printed *Athenian Letters* of her Cambridge student friends, Philip and
Charles Yorke. Private printing maintained the connection with old aristocratic habits of circulating manuscripts within an elite, self-selected group.
But books, and therefore customs of writing and circulation, had been
transformed by the expansion of the printing and publishing industry. No
longer semi-precious objects, beautifully bound and read mostly by the
well-off, they were becoming plentiful everyday objects. A public with

purchasing power made available new social roles for writers which complicated old social hierarchies. 'Low' could become 'high'; or it could appear
'high' but really be 'low'. Old categories were collapsing, old boundaries
dissolving.

Charlotte Lennox's *Shakespear Illustrated: or The Novels and Histories on
Which the Plays of Shakespear are Founded, Collected and Translated from
the Original Authors* was an appropriate work to follow *The Female Quixote*
and was very likely already in progress at the same time as *The Female
Quixote* was being written. The two books can be seen as companion pieces.[28]
Both seek to undo the layers of fiction out of which literary texts are
constructed. Both seek to find what one text owes to another in order to
deconstruct what the reader has received in reading. *Shakespear Illustrated*
is textual criticism of a sort entirely recognisable to any literary scholar
today. As well as discovering the sources of Shakespeare's plays, the histories
and novels from which he drew his plots, it offered comments – 'Critical
Remarks' – on his use of those sources.

In 1753 such a conception was both original and bold. Shakespeare's
position as pre-eminent British poet was already assured, a fact which made
the project of a book with his name in the title a likely commercial success.
But Shakespeare criticism tended to be of the adulatory, self-congratulatory
sort – of a piece with the way Britons congratulated themselves for God's
goodness to them. Shakespeare's existence in Britain, like God's, was a
measure of British worth. Few were so ungrateful as to find fault. However,
it was as a fault-finding exercise, as a venture into negative criticism, that
readers and critics alike received *Shakespear Illustrated*. The *Monthly Review*,
in a favourable notice, observed: 'Her remarks, which are very judicious,
and truly critical, are chiefly intended to prove, that Shakespeare has
generally spoiled every story on which the above plays are founded, by
torturing them into low contrivances, absurd intrigue, and improbable
incidents.'

Since then, most people have dealt with *Shakespear Illustrated* by ignoring
it altogether. Elizabeth Montagu made no reference to it when she brought
out her *Essay on the Writings and Genius of Shakespeare* fifteen years later.
There is in *Shakespear Illustrated*, as there is in *The Female Quixote*, a
half-spoken question driving the text which has to do with writerly formation,
and it asks: what kind of reading and writing has formed this self, this writer
Charlotte Lennox? And what might she have it in herself to be? In other
words, as in *The Female Quixote*, Lennox can be seen working out issues
that were fundamental to her development, issues that concerned gender
and genre and which were not easy to separate. Ostensibly the book is about
the romance-sources of Shakespeare's plays and his relationship to those

sources. The starting point is the fact that, like Arabella in *The Female Quixote*, Shakespeare lived a life of imaginative engagement with fantastical figures and unbelievable adventures. Romance, that female genre par excellence, was an important source of his writings. Romance was 'low' but Shakespeare was 'high'.

For a woman writer, the status of romance-writing, and the world view which romance purveyed, as well as – more ambiguously – the representation of women in romance, made it a troubling inheritance in ways which Lennox had explored in *The Female Quixote*. New forms had taken the place of enchanted isles and castles – as the good doctor was shown telling Arabella. The crucial fact, however, was that the doctor had read his romance texts; in order to argue Arabella out of her literal beliefs, he showed an equal knowledge. It was the recognition that these stories had been important to men and women alike, including the most respected male authors like Shakespeare and Johnson, that lay behind *Shakespear Illustrated*. Playing through the discussion of romance is the question of gender: to what extent is fantasy and imagination subject to the constraints of gender? Can a woman be what she is capable of imagining herself? Can she live through mind on the same terms as men?

In this sense, the whole of *Shakespear Illustrated* is an extension of the discussion with the divine in the long penultimate chapter of *The Female Quixote*. In it, the handling of the Johnson-like figure, brought in to speak words Johnson undoubtedly endorsed if he didn't actually write, is overtly deferential. But there is nothing deferential in the handling of Shakespeare in *Shakespear Illustrated*. Vigorous and engaged, Charlotte Lennox pursued the argument that many have chosen to see as closed by Arabella's 'capitulation' to marriage at the end of *The Female Quixote*. How should we read romances? How did Shakespeare read them? How do we read Shakespeare? What do these writings mean in mid eighteenth-century England? The questions multiply as the text proceeds. What does fiction mean? What is the place of the imagination? What use do we make of the past? Shakespeare, she demonstrated, frequently made poor use of his fictional sources. But Shakespeare had become a venerated figure whose name was a byword for English literature. What, then, were the terms of the growing Shakespeare idolatry?

A Shakespeare idolised and 'appreciated' was also a Shakespeare whose representations of women were read as versions of the real. It was already a commonplace that Shakespeare, as Johnson expressed it (taking his image from *Hamlet*), 'holds up to his readers a faithful mirror of manners and of life'. In this 'mirror', so it was widely believed, could be seen 'human nature'. With scorn and sarcasm, Charlotte Lennox took issue with this notion, pointing out the ways in which the double standard operated in favour of men and to the detriment of women. Most of her observations on Shakespeare's plays in fact concern his characterisation of women. (She was the first in a long line of female critics to address themselves to this theme.) Over and over again she pointed out that the representation of the woman in the original source story – those romance stories dismissed by her contemporaries as 'old' and 'paltry' – showed a woman who was 'prouder, freer, stronger, and more effective' than Shakespeare would allow in his version of the character. Whereas the romances showed women as rulers, capable of good leadership, Shakespeare was bent on showing them as pathetic. Helena in *All's Well That Ends Well* was typical: 'The character of the heroine is more exalted in the original than the copy.'

Shakespear Illustrated is a pioneering work, overtly polemical and feminist, and full of critical energy. As an early essay in English literature (possibly the first of its sort by a woman), it deserves far more attention than it has ever received; likewise, it deserves attention as probably the first study by a feminist critic of an already canonical author. There is a fury in its tone which probably reflects some of the tension in the position Charlotte Lennox occupied: uncomfortably allied with men, convinced of her entitlement to form and express authoritative opinion on exactly the same terms as men, aware that she knew better about certain areas of experience than they did, but subject to the social constraints of being a woman.

The strain of this position, or perhaps just sheer exhaustion after the effort of producing *The Female Quixote* and *Shakespear Illustrated* in quick succession, seems to have brought about a collapse of confidence. By 1753 Charlotte Lennox – probably not yet thirty – had published a volume of poems, two very well-received novels, and a work of substantial literary criticism. She had tried her hand (unsuccessfully, it would appear) at acting. She was established in London, living as she did throughout her life at a succession of lodgings: at Mr Austin's Engraver, Great George Street, Hanover Square; at the Mineral Water Warehouse in Bury Street, Saint James's; at the cabinet makers in Dartmouth Street, Westminster. Her circle of friends and acquaintances was extensive, including the more raffish theatrical element that the actress Mrs Yates moved in, as well as the varied society around Johnson.

All the evidence is that she spent little time socialising, however, and extremely long hours at her desk. This is probably the simple explanation of Bishop Warburton's remark in a letter to publisher Andrew Millar: 'Nothing is more public than her writings, nothing more concealed than her person.' Lennox's capacity for hard work is humbling, especially when we consider the relative lack of reward. She had found good patrons and appreciative fellow writers. Even the critical critics acknowledged her genius. What Johnson assured her of in his 1756 letter about the *Memoirs of the Countess of Berci* was already true: the critics mentioned her 'with great respect'; she had acquired 'a degree of reputation' sufficient to 'secure you from any neglect of readers or stationers'.

But after *Shakespear Illustrated* she became despondent and experienced doubts about the direction her writing should go. We know this because Giuseppe Baretti wrote a poem about it, which was found in a notebook at Casale, Italy, and dated London 30 May, 1754.[29] Baretti's poem, 'Alla Signora Carlotta Lennox. Oda' (or Ode to Charlotte Lennox) began by asking why she was so downcast, and why she should be thinking of giving up in the very moment of her success:

> Or, che ti sei condotta
> Quasi all' Aonie Cime,
> Di retroceder pensi?
> Come questi, Carlotte,
> In menti si sublime
> Pusillanimi sensi?
>
> Or che piu pochi passi
> Ti rimangono a fare
> Su pel difficil Monte,
> Rivolgere vedrassi
> Una Donna tua pare
> Sbigottita la fronte?
>
> Or che la stessa Clio
> Ti viene incontro, e vuole
> Teco cambiar di cetra
> Or che il lucente Dio
> T'apre sue dolci Scuole
> Carlotta il passo arretra?*

The speaker of the poem had no doubts about what she should do and

---

* Now that you have nearly reached the Aonian summit, do you think of turning back? How do such cowardly thoughts arise in so sublime a mind, Charlotte?

    Now that only a few steps remain to be taken up the difficult hill, shall we see a woman like you change her mind and turn back with despondent face?

    Now that Clio herself comes to meet you and wishes to change lyres with you; now that the shining God opens to you his sweet schools, Charlotte, will you turn back your step?

what she should write. She should return to the subject-matter and style of her earliest writings. She should write of love:

Bestir, bestir yourself, return and tread with light step the first pathways. You fearful? You downcast on a way now so short? Ah no, that must never be true!

Return to sing of love on the calm waters of your native river; return to the nymphs to fill your heart with sweetness.

The suggestion induces a troubled response. The poet addresses his subject, dramatising a conversation between himself and 'Charlotte Lennox' in which he insists that he knows the meaning of her troubled feelings:

Ma tu non dai aseolto
Al dritto mio consiglio,
Non parli, non respondi?
Anzi arrossendo in volto
Chini turbata il ciglio,
E al mio dir ti confondi?

E che vuol quel silente
Insolito contegno,
Che vuol, Carlotta dire?
Perche chiudi tua mente
A chi ver l'alto segno
Ti vuole incoraggire?

E che? Ma gia indovino
Di tanta vitrosia
La segreta cagione.
So chi dal bel cammino
Distoglier ti vorria;
So, so chi a me s'oppone.

Johnson, rigido Inglese,
Che un grazioso nulla
Crede peccato, e vizio;
Che sta pesando un mese
Ogni sua riga sulla
Bilancia del guidizio;

Johnson, che pieno ha il petto
D'austere cose, e il capo,
Filosofante grave;
Che un innocente afetto
Del tiempo di Priapo
Teme non sia la chiave;

> Johnson, Johnson e quello
> Che intorno a te s'e messo
> Col suo parlar feroce;
> E la mente, e'l cervello
> Sento intronarmi io stesso
> Dalla severa voce ... *

This angry, rivalrous poem continues for another fourteen stanzas to argue in favour of 'the beautiful road' of love and against 'austerities' and 'serious philosophy'. It is a rare example of a male author taking as his subject matter the question of a female author's professional development.

The tradition Baretti wanted Charlotte Lennox to write in was the pastoral tradition, full of classical allusions to Diana and Dido, with shepherds, lyres, langorous love and breezes through the trees. As can be seen, the argument was rather with Johnson than with Lennox – 'I myself feel his austere voice lording it over my own mind and senses' – and says more about Baretti, perhaps, than Lennox. The poem usefully highlights, however, some of the dilemmas a woman faced in making choices about the kind of writing she might attempt. Italian literature, especially the Italian pastoral tradition, was very popular in England. Elizabeth Carter's enthusiasm for the Italian poet Metastasio is a good example of the way respectable English ladies accessed the pleasures of the pastoral with its undercurrent of the erotic and its Romantic endorsement of solitary walks with a slim volume of poetry in one hand.

Poets like James Thomson were patronised by aristocratic ladies who had cultivated their sensitivity to nature in part by reading Italian pastoral like

---

* But do you not yield attention to my honest advice, do you neither speak nor reply? Rather with blushing cheek, and downcast, troubled eye, are you perturbed at my words?

And this silent, strange behaviour, what does it mean, Charlotte? Why close your mind to him who wishes to encourage you to the lofty goal?

What? But I already divine the secret cause of all this waywardness. I know who it is would dissuade you from the beautiful road. I know, I know who is opposed to me.

Johnson, inflexible Englishman, who thinks a graceful nothing a sin and a vice; who weighs for a month in the balance of his judgement every one of his own lines.

Johnson, whose heart is full of austerities, whose head is filled with serious philosophy; who fears that an innocent feeling can only be the key to the temple of Priapus;

Johnson, Johnson, it is he who has been at you with his terrible words, and I myself feel his austere voice lording it over my own mind and senses.

Il Pastor Fido by Guarini – the text on which Charlotte Lennox based her 1757 dramatic pastoral, *Philander*. Thomson's *The Seasons* was hugely popular. Johnson made fun of the pastoral in two *Rambler* essays and also tricked one enthusiast by reading aloud to him from *The Seasons*, eliciting agreement that the verse was wonderful before revealing that in his reading he had deliberately read only alternate lines.

Of the pastoral tradition in general, Johnson objected that it was narrow and trite. He argued that it had become debased, and that pastoral poets, by merely bringing on the shepherds, could 'make the clouds weep, and lilies wither, and the sheep hang their heads, without art or learning, genius, or study'. As a form, he argued, the pastoral did not offer opportunity for intellectual or imaginative growth. It was full of 'absurdity'. Pastoral poets wrote 'with an utter disregard both of life and nature, and filled their productions with mythological allusions, with incredible fictions, and with sentiments which neither passion nor reason could have dictated'. Under Johnson's influence, the pastoral as a form for sexual expression, available to women and men alike, was to lose whatever was left of its credibility. The separating out of minds (good) and bodies (bad) was at work here as elsewhere. Baretti was equally capable of being satirical at the expense of pastoral poetry, but he identified something else in Johnson's response and that was the 'fear' in Johnson's rejection of the erotic. In an extempore poem, the 'Verses for Baretti', Johnson answered this charge, claiming to feel as much eroticism as the next man:

> At sight of sparkling bowls or beauteous dames,
> When fondness melts me, or when wine inflames,
> I too can feel the rapture, fierce and strong;
> I too can pour th'extemporary song

Wine, women and song produce erotic feeling and its accompaniment: poetic expression. However, Johnson's verses continued:

> But though the numbers for a moment please,
> Though music thrills, or sudden sallies seize,
> Yet, lay the sonnet for an hour aside,
> Its charms are fled, and all its powers destroyed.
> What soon is perfect, soon alike is past;
> That slowly grows, which must for ever last.

Denying the rapture and silencing the song that rises, Johnson gave a characteristically emphatic and pessimistic turn to his feelings; the iron fist of the moralist came down. (The gist of that final couplet found better expression in the later *Preface to Shakespeare* where it appeared as follows: 'the pleasures of sudden wonder are soon exhausted, and the mind can only repose on the stability of truth'.) Baretti's argument with Johnson, his insistence, 'it is not true that the Apollonian art must be consecrated wholly to virtue', was carried on in the 'Ode to Charlotte Lennox'. Poetry, according to Baretti, should not become wholly engrossed by morality; it should not lose its gentle dreams and fantasies, the playful erotic, the tears and tenderness, pleasurable sorrows and sentiments. The idea of the playful erotic could thus be shared between men. Its meaning was different for women. Johnson's expressed preference for the stability of mind and virtue was a large part of his appeal to women.

It was, of course, in Baretti's interest to keep alive English enthusiasm for Italian poetry. For Charlotte Lennox, the issue was more complicated. Women writers of the previous generations had used pastoral conventions widely, from Aphra Behn to the pious Elizabeth Rowe. But like the old romances, pastoral now looked fusty. As for the erotic, that figured more in urban narratives such as actresses' memoirs as well as racy novels like John Cleland's *Fanny Hill*, and explicit pornography of which there was a great deal. The modern, forward-looking writing woman identified herself with intellectual acquirements. She sought to expand the nation's store of wealth by making sources of knowledge available.

Witty women like Laetitia Pilkington brought pornography and learning together. In her 1748 *Memoirs*, Pilkington explained that her husband tricked her into a divorce after she was discovered by twelve watchmen with a strange man in her bedroom in the middle of the night. This, she conceded, had been 'indiscreet'; her excuse, directed at 'lovers of learning' was an original one:

> I own myself very indiscreet in permitting any man to be at an unseasonable hour in my bed-chamber: but lovers of learning will, I am sure, pardon me, as I solemnly declare, it was the attractive charms of a new book, which the gentleman would not lend me, but consented to stay till I read it through, that was the sole motive of my detaining him.[30]

It was increasingly agreed that those who had talent, male and female, had a duty to share it – a view promulgated in the highest circles in the land. When Frederick, Prince of Wales, thanked Lady Hertford for some poems in 1731, he wrote to her: 'I think people are vastly to be blamed, who won't show their parts, and whose talents must be lost to the world.'

Such a rage for improvement lent weight to translation projects such as the historical memoirs Charlotte Lennox undertook. There was credit and money in this work. Baretti might urge the pastoral (and *Philander*, in 1757, showed that she was willing to try) but it was with Johnson and what Johnson embodied and represented that Charlotte Lennox continued

1. Samuel Johnson (1709–1784), Sir Joshua Reynolds, *c.* 1756. (*National Portrait Gallery*)

2. Eva Garrick (1724–1822), by Nathaniel Dance, 1771. (*National Portrait Gallery*)

3. Elizabeth Carter (1771–1806), by Sir Thomas Lawrence. (*National Portrait Gallery*)

Sir J. Reynolds Pinx.   H.P. Cook Sculp.t

4. Charlotte Lennox (*c.* 1727–1804), engraving by H. P. Cook after Sir Joshua Reynolds.

5. Elizabeth Montagu (1720–1800), after Sir Joshua Reynolds. (*Courtauld Institute*)

6. Hester Thrale, neé Lynch, later Piozzi (1741–1821), by George Dance, 1793. (*National Portrait Gallery*)

7. Fanny Burney, later d'Darblay (1752–1840), by Edward Francis Burney, *c.* 1784–85. (*National Portrait Gallery*)

8. Hannah More (1745–1833), by Frances Reynolds. (*City of Bristol Museum and Art Gallery*)

to throw in her lot. Johnson's authority derived in part from his compendious knowledge of a number of foreign literatures: French, Italian, Latin and Greek. It was reasonable to think that making these literatures more widely available was a route to sharing in some of the authority. With one or two exceptions, the translations Charlotte Lennox undertook between 1753 and 1760 were serious works of scholarship. The *Memoirs of the Duke of Sully*, for example, is good history. A respected text in the original, her translation was to be reprinted many times and it remained the standard translation well into the nineteenth century. It was expensively produced, and immediately identifiable as a leading title.

Charlotte Lennox was what Elizabeth Montagu dreamed of being: 'an author in form'. More than that, she was sufficiently prominent to be considered by publishers and other writers as one who could take on leadership. That she was trusted to lead and coordinate large-scale publishing ventures is demonstrated by *The Greek Theatre of Father Brumoy*. This was a massive and prestigious undertaking. A learned project in three huge volumes which came out under Charlotte Lennox's name, dedicated to the Prince of Wales, and financed by a congerie of booksellers, much as was Johnson's *Dictionary*: Millar, Vaillant, Baldwin, Crowder, Johnston, Dodsley, and Wilson and Durham are all listed on the title page. The work was a translation into English of Brumoy's French edition of ancient Greek plays by Sophocles, Euripides, Eschylus and Aristophanes. It included Brumoy's Introductory Discourses and his General Conclusion, both of which Lennox delegated: to Orrery and to 'the celebrated author of the *Rambler*'. Other assistants whose contributions were properly acknowledged were: 'a young gentleman'; 'Dr Grainger, author of the translation of Tibullus'; and 'the learned and ingenious Dr Gregory Sharpe', who tackled Aristophanes.

Brumoy's was the most readily available scholarly edition for readers of ancient Greek dramatic texts and for wide-ranging critical discussion of dramatic theory. (It was in the French of Brumoy that Elizabeth Montagu read Sophocles.) Charlotte Lennox herself translated all of volume two, a great deal of volume three and at least two-thirds of volume one. She was ill by the end of it, and anybody who leafs through these volumes is unlikely to be surprised. The responsibility of seeing the project through to completion, coordinating contributions from scholarly men, editing and checking proofs, not to mention producing her own translations, must have weighed very heavily. For Catherine Talbot, the mammoth three-volumes – with a splendidly gilt-edged version for the King's library, now in the British Library – were themselves sufficient to disprove 'the foolish assertion, that Female Minds are not capable of producing literary Works, equal even to those of Pope'. She heralded the Brumoy as a female production that would enable the next generation to be 'taught by our pens that our Geniuses have been hitherto smothered, but not extinguished'. This translation appeared in 1759, one year before Elizabeth Montagu slipped anonymously into print under the protection of George Lyttelton. The contrast is striking. Mrs Montagu may have been 'Queen of the Blues' but Charlotte Lennox, crowned queen at the Devil tavern by her peers, was the reigning monarch of the booksellers in the 1750s.[31]

It is no wonder that scholars have been at a loss to know how to understand Charlotte Lennox's career as a writer. No other woman occupied such a position at the mid century. Her ability to work collaboratively and take the lead in major projects is not just unusual; it also offers a contrast to her well-documented appeals for help and explosions of rage. While it is true that she voiced complaints and did not accept criticism gracefully, tending to be 'rather too full of wrath for the provocation', as Johnson bluntly told her after her furious response to criticism of her 1756 translation, *The Memoirs of the Countess of Berci*, it is also true that she had cause for complaint and that her position made her liable to a number of provocations. Chief amongst those, and what must have been most galling, was the under-appreciation of the real nature and extent of her work and achievement; although again, as Johnson pointed out, the critics were actually very respectful of what she had done. Similarly, all those with whom she worked collegially had a great respect for her as a fellow professional. It may be that she was best in a leadership role, such as that which she developed whilst working on *Shakespear Illustrated* at the beginning of the 1750s and consolidated with *The Greek Theatre of Father Brumoy* at the end. But full social recognition of that aspect of her working life was denied. It seems reasonable to read some frustration on that account into her ventings of 'indignation'.

By any reckoning, the 1750s were an immensely hard working and successful decade for Charlotte Lennox, which makes it all the more surprising to discover that 'distress' and 'failure' accompanied her name even during these years. There are recurring motifs: desperate penury, failure of expectations, a turning this way and that for the means of survival. Lennox herself was the source for much of this rhetoric. In 1760, writing to the Duchess of Newcastle asking permission to dedicate a new edition of the novel, *Henrietta*, she thanked the Duchess for her goodness in having generously 'relieved my distress last Winter', and assured her she had been 'restored ... to a very tolerable degree of health'. This health, acquired by the benevolent gift of the Duchess's money, combined with country air and exercise, was set against a way of life always liable to reproduce the conditions of distress:

'my present slavery to the Booksellers, whom I have the more mortification to see adding to their heaps by my labours, which scarce produce me a scanty and precarious substance'. The letter, we should note, was designed to flatter and persuade.[32]

Henry Fielding, whose review of *The Female Quixote* in the *Covent Garden Journal* of 24 March 1752 is not only the most thorough and favourable review of the book but also considered by many the best book review Fielding ever wrote, became a friend at the time. In his *Journal of a Voyage to Lisbon*, published in 1754, he referred to Charlotte Lennox as 'the inimitable and shamefully-distress'd author of *The Female Quixote*'. All those who have written about Charlotte Lennox quote these words. They demonstrate that she had the respect and sympathy of one of the most brilliant writers of the day. That she, a woman, should fail to thrive economically fits preconceptions of a male-dominated literary marketplace. Yet it is neither foolish nor naive to ask: why was Charlotte Lennox so 'shamefully-distress'd'? She had patrons, friends, a husband, work. She was paid for everything she did. There are several reports of her receiving very handsome presents in addition to her earnings. She courted all who could help her and found support for her genius at the highest levels of society and in literature. Her patrons were leading aristocrats: the Duke and Duchess of Newcastle, for example, as well as accepting the dedication to *Henrietta*, and helping her out with money, also arranged for her to live in apartments in Somerset House for some years until 1773, when the building underwent renovation and she had to leave.[33]

The Duke of Newcastle was Prime Minister in 1756 when the translation of the *Memoirs of the Duke of Sully* was dedicated to him, and he responded with 'a most liberal present' and the promise that he would recommend her to the King as someone worthy of being granted a pension. This would appear to be the epitome of success: a present and a promise – the point of a dedication, the fairy-tale ending for the writer of a book. In 1759 *The Greek Theatre of Father Brumoy* was dedicated to the Prince of Wales who was shortly to become George III. He responded, it is said, with 'a munificent present'. Meanwhile, the booksellers paid reasonable money for her translations: the *Memoirs for the History of Madame de Maintenon and of the Last Age*, dedicated to that active patron of the arts, the Countess of Northumberland, whose family had for a number of generations been a support to women writers, earned her £86 17s. 6d. from the booksellers. It might not have been riches beyond the dreams of avarice, but it was more than most were getting: in 1772, Mrs Montagu was interested to learn that the Scottish clergy were living comfortably on £40 p.a.

It may be that there was a disparity between the amount of work involved for each book and the fees she received. It may also be that she was expensive and pitched her expectations high. The fact is that large sums of money passed periodically through her hands. From *The Female Quixote* to *The Greek Theatre of Father Brumoy*, she published eight books with Andrew Millar, a publisher who had the reputation of being generous to authors. He went bankrupt at the end of the 1750s. She moved to John Newbery, who immediately gave her a sum of money. Her ability to solicit money and help from people was well developed. From the limited surviving evidence it appears that she could employ a range of tones, from begging to demanding, but the rhetoric of outraged, undeserved distress was a favourite.

Publishers and writers alike were having a hard time throughout the 1750s. Publication was expensive, reading and buying habits unreliable, and publishers paid as little as they could get away with. The poverty of writers was a subject much bemoaned, especially by writers. James Ralph declared there was 'no difference between the writer in his garret, and the slave in the mines', whilst Oliver Goldsmith in 1759 objected to the new practice of blaming writers for their poverty:

> The poet's poverty is a standing topic of contempt. His writing for bread is an unpardonable offence. Perhaps of all mankind an author in these times is used most hardly. We keep him poor, and yet revile his poverty. Like angry parents who correct their children till they cry; and then correct them for crying, we reproach him for living by his wit, and yet allow him no other means to live.[34]

The literary world simply could not sustain the mixed community of different working folk who looked to it for an income. The income-generating base was too small, the transition from patronage to print markets still patchy. In this, as in other respects, Charlotte Lennox was typical rather than unusual. Henry Fielding, who described her as 'shamefully distress'd', was frustrated at failing to make literature support him, too – and he had been trying most of his life, and, like Lennox, had help from some of the best patrons. He only turned to novel writing after the 1737 Licensing Act closed his theatre – always his best source of income. From his point of view, writing as an author about another author and addressing the same reading public both authors looked to for support, the rhetoric of shameful distress might have appealed because it was additionally compelling applied to a female, especially one of such acknowledged achievement. If so, we should read such constructions as political and emblematic: Lennox represented the 'distressed' state of the profession. We can then separate what appears to have been a relative financial failure from a more generalised (and moralised) 'failure' that has clouded Charlotte Lennox's reputation.

Or, to put it another way, we can separate the 'shameful' from the 'female' and recognise that Fielding's purpose was to shame the institutions of literature for failing to support their own.

Writers like Charlotte Lennox, Henry Fielding, and Samuel Johnson saw themselves as having something very valuable to offer respectable society: their learning and their willingness to work hard to help improve the nation. This was a form of virtue; they gave themselves in benevolent, even self-sacrificial ways. Stories of Herculean work efforts or mountains of drudgery were a part of this self-mythologising construct. Pumping propaganda into the press was a survival strategy. But respectable society failed to give writers in return the means of a comfortable existence. Respectable society invited a select few into its homes and salons and country retreats: in the form of patrons it promised to subscribe and support; in the form of booksellers it promised to provide work and pay. But writers seeking protection fell into the gaps: patrons who only seemed to support and booksellers who provided work but not enough pay. The old aristocratic traditions of patronage in which a writer might be domesticated for much of his life with a family – as Isaac Watts in the previous generation had been domesticated at Abney Park under the protection of the Somersets – were changing (although, as Johnson demonstrated in his willingness to be domesticated with the Thrales, it continued to have an appeal). Protection of that sort was becoming a minor theme in the face of the expansion of printing and the growth of a buying public.

During the 1750s Charlotte Lennox, like Johnson and others, was often chronically short of funds. She may have been extravagant, and we know she was a poor manager. She made some expensive bad decisions, as for example when she declined the offer of the pension for herself 'in favour of her husband, for whom she solicited a place, which the Duke promised to procure him the first opportunity'. Alexander Lennox was duly given various lowly positions in the 1760s and 1770s. If Johnson's 1761 pension is anything to go by, Charlotte Lennox might have been in receipt of £200 to £300 per annum had she had a pension, enough to keep her in comfort. Instead, she continued writing whatever suited the times. In the early 1760s she wrote and produced a periodical, the *Lady's Museum* in which she serialised her own fiction amongst other things; another novel, *Sophia*, featured a heroine who was always at her books, and who exhibited 'a dignity which she derived from innate virtue and exalted understanding'. In the 1770s she behaved with impeccable politeness towards Garrick, revising her proposed dramas according to his suggestions, and having some success with the adaptation of Jonson, Chapman and Marston's *Eastward Ho*, renamed *Old City Manners: A Comedy*. Her novels were generally well received: *Henrietta* in 1758 was 'one of the best and most pleasing novels that has appeared for some years'.

Though it pleased the critic of the *Critical Review*, *Henrietta* did not please Elizabeth Carter and Catherine Talbot when they read it. Neither of them relished the pointed satire in *Henrietta* which is directed at learned ladies, particularly the learned lady who reads Seneca and Epictetus. Of this hypocritical creature we are told:

> Her own sex are the objects of her scorn, because they are subject to such weaknesses as tenderness and pity. She reads Seneca on friendship in the morning; and exclaims, O! the exalted passion! How divinely he treats it! What noble sentiments! In the afternoon she overreaches her friend and applauds her own wisdom. Epictetus is studied with great care. She will preach a moral sermon out of Epictetus that will last two hours. Epictetus teaches her to regulate her passions. She reads him intently while her maid is combing her hair, and closes her book to storm at the poor trembling creature for accidentally hurting her with a comb.

The character is not meant for Elizabeth Carter, but since *Henrietta* came out in the same year that Elizabeth Carter's *Epictetus* appeared, her presence is unflatteringly invoked. The passage suggests an almost compulsive desire to offend. If we seek the sources of what has been well described as 'the feminine disapprobation which is steadily and impressively cumulative throughout [Lennox's] life' (and which contrasts with widespread male approbation), we can find it in passages like this. Speaking of the heroine, Catherine Talbot disapproved of what she called the 'bits of pride and sauciness in Henrietta' but admitted that the novel 'has been useful to us here' (in the country); adding, 'there are many things in it that I dislike, and that tally with my opinion of the writer.'[35]

Talbot's 'opinion of the writer' was inevitably formed according to class assumptions – what in eighteenth-century parlance would have been represented as degrees of 'politeness', the being or not being 'well-bred'. We can be sure that the movement of class antagonism worked in both directions and was a potent brew, since Lennox's identifications were with the aristocracy to which she did not belong and whose advantages she did not share. The Epictetus-reading lady perhaps serves as an indirect riposte to the genteel women who took pleasure in tut-tutting about Charlotte Lennox's foul temper and bad habits: *she* might have been demonstrably violent and unwashed; *they* were hypocritical and violent and unclean in secret. 'Politeness' as the author observes in *Henrietta*, 'is sometimes a great tax upon sincerity.'

Mocking learned ladies, or pseudo-learned ladies, was standard practice. Fanny Burney took up the well-worn subject twenty years later in *The*

Witlings. Presenting men and women of society as vain, shallow and mercenary was also standard; as was a heroine full of virtue and distress who triumphs over the sins of the world so that 'her beauty, her sufferings, her virtue, and her good fortune' become the talk of the town. But it is misleading to think of *Henrietta* as a realistic novel of genteel life, even if contemporary reviewers elected to receive it in those terms. The *Critical Review* described it as, 'simple, uniform, and interesting; the stile is equal, easy, and well kept up, sinking nowhere below the level of genteel life', adding that, to describe it thus was a 'compliment which cannot be paid to one of the most celebrated novel-writers we have'. The 'celebrated novel-writer' was probably Fielding and the remark partly alludes to Fielding's 'low life' characters and partly to his exuberantly satirical and knowing narrative voice. Lennox's 'simple', 'uniform', 'interesting', 'equal', 'easy', 'well kept up' style (heroically moderate terms of praise) is supposedly superior to Fielding.

In fact the satire in *Henrietta* does not always rise beyond sarcastic or cruel sneering. A good example is a scene in which Henrietta sits at table with an old baronet whom her aunt wants her to marry. This 'superannuated enamorato' with the 'hideous ogle which he designed for a languish' is of course disgusting, as well as being foolish to think his riches will procure him her hand. Henrietta shows him her 'infinite contempt'. So far so familiar. But an extra kick is given to the contempt. The baronet has no teeth, and Henrietta notices the difficulty he has in chewing his meat: 'I was resolved to mortify him, by letting him perceive that I observed it, looking at him several times with a kind of sensibility for this so unavoidable misfortune.' The author's pleasure in this scene recalls the acknowledged pleasures of sadism in *Harriot Stuart*; it also evokes rhetorical codes from sexually explicit or pornographic novels like *Fanny Hill* where the quintessential young female experience involves selling the body – often, sadly, to disgusting but rich old men.

Henrietta begins with great brio. A strange young lady bursts from behind a roadside tree and begs a coachman to let her on the coach to London. Once aboard the coach she discovers another young lady and 'a violent friendship' immediately suggests itself. They must call each other Clelia and Celinda, the young lady insists, since 'Romantick names give a spirit to the correspondence between such friends as you and I are ...' They must 'correspond every hour – Oh! What a ravishing pleasure it is to indulge the overflowings of one's heart upon paper!' All this within a few minutes of meeting, for these are modern women committed heart and soul to sentimental friendship. The satirical targets in *Henrietta* are drawn mostly from literature and – not surprisingly considering the huge impact of Samuel

Richardson's *Pamela* and *Clarissa* – especially from contemporary novels that foregrounded the experiences of young females. The moment-by-moment communication of sensibility supposed to be achieved by letter-writing – taken to extreme lengths in Clarissa where it is calculated that Clarissa must have written non-stop for twenty-four hours to cover the number of pages devoted to her narrative of certain events – is mocked; as are the trite clichés of pastoral verse. Miss Woodby, the ugly foil to clever, beautiful, resourceful Henrietta, declares that 'a cottage, with the person we love, is to be preferred to a palace with one to whom interest and not affection has joined us. I know I could be contented to keep sheep with the man I loved.' Henrietta knows she could not. This is the cant of the times. She describes having once had the same romantic notions of shepherds and shepherdesses until she went to stay on a farm and discovered a real shepherd and his 'lovely nymph': they were an old man, ragged and miserable, and a witch-like old woman sitting under a hedge mending old stockings. The picture is not offered to arouse sympathy for 'real' shepherds: 'How diverting,' she laughs, 'it would have been to have heard this enamoured swain sigh out soft things to this lovely nymph!'

Henrietta reads as partly a copy of and partly a commentary on *Clarissa*. There is a chapter titled, 'In Which our Heroine is in Great Distress', which it has been remarked might serve as a description of the whole book, but it could equally serve to describe the whole of *Clarissa*. Our heroine is in distress because she is a female and unprotected. She moves virtuously (but with considerable ill-nature) through different levels of society, learning and dispensing wisdom of various kinds. She is told she must expect to be envied because she is pretty and clever, and 'those who are remarkable for any shining qualities will be more envied than admired, and frequently more calumniated than praised'. Unlike Arabella in *The Female Quixote*, Henrietta is depicted as having an appropriate understanding of the world she finds herself in, though she is naturally superior (a sign of her gentle birth). That she is an advance on her other fictional predecessor, Harriot Stuart, is shown by her taste in novels. As Arabella symbolically lets go of childish things and becomes an adult by abandoning immature fictions, so Henrietta is shown at an early stage refusing to fill her mind with the frivolous female romances Harriot loved. The scene is a boarding house which, unbeknownst to Henrietta, discreetly serves pregnant women: a place where they might 'lie-in privately, and be properly attended' for a certain sum. Some books belonging to the landlady are lying about and Henrietta picks one up. It is the *New Atalantis*, by Delarivier Manley. She puts it down. The landlady offers her something by Mrs Haywood: 'the finest love-sick, passionate stories. I assure you, you'll like them vastly: pray take a volume of it upon my recommendation'. Henrietta counters with the superior quality of Fielding's *Joseph Andrews*, 'one of the most exquisite pieces of humour in our language'. It is a novel she has already read three times but is willing to read again. Fielding's kind words about Charlotte Lennox in his *Journal of a Voyage to Lisbon* are repaid by her kind words about him in *Henrietta*.

Not Johnson, then, and not the coquette tradition of Delarivier Manley or Eliza Haywood, but some mixture of Fielding and Richardson served as the desired ideal for the novelist. By 1758 they represented the best in fiction and Charlotte Lennox scorned to align herself with anything less than the best. 'Scorn' is indeed, along with 'pride', 'indignation', 'impertinencies', and 'contempt' a recurring word in this novel – the scorn and pride of the sexually confident woman of the coquette tradition, the indignation of a woman who has not received her due. Henrietta's scorn is of a piece with her consciousness of virtue and it is directed at others less virtuous (or less young and beautiful) than herself. The effect is often simply unpleasant. Charlotte Lennox's scorn bursts through the 'politeness' of the genteel novel she attempted to write and which reviewers lavishly praised her for. The polite world registered the scorn. She remained true to the laws of coquetry, since the figure of the author (not just the female author) was so evidently aligned to the figure of the coquette: each sought to please, learning the hard way that other appetites than her own were the ones to be gratified. Appetites and powers locked and struggled in the dynamic between author and reader or author and patron. In an essay in her journal, The *Lady's Museum*, Charlotte Lennox spelled it out:

> The desire of fame, or the desire of pleasing ... in my opinion, are synonymous terms ... The poet's inspiration, the patriot's zeal, the courtier's loyalty, and the orator's eloquence. All are coquets, if that be coquetry.

It is no accident that *Henrietta* evokes novels like *Fanny Hill* and the tone of memoirs like those of Laetitia Pilkington and Constantia Phillips, nor that Eliza Haywood should be symbolically cast aside in a setting devoted to obscuring the effects of 'love-sick' passions: a boarding house where women seek the help of other women, either for secrecy, or to abort and dispose of the products. Working through *Henrietta*, often accounting in some measure for its awkward transitions or poorly integrated passages, is a struggle between different representations of female life, and different traditions of writing. Pilkington's combative collusiveness with the reader about life, literature, sex and rage belonged to a model that had become outdated. The areas of everyday experience considered fitting for fiction had narrowed. The range of acknowlegeable emotions had shrunk. When

Charlotte Lennox read books by women of an earlier generation which had been outspoken (up to a point) about the connections of sex and power, and women's use of sex for power, she was also able to remark the way these forces operated in a not dissimilar way upon men. The desire for fame, poetic inspiration, patriotic zeal, loyalty to a king or patron, eloquence to move listeners and gain supporters, were all forms of coquetry. That is to say, they were all female arts.

4

Hester Thrale and Elizabeth Montagu

Boswell followed up his bruising first encounter with Johnson in Tom Davies's bookshop by paying him a visit at home. Davies had reassured him, 'Don't be uneasy, I can see he likes you very well'. Like other new young friends, among them Charles Burney, Bennet Langton and Joshua Reynolds – who described how Johnson sat in a broken three-legged chair, after placing it 'with great composure against some support, taking no notice of its imperfection to his visitor' – Boswell was struck by the contrast of squalid surroundings and sparkling talk:

> It must be confessed that his apartment, and furniture, and morning dress, were sufficiently uncouth. His brown suit of clothes looked very rusty; he had on a little old shrivelled unpowdered wig, which was too small for his head; his shirt-neck and knees of his breeches were loose; his black worsted stockings ill drawn up; and he had a pair of unbuckled shoes by way of slippers. But all these slovenly particularities were forgotten the moment that he began to talk.

Boswell's company was agreeable to Johnson. They walked the streets of London together talking about everything (Johnson declining the solicitations of a prostitute on behalf of them both); they had an idyllic day out at Greenwich; and when the time came for Boswell to leave for Holland, where he was going by his father's command to study civil law, Johnson decided to see him off at Harwich. Already in the habit of recording everything he could remember of what was said – a task which sometimes kept him up all night – Boswell now had opportunity to observe Johnson's manners among strangers. On the coach, the ill-dressed philosopher startled the other passengers by his provocative views: he defended the Spanish Inquisition, and found good reasons why governments might torture prisoners to obtain confessions, a practice which was still legal in Holland. Boswell was used to this sort of thing, but Johnson's gross table manners transfixed him:

> When at table, he was totally absorbed in the business of the moment; his looks seemed rivetted to his plate; nor would he, unless when in very high company, say one word, or even pay the least attention to what was said by others, till he had satisfied his appetite, which was so fierce, and indulged with such intentness

that while in the act of eating, the veins of his forehead swelled, and generally a strong perspiration was visible.

Johnson was a man of extremes. He had given up alcohol because he felt incapable of drinking moderately: he could abstain but he couldn't be temperate. The rigidities of a complete refusal came more easily to him than the self-control required in moderate use. In place of alcohol he put tea, becoming, as he happily described himself, 'a hardened and shameless tea-drinker ... whose kettle has scarcely time to cool; who with tea amuses the evening, with tea solaces the midnight, and, with tea, welcomes the morning'. The sexual imagery in these descriptions of uncontrollable appetite suggests that food and tea served to some extent as a substitute for sex. According to Boswell, Johnson's 'amorous inclinations' were 'uncommonly strong and impetuous'. Since we know of no serious attempt to marry again after Tetty's death, it seems likely that, as with alcohol, he chose rigid abstention rather than moderate use of what he evidently thought of as 'criminal' indulgences. Boswell secretly read much of the private diary which Johnson destroyed before his death, and he believed that in his early days in London, 'Johnson was sometimes hurried into indulgences which he thought criminal'. With the 'vagrant' poet Richard Savage, Johnson had mixed much with women of the streets, taking them to taverns and hearing their stories. He was sympathetic, making it his business to understand what had brought 'those forlorn creatures' – often children as young as ten or twelve – to the condition they were in; and he was prepared to point the finger of blame:

How frequently have the gay and thoughtless, in their evening frolics, seen a band of these miserable females, covered with rags, shivering with cold, and pining with hunger; and, without either pitying their calamities, or reflecting upon the cruelty of those who perhaps first seduced them by caresses of fondness, or magnificence of promises, go on to reduce others to the same wretchedness by the same means?[1]

After Tetty's death (and sexual relations between them had stopped some years before she died) he prayed against 'unchastity, idleness, and neglect of public worship'. He thought about marrying again, and worried that he was being disloyal to her memory: 'I know not whether I do not too much indulge the vain longings of affection'. Nothing came of it. He was plagued by feelings of guilt. The need for restraint obsessed him. He made lists and lists of resolutions: 'Resolved ... To apply to study ... To reclaim imagination ... To study Religion. To go to Church ... To oppose laziness, *by doing what is to be done.*'

Frances Reynolds claimed that Johnson was jealous of Samuel Richardson for having gained the attentions of Elizabeth Carter and Hester Mulso: 'he thought himself neglected by them on his account. Dr Johnson set a higher value upon female friendship than, perhaps, most men'. In fact, Johnson was never close to Hester Mulso, who disliked him, and Elizabeth Carter was never integrated into Samuel Richardson's circle. But Frances Reynolds, his 'dear Renny', was in a good position to appreciate the value Johnson put on friendship with females like herself. She was often in his company. A painter, like her brother, and also a poet whose verses Johnson helped correct, she was less interested in recording what Johnson said than in describing the visual impressions she received. For example, she was the only friend to describe his compulsive ritual movements, and she did so with sly comedy:

> I believe no one has described his extraordinary gestures or antics with his hands and feet, particularly when passing over the threshold of a door, or rather before he would venture to pass through any doorway. On entering Sir Joshua's house with poor Miss Williams, a blind lady who lived with him, he would quit her hand, or else whirl her about on the steps as he whirled and twisted about to perform his gesticulations; and as soon as he had finished he would give a sudden spring, and make such an extensive stride over the threshold, as if trying for a wager how far he could stride, Mrs Williams standing groping about outside the door, unless the servant took hold of her hand to conduct her in, leaving Dr Johnson to perform at the parlour door much the same exercise over again.[2]

At Sir Joshua's house, these oddities went unremarked. Out of doors, however, it was another matter:

> One Sunday morning, as I was walking with him in Twickenham meadows, he began his antics both with his feet and hands, with the latter as if he was holding the reins of a horse like a jockey on full speed. But to describe the strange positions of his feet is a difficult task; sometimes he would make the back part of his heels to touch, sometimes his toes, as if he was aiming at making the form of a triangle, at least the two sides of one ... I well remember that [these gestures] were so extraordinary that men, women, and children gathered round him, laughing.

People gathered to watch whenever he emerged from Bolt Court to show a female visitor to her carriage in Fleet Street. It was his custom to accompany such visitors all the way and then stand until they drove off, a practice which was likely to draw a 'mob':

> indeed, they would begin to gather the moment he appeared handing the lady down the steps into Fleet Street. But to describe his appearance – his important air – that indeed cannot be described; and his morning habiliments would excite the utmost astonishment in my reader, that a man in his senses could think of

stepping outside his door in them, or even to be seen at home. Sometimes he exhibited himself at the distance of eight to ten doors from Bolt Court, to get at the carriage; to the no small diversion of the populace.

The female visitor, at such moments, probably also experienced some hard-to-describe feelings.

Another anecdote Frances Reynolds, Sir Joshua's sister, told reveals both the unexpected charms of Johnson's company and his odd unpredictability, as well as his unceasing competitive drive to measure himself against others – including young females – and to win:

> at a gentleman's seat in Devonshire, as he and some company were sitting in a saloon, before which was a spacious lawn, it was remarked as a very proper place for running a race. A young lady present boasted that she could outrun any person; on which Dr Johnson rose up and said, 'Madam, you cannot outrun me' and, going out on the lawn, they started. The lady at first had the advantage; but Dr Johnson happening to have slippers on much too small for his feet, kicked them off up into the air, and ran a great length without them, leaving the lady far behind him, and, having won the victory, he returned, leading her by the hand, with looks of high exultation and delight.

Some years after Johnson's death, and perhaps out of loyalty to her old friend, Frances Reynolds took Charlotte Lennox in under her own roof. It is not known for how long they cohabited, and they seem an unlikely pairing if we trust Johnson's version of Frances Reynolds – a woman all 'goodness of heart and sweetness of temper'. But there are other versions. Hester Thrale remarked on her 'odd, dry manner, something between malice and simplicity' and mused at some length on Frances Reynolds's relationship with Sir Joshua. The unmarried younger sister kept house for the celebrated painter, as well as developing her own artistic skills, especially in portraiture, and found the time and courage to write on aesthetics. Mrs Thrale identified strong sibling rivalry which reminded her of similar tensions between Henry Fielding and his sister, Sarah. Fielding's behaviour she thought an instance of 'narrowness':

> While she only read English books, and made English verses it seems, he fondled her fancy and encouraged her genius, but as soon as he perceived she once read Virgil, farewell to fondness, the author's jealousy was become stronger than the brother's affection ... I have fancied lately that there was something of this nature between Sir Joshua and Miss Reynolds; he certainly does not love her as one should expect a man to love a sister he has so much reason to be proud of; perhaps she paints too well, or has learned too much Latin, and is a better scholar than her brother; and upon more reflection I fancy it must be so, for if he only did not like her as an inmate why should not he give her a genteel

annuity, and let her live where and how she likes: the poor lady is always miserable, always fretful; yet she seems resolved – nobly enough – not to keep her post by flattery if she cannot keep it by kindness: – this is a flight so far beyond my power that I respect her for it, and do love dearly to hear her criticise Sir Joshua's painting, or indeed his connoisseurship, which I think she always does with justice and judgement – mingled now and then with a bitterness that diverts one.[3]

Fanny Burney, whose observations were often tinged with malice, found Frances Reynolds tiresome. She described a fussy, tediously indecisive spinster, whose 'habitual perplexity of mind and irresolution of conduct' were irritating, or, in her own words, 'restlessly tormenting' and 'teasingly wearisome'.[4] Typically of Johnson, he made a friend of Frances Reynolds without becoming drawn into questions about female independence or sibling rivalry, and if such had been forced upon him he would certainly have taken Sir Joshua's part.

Burney's words serve very well to describe the dark side of Johnson's psyche: phrases like, 'habitual perplexity of mind', 'restlessly tormenting', could easily be applied to him. This may explain some of Johnson's special feeling for Frances Reynolds. It was no secret to Johnson's friends that he was a man of deeply troubled mind. He made sure that most of his private writings – diaries, autobiographical jottings and reflections – were burned, but in those that survived and from other evidence such as prayers and end of year summaries of the state of his soul, it can be seen that he judged himself harshly; indeed, that he habitually turned a profound and corroding anger upon himself. Speaking of the period that followed completion of the *Dictionary*, Arthur Murphy writes:

> His mind, at this time strained and over-laboured by constant exertion, called for an interval of repose and indolence. But indolence was the time of danger: it was then that his spirits, not employed abroad, turned with inward hostility against himself. His reflections on his own life and conduct were always severe; and, wishing to be immaculate, he destroyed his own peace by unnecessary scruples. He tells us that when he surveyed his past life, he discovered nothing but a barren waste of time, with some disorders of body, and disturbances of mind, very near to madness. His life, he says, from his earliest years, was wasted in a morning bed; and his reigning sin was a general sluggishness, to which he was always inclined, and, in part of his life, almost compelled, by morbid melancholy, and weariness of mind.[5]

In a poem, 'Know Thyself',* written in Latin, Johnson gave full vent to his rage, his 'scant sense of achievement' after such 'prolonged toil':

* Translated here by John Wain

my task finished, I find myself still fettered to myself:
The dull doom of doing nothing, harsher than any drudgery,
Stays with me, and the staleness of slow stagnation.
Cares beget cares, and a clamouring crowd of troubles
Vex me, and vile dreams, the sour sleep of an empty mind.
What will refresh me? The rattle of all-night roisterers,
Or the quiet of solitary spaces? Oh, sleep, sleep, I call,
Lying where I fret at the lingering night, but fear day's cold finger.

In 1756, a year after finishing the *Dictionary*, he signed a contract for the annotated edition of Shakespeare which had been announced by published proposals some ten years earlier. Sir John Hawkins congratulated him 'on his being now engaged in a work that suited his genius.' Johnson's response was in keeping with the depressed mood of the poem: 'I look upon this as I did upon the *Dictionary*: it is all work, and my inducement to it is not love or desire of fame, but the want of money, which is the only motive to writing that I know of.' This gruff denial of interest in the prestige of the subject was almost certainly untrue. Want of money, however, probably induced him to promise to produce the eight volume edition within an unrealistic time frame of eighteen months. In the event it was to be another ten years before Johnson's edition of Shakespeare appeared, and some of this delay can be ascribed to the sorts of feelings Sir John Hawkins assumed and which Johnson denied: a 'torpor' that 'seized his faculties'; a paralysis based on high self-expectations and a consciousness of public expectation. 'Dictionary' Johnson had undertaken to provide the definitive edition of the national poet. Hawkins recalled that it was 'provoking to all his friends to see him waste his days, his weeks and his months so long, that they feared a mental lethargy had seized him out of which he would never recover'. The public – at least, the writing fraternity – were not less provoked and were not silent during this wait. Charles Churchill's gibe, 'He for subscribers baits his hook, and takes their cash – but where's the Book?' circulated widely.

On its appearance in 1765, it was immediately apparent that Johnson's edition of Shakespeare was a work of profound scholarship. As well as the editing and critical annotation of the plays, there is a preface which many consider one of the finest things he ever wrote. Johnson's Shakespeare at times evokes Johnson. He was a man who knew the world by 'mingling as he could in its business and amusements'; he had to make his own opportunities; he immersed himself in the social, he did not hold fast to the comfort of his 'closet', and he did not let 'narrow' circumstances constrain his ambitions:

Shakespeare ... came to London a needy adventurer, and lived for a time by very mean employments. Many works of genius and learning have been performed in states of life that appear very little favourable to thought or to inquiry ... The genius of Shakespeare was not to be depressed by the weight of poverty, nor limited by the narrow conversation to which men in want are inevitably condemned; the encumbrances of his fortune were shaken from his mind ...

For Johnson, Shakespeare was the writer who brought English literature to maturity and made it available to the people. Previously, learning and elegance had been confined to 'professed scholars, or to men and women of high rank.' Like Shakespeare he, too, had felt the weight of poverty, and had run the risk of being limited by 'the narrow conversation to which men in want are inevitably condemned'. By the time his edition of Shakespeare appeared, however, all that had changed, and a new era had opened in Johnson's life.[6]

Of all Johnson's friends, male and female, none was brought into so close a communion with his troubled inner life as the new friend he made in January 1765 when Arthur Murphy, after introducing him to his boon-companion, Henry Thrale, took him to dinner at Thrale's house across the river in Southwark, where Hester Thrale awaited the arrival of the famous writer. It was she who had urged the invitation. She was only twenty-three, new to marriage and motherhood; emotionally, intellectually, and erotically unsatisfied; a woman whom Boswell later (when they became enemies) described as having 'the insolence of wealth and ... the conceit of parts'. She was already a thoughtful reader of Johnson, eager to please and to shine, and he was to become virtually a member of the family for the entire length of her marriage to Henry Thrale. Her wealth and her 'parts' were a significant factor in Johnson's eagerness to put himself under their protection. His expectations of what might be given and owed in return between himself and the young couple who took him up were shaped within the assumptions of patronage.

Hester Thrale was profoundly marked by her long and close relationship with Johnson. Far more than Boswell, she came under his influence and was formed by him. She felt the willing love of a pupil for an admired teacher. She dwelt pleasurably on,

> our mutual regard ... founded on the truest principles, religion, virtue, and community of ideas ... He has fastened many of his own notions so on my mind ... that I am not sure whether they grew there originally or no: of this I am sure, that they are the best and wisest notions I possess; and that I love the author of them with a firm affection.[7]

She reproved herself for this grandiosity: 'saucy Soul! Community of Ideas with Doctor Johnson'. How dare she! But it was this experience, eagerly grasped, gratefully and self-approvingly recorded, which later modulated into the resentful reflection on her loss of self: 'in Dr Johnson's mind mine was swallowed up and lost'. He was a powerful formative influence. He moulded her mind. She emerged fully as a writer only after his death (and after the death of her first husband), publishing under her new married name of Piozzi; and not only was her first book an account of her life with Dr Johnson, it could be said that all her writing was a continuation of the conversation which began when he first came to dinner in January 1765, when they liked each other so well that further dinners were immediately arranged. His large presence haunted her intellect and imagination. No more peaceable a soul than he was, the conversation Hester Thrale went on having with Dr Johnson was a quarrelsome and rancorous one.

Henry Thrale, worldly and a *bon vivant*, liked to entertain lavishly. Although not himself a great talker, he enjoyed nothing better than argumentative conversation. Fanny Burney noted his 'singular amusement in hearing, instigating and provoking a war of words, alternating triumph and overthrow, between clever and ambitious colloquial combatants'. Johnson's conversational style, his liking for 'rough dispute', was much to Thrale's taste. Ambitious to increase his consequence as well as his business, with his sights set on becoming MP for Southwark, Thrale understood the advantage of being known to have so famous a man at his table. Mrs Thrale meanwhile, allowed little freedom or scope in a marriage entered into in a spirit of business rather than love, found her role as hostess to her husband's friends enlivened by a writer she admired; a writer, furthermore, who immediately encouraged her into literary activity.

Brought up to believe herself 'half a Prodigy', Hester Thrale had literary ambitions. She was fiercely intelligent, with a sharp critical mind, contentious and revisionary like Johnson's. She had been well-educated in the usual subjects and some unusual ones, such as Latin, logic and rhetoric. Until her marriage, she had been taught to value herself for her wit: her head, she wrote later, was 'full of authors, actors, literature in every shape'. She was saturated in books, her passion for literature every bit the equal of Johnson's. Like Elizabeth Carter, whose name and fame for learning she undoubtedly knew of through her Latin tutor Arthur Collier, who was a friend of Sarah Fielding, she began sending pieces to the newspapers under various signatures; her first identified article being in the *St James's Chronicle*, 1762. Like Carter also, she was attracted to Pope's *Essay on Man*, had a command of many languages, and was a poet. Marriage cut short this budding career just as she completed an 'Ode on the Blessings of the Peace' to celebrate the end of the Seven Years War, which she had submitted to Thomas Arne in hopes it might be set to music and sung at Ranelagh.

Marriage was a disappointment in other ways. Henry Thrale worked hard at his brewery business, took command of every aspect of household affairs including planning the menus and ordering dinners to his taste (priding himself on being a gourmet), and continued to keep mistresses in the city. His notion of proper wifely behaviour was narrow: not only did he not want her meddling in the kitchens, he discouraged her from paying visits and preferred her not to ride (she was an excellent horsewoman). Her place was in the drawing-room, where she was a pretty and accomplished hostess, and in the bedchamber.

Hester Thrale was typical of the women Johnson was attracted to: well-informed, vividly intelligent, and playful but respectful. Her independence of mind pleased him so long as it remained 'feminine': he disliked what he called 'honeysuckle wives' but approved of female subjugation in marriage and would not allow Mrs Thrale to complain to him of her husband's coldness. He would take the husband's side in any quarrel – on principle, for the husband was master. (He enjoyed the idea of Henry Thrale as Master, and frequently referred to him as such.) Nevertheless, he could also say: 'It is a paltry trick indeed to deny women the cultivation of their mental powers, and I think it is partly a proof we are afraid of them, if we endeavour to keep them unarmed.'[8]

He did not wish to be thought afraid of women; it was among Hester's charms that she was well-armed in wit and mental prowess. Intimacy between all three developed quickly. Henry Thrale had little interest in literature, but he was kind and generous, an amiable, unimaginative, easy-going gentleman. Hester Thrale sought affection as well as intellectual recognition from Johnson. They translated the 'Odes' of Boethius together, each taking alternate verses. She also, by his invitation, contributed to Anna Williams's *Miscellanies* (which perhaps needed some padding out) which finally appeared in 1766. This brought her something of a literary reputation: her ballad, 'The Three Warnings', went on being reproduced into the nineteenth century. But it was as a conversationalist that Johnson mostly appreciated her, finding her 'one of the wisest women in the world'. Frances Reynolds bore witness:

> On the praises of Mrs Thrale he used to dwell with a peculiar delight, a paternal fondness, expressive of conscious exultation in being so intimately acquainted with her ... expatiating on her various perfections – the solidity of her virtues, the brilliancy of her wit, and the strength of her understanding.

Over the years, continuous pregnancy and child-bearing made regular literary work impossible. The 'pleasures' of her marriage, as she put it, consisted in 'holding my head over a Bason Six Months in the Year'. Twelve children were born to Hester Thrale of whom eight died, including a much-loved son at the age of nine. There were also a number of miscarriages. It is a terrible catalogue of misery and she often had cause to note, 'This house smells like a hospital'.

Whatever went on in the nursery, however 'big with child' she might be, or sick, or devastated by grief, the dinners continued and the conversation flowed. Streatham talk was relentlessly literary. Fanny Burney found it impossible to keep up: 'I hardly ever read, saw, or heard of any book that ... has not been mentioned here.' A room was assigned to Johnson, and as well as making some long extended stays he fell into the habit of spending the middle part of the week at Streatham, returning to London at the weekends. He was not engaged in a major literary task. What he wanted was talk. Sleeping late, drifting from his room to the library, from the library to the nursery (he was attentive to children and believed they should be treated with respectful indulgence), from the nursery to the garden, muttering aloud, perhaps, as was his wont, gesticulating oddly, eating 'grossly', he appeared

> the idlest of all human beings; ever musing till he was called out to converse, and conversing till the fatigue of his friends, or the promptitude of his own temper to take offence, consigned him back again to silent meditation.

Hester Thrale's acquaintance with him, she wrote, 'consisted in little else than talking'; under his guidance she trained herself so well that she became one of the most famous female talkers of her time. It was Johnson's view that 'nothing promoted happiness so much as conversation'. Later she recalled the contempt he expressed for a pretty woman who sat in a room and had nothing to say. Such a woman, he complained, 'adds nothing to life, and by sitting down before one thus desperately silent, takes away the confidence one should have in the company of her chair if she were once out of it'. To be his chosen companion was not easy: 'Mr Johnson had a roughness in his manner which subdued the saucy, and terrified the meek: this was, when I knew him, the prominent part of a character which few durst venture to approach so nearly.' [9]

In his idleness and melancholy, he could also be mischievous. One of the problems Mrs Thrale faced after she brought him to Streatham in a state of mental collapse in 1766 was the mutual dislike between him and her mother, Mrs Salusbury. Johnson, fearing the complete loss of his reason, had been unable to leave his rooms off Fleet Street for months. His mind was in a 'horrible condition', 'nearly distracted'. The 'perverse opposition, petty contentions, and mutual complaints' that instantly sprang up between Johnson and Mrs Salusbury made Hester's task of caring for Johnson more difficult. He, however, found entertainment. Annoyed by what he considered Mrs Salusbury's obsessive reading of foreign politics in the newspapers and her insistence on talking about these and other matters he had no interest in, he planted fictitious stories in the press: 'he teased her,' Mrs Thrale recalled, 'by writing in the newspapers concerning battles and plots which had no existence, only to feed her with new accounts of the division of Poland perhaps, or the disputes between the states of Russia and Turkey'.

His mischievous impulses might be preferable to hypochondria and self-pity: reading aloud in company one day from his own lines in 'The Vanity of Human Wishes' about the 'ills' that assailed the scholar's life, he burst into tears. Mrs Thrale describes a period of depression when he became convinced he was dying:

> when he had lamented in the most piercing terms his approaching dissolution, and conjured me solemnly to tell him what I thought, while Sir Richard Jebb was perpetually on the road to Streatham, and Mr Johnson seemed to think himself neglected if the physician left him for an hour only, I made him a steady, but as I thought a very gentle harangue, in which I confirmed all that the Doctor had been saying, how no present danger could be expected; but that his age and continued ill health must naturally accelerate the arrival of that hour which can be escaped by none. 'And this (says Johnson, rising in great anger) is the voice of female friendship I suppose, when the hand of the hangman would be softer.' [10]

Henry Thrale was rarely treated to these performances. Johnson deferred to him as the master of the household. Mr Thrale's influence was powerful enough 'to make him suppress many rough answers: he could likewise prevail on him to change his shirt, his coat, or his plate, almost before it came indispensably necessary to the comfortable feelings of his friends'. Mr Thrale appointed a valet to be ready with a clean wig for Johnson when he came down to dine. Keen travellers, the Thrales took Johnson on many trips with them. He enjoyed travelling for its own sake, but could be a wearisome companion with his habit of contradiction and tendency to take offence. After Henry Thrale's death in 1781, it became 'perplexing and difficult to live in the house with him'. Much of his time was spent in blaming Hester Thrale for this or that. His miseries increased with age and ill health and perhaps with the completion of his last major work, *The Lives of the Poets*. Convinced of the fundamental vacuity of life, he had never been able to take pleasure in achievement; and though berating himself for idleness was, in fact, most happy when most at work:

> Mr Johnson's knowledge of literary history was extensive and surprising; he knew every adventure of every book you could name almost, and was exceedingly pleased with the opportunity which writing the Poets Lives gave him to display

it. He loved to be set at work, and was sorry when he came to the end of the business he was about.[11]

Hester Thrale summed up her 'candle-light picture' of his latter days with a summary of her relationship with Johnson in which she awarded herself full credit for her services to English Literature:

> Veneration for his virtue, reverence for his talents, delight in his conversation, and habitual endurance of a yoke my husband first put upon me, and of which he contentedly bore his share for sixteen or seventeen years, made me go on so long with Mr Johnson; but the perpetual confinement I will own to have been terrifying in the first years of our friendship, and irksome in the last; nor could I pretend to support it without help, when my coadjutor was no more. To the assistance we gave him, the shelter our house afforded to his uneasy fancies, and to the pains we took to sooth or repress them, the world is perhaps indebted for the three political pamphlets, the new edition and correction of his Dictionary, and for the Poets Lives, which he would scarce have lived, I think, and kept his faculties entire, to have written, had not incessant care been exerted at the time of his first coming to be our constant guest in the country; and several times after that, when he found himself particularly oppressed with diseases incident to the most vivid and fervent imaginations.[12]

Hester Thrale's *Anecdotes of the Late Samuel Johnson*, published under her married name of Hester Piozzi, carried an unexpected Postscript, dated at Naples, where she then was and where she had written much of the book. It read as follows:

> Having seen a passage from Mr Boswell's *Tour to the Hebrides*, in which it is said, that *I could not get through Mrs Montagu's Essay on Shakespeare*, I do not delay a moment to declare, that, on the contrary, I have always commended it myself, and heard it commended by everyone else; and few things would give me more concern than to be thought incapable of tasting, or unwilling to testify my opinion of its excellence.

It was no news to Hester Thrale that Johnson, who famously gutted books but did not read through them, was lukewarm about Mrs Montagu's *Essay on Shakespeare* which came out in 1769, four years after Johnson's edition. James Beattie, the moral philosopher who was among the group of Scottish intellectuals, including Robertson, Blair, Kames and Gregory, who seem to have found it easier to accept Montagu's brilliance than their English counterparts (though Beattie was, of course, her protégée) summarised what was a widely shared view in the Montagu camp:

> Johnson's harsh and foolish censure of Mrs Montagu's book does not surprise me, for I have heard him speak contemptuously of it. It is, for all that, one of the best, most original, and most elegant pieces of criticism in our language, or

any other. Johnson had many of the talents of a critic; but his want of temper, his violent prejudices, and something, I am afraid, of an envious turn of mind, made him often a very unfair one. Mrs Montagu was very kind to him, but Mrs Montagu has more wit than any body; and Johnson could not bear that any person should be thought to have wit but himself.[13]

Montagu herself had an acute consciousness of the tendency of talent to expose women to envy – 'It is hard to say whether women remarkable for their understanding suffer most from the envy of their own sex or the malice of the other, but their life is one continual warfare' – and she did not think it was confined to Johnson. She knew also that she had set out to contradict 'established prejudices' about Shakespeare which would draw down wrath upon her. She fed on that warfare to some extent – and perhaps she was consciously echoing Pope, giving a gendered turn to his words about the life of a wit being a warfare on earth. Nevertheless, the writer whose prejudices she most set out to contradict was Johnson; her *Essay on Shakespeare* was in part provoked by dissatisfaction with his preface to the edition of 1765.

Johnson's *Preface* falls into four sections: Shakespeare's virtues are canvassed; his 'faults' arraigned but not so as to call into question his greatness; he is defended against the charge that he disregarded the unities of time and place, which Johnson dismisses as worthless anyway; the question of his learning and understanding is explored and an account is given of the history of the editing of Shakespeare before Johnson. Some of these points had appeared in the dedication of *Shakespear Illustrated*, which Johnson wrote for Charlotte Lennox, and some in Johnson's own proposals for his edition. For all its strengths – and it still reads as a vigorous and engaged piece of historiographic criticism – one element is strikingly absent from the preface: there is no consideration of the texts in terms of their dramatic qualities. Elizabeth Montagu seized on this. She wrote to Elizabeth Carter that Johnson had not

pointed out the peculiar excellencies of Shakespear as a *Dramatic* poet, this point I shall labour as I think he therein excels everyone. I have been very busy in writing upon the Tragedy of Macbeth, which opens a large field for criticism, as I have there taken notice of how he employs his supernatural Beings (who, by the by, other poets have not made at all supernatural). I have compared the Manes of Daniis with the Ghost of Hamlet, and have, asking your pardon, spoken a little irreverently of the Minerva in the Ajax of Sophocles … I think poor Shakespeare is like an unfortunate maid, whom many lovers have betrothed and none has married. The subject is a little contaminated …[14]

Contaminated or not, 'poor' Shakespeare was the subject she proposed for the display of her own abilities.

Throughout the 1760s, Elizabeth Carter had been encouraging Montagu in her literary progress. She received and responded to pages of thoughtful discussion in letters: essays on the Chorus in Greek tragedy, analyses of the merits of Sophocles and Euripides, of Dryden, Cowley and Milton, and, above all, of Shakespeare as the greatest natural genius of all time. Montagu was an enthusiast for drama in general to a degree which Carter did not share and for Shakespeare in particular. She followed Shakespeare criticism as it developed: in 1747 she was scathing about Warburton's 'nonsense'; and in 1755, she expressed outrage at Voltaire's comments on Shakespeare. The 'saucy frenchman' had no right, in her opinion, to attack 'fancy's sweetest child' and she wished she could be as sure that 'our fleets and armies could drive the French out of America as that our poets and trage-dians can drive them out of Parnassus'. Like Johnson, who boasted that, alone, he would be able to compile a dictionary of the English language in three years, even though the French academy with forty members took forty years to produce the equivalent for the French language, because the proportion of an Englishman to a Frenchman was as 'three to sixteen hundred', so Elizabeth Montagu considered herself one of the leaders of the winning side in the culture wars. The defence of Shakespeare was a defence of national honour and she was equal to it. To be outraged by Voltaire was not original: in 1744 Catherine Talbot objected to his 'French impertinence' in asserting the utter incapacity of 'our nation' for music, painting and dramatic poetry.

Voltaire and Johnson both served as targets. Johnson's edition stirred Montagu to a flurry of studious critical activity. Throughout 1766 she worked hard on her own book. It allowed a free flow of her natural combativeness. Reading and rereading Johnson's preface, Montagu became more critical, more confident of her own opinions, and less inclined to be polite even to his loyal friend Miss Carter:

> My Dear Friend, I am quite of your opinion that our last commentator of Sha-kespear [Johnson] found the piddling trade of verbal criticism below his genius and I am much at a loss when I would account for his persisting in it, through the course of so many volumes. It has been lucky for my amusement, but unfor-tunate for the public, that he did not consider his author in a more extensive view. I have so much veneration for our poet, and so much zeal for the honour of our country, and I think the theatrical entertainments capable of conveying so much instruction, and of exciting such sentiments in the people, that if I am glad he left the task to my unable hand, I dare hardly own it to myself.[15]

If she was glad, she hardly dared own it to herself. It is an interesting formulation, especially when associated with her description of the activity she was thoroughly engrossed in at that time: 'the piddling trade of verbal criticism'. Criticism, as a literary activity, was so much more nakedly about the sense of superiority than, for example, novel-writing or translation and adaptation. Critics ranked authors. On the basis of their 'perfect judgement' or impeccable taste, they asserted the superiority of this author over that and drew upon themselves a like response: George Lyttelton reported to Montagu that Sir James Macdonald 'declared at once that you were a critic as much superior to Brumoy, as he is to most others'. Competition for the heights of critical authority was fierce. This may be why, in spite of Montagu's immersion in Brumoy – most likely in its original French, not in Lennox's English translation – and her major project on Shakespeare (staying in Suffolk she thought it best to work in her bedroom rather than 'sit with my Shakespear and Brumoy in public'), she seems not to have addressed the connection with Charlotte Lennox as a predecessor in the field. She certainly knew about *Shakespear Illustrated*. Probably her work occupied a completely different realm in the imagination, as she herself occupied a grander social world in life. Probably Charlotte Lennox represented 'the piddling trade' side of things which contributed to Montagu's ambivalence, which in turn needed so much bolstering with concepts like 'veneration', and 'zeal for the honour of our country'.

Convinced that critics could 'make no honey' – 'Critics make no honey, when angry they are wasps and when softer they are drones' – Montagu was more comfortable as a wasp than a drone. She returned to the attack on Johnson:

> It is strange that Mr Johnson should so superficially examine the merits and faults of his author's plays: he should have said more or have said nothing. If he had given attention to the dramatic genius of Shakespear he might have done him justice, and I wonder he did not enter with pleasure into a task that seemed peculiarly suited to him, he has taste and learning, therefore is a capable critic; he wants invention, he wants strength and vigour of genius to go through a long original work. I will own he gives smart correction to former commentators, but the last commentator deserves the least indulgence, as he had most opportunity of seeing the futility of the thing.[16]

And even more scornfully:

> I cannot imagine what these wise men mean by denying the third part of *Henry VI* to be Shakespear's. I agree with Mr Johnson as to the French scene in the courtship, but it seems to me he has very superficially treated of the play of *Henry V*. It made me laugh heartily to read a parcel of litterati, some of them desiring the reading might be *accurs'd* others *a scursed*, others *a crude*, others a *crush'd* neccesity, a mighty pretty amusement truly writing such notes. Is this the

infant sporting or dotage of criticism? I think the latter. There is an imbecility in it that argues parts worn out.[17]

The establishing of reliable editions of Shakespeare's texts was in its infancy and some passages had been rendered in highly disputed ways. Like all critics, Montagu criticised other critics. Partly this enabled her to create a space where she could insert her own work, and partly it served as a foil or irritant to keep herself going. Disagreement quickly turned to sarcasm:

> Do you agree with Mr Johnson and Pope that the style of the *Two Gentlemen of Verona* is less affected than almost any play of Shakespear? Johnson adds, it has as many fine lines and passages as any of his. Where are they? It is a little unlucky that the note remarking the pure and unaffecting style of this play should be placed under the following words
>
> > Wer't not, affection chains thy tender days
> > The sweet glances of thy honoured love &cc
>
> Affection chaining tender days to sweet glances of an honoured love is surely a very easy natural mode of expression! [18]

Although not planning to include *Henry V* in her book, she could not resist elaborating her own observations on it and did so with her usual fluency. Her ideas tumbled over one another as she chased them, full of excited responsiveness:

> Shakespear deserved some praise for contriving to make his Henry so naturally arise from Prince Hal. The hint thrown out of his having studied mankind and their various occupations and duties in the promiscuous company he had kept, is artful. His speech to the conspirators divine the long political discussions of his right to the realm of France is undramatic, and therefore imperfect on the stage. His reflections at his return from his midnight walk round the camp admirable, the conversation of the soldiers natural. By the by, I think Shakespear has therein excelled our darling Tacitus, who imagines Germanicus on the like occasion to hear nothing but his own praises.[19]

Tacitus was the author Carter and Montagu had agreed to read in a systematic way and exchange thoughts about. What Carter thought about all the ire against Johnson is not recorded, but she did now and then reiterate the high value she put on him and his writings. She received Montagu's drafts as they were produced; she read and annotated with comments and corrections. We have nothing but the blandest records of what she thought about it, although the intellectual engagement between the two women was always strong. Elizabeth Montagu's energy, her vigorous – even contemptuous – speech as she committed herself and her genius to a kind of writing she found it necessary to disparage, contrasts dramatically with Carter's preference for acquiescent calm and loyalty to both her literary friends.

In May 1769, Dodsley printed the *Essay on the Writings and Genius of Shakespear, Compared with the Greek and French Dramatic Poets: With Some Remarks upon the Misrepresentations of Mons. De Voltaire.* The first run of a thousand copies sold out quickly. The work was enormously popular, both amongst Montagu's friends and amongst the critics. The 'pert news-writers', she was glad to see, 'have not sneered at the lady critic'. Pert or not, she read the critics avidly, taking seriously the potential impact of her writings on the minds of the reading classes throughout the land:

> The Critical Reviewers have most graciously extolled a certain essay … As many good people in all the towns in England regulate their opinions by this review it is lucky. The rich grocer, the substantial manufacturer sits and reads this literary gazette with implicit faith, and the curate (who dictates in matters of learning to the farmer's heiress, who at boarding school learnt to read novels) takes his opinions and derives his knowledge from the monthly papers.[20]

Mrs Montagu, the 'Queen of the Blues', was unambivalently interested in the widest extension of her new sovereignty. By the fourth edition in 1777, her name appeared on the title page though her identity as the author was well established before then.

Hester Chapone (the former Miss Mulso) wrote to Elizabeth Carter soon after the appearance of the *Essay on Shakespeare* confessing that she had slipped up in not writing to Mrs Montagu about it: 'my friends at Knight's tell me I ought to have written to her on the subject of her book.' Some token praises followed. Mrs Chapone had been depressed, 'rather shabby of late since the wet weather came.' She must have pulled herself together sufficiently to satisfy Mrs Montagu with her comments, for by the summer of 1770 she was holidaying with her at Denton in Northumberland and drawing on her support for her own writing. Her confidence was high: 'I am grown as bold as a lion with Mrs Montagu, and fly in her face whenever I have a mind; in short I enjoy her society with the most perfect *gout*, and find my love for her takes off my fear and awe, though my respect for her character continually increases.' Mrs Chapone's 'little publications', which followed a few years later and which Montagu helped her edit, went some way to 'appease … that uneasy sense of helplessness and insignificancy in society, which has often depressed and afflicted me'. Mrs Montagu's patron-age and support served her well; or, to put that the other way, Mrs Chapone knew how to make good use of it. The combination of critical boldness with 'awe' for one so much her superior in rank, as well as a willingness to feel her own helplessness and insignificancy, struck the right balance.[21]

Johnson's opinion of Montagu's work was a matter of considerable interest. Her *Essay* brought the two most powerful figures in literary London into direct competition with each other over intellectual possession of the national bard. (Meanwhile, 1769 was also the year of Garrick's Shakespeare Jubilee, which helped advertise the *Essay*, and Garrick later published a poem praising it.) Johnson, as Boswell put it, was 'not apt to encourage one to *share* reputation with himself' and he was not inclined to give place to Mrs Montagu, who, coming after him and basing her reputation on a book about Shakespeare, was rather seizing than sharing. Montagu expected criticism from Johnson. She knew, too, that the other surviving men who had published on Shakespeare – Warburton especially, who was a notorious controversialist – would not receive her work silently. Like Charlotte Lennox, Mrs Montagu went to war when she picked up her pen, and although she often hid it successfully (hence the elaboration of defensive flatteries that can make her letters unreadable) she was, nonetheless, aware of her aggressive impulses and of their impact on others. How could she not be? She was a woman who was used to command and rule. The critical aggression in her book would, she well knew, bring aggression back upon her; she was laying imperious claim to what had hitherto belonged to men. In a long letter to her father – who, like her husband, welcomed the book wholeheartedly – she explained her reasons for not having told him about it earlier, especially since he had always encouraged her in her studies. She did not want him to think she was ungrateful. She wrote:

there is in general a prejudice against female authors, especially if they invade those regions of literature which the men are desirous to reserve to themselves. While I was young, I should not have liked to have been classed among authors, but at my age it is less unbecoming. If an old woman does not bewitch her neighbours' cows, nor make any girl in the parish spit crooked pins, the world has no reason to take offence at her amusing herself with reading books or even writing them. However, some circumstances in this particular case invite secrecy. Mr Pope our great poet, the Bishop of Gloucester our great Critick, and Dr Johnson our great scholar, having already given their criticisms on Shakespear, there was a degree of presumption in pretending to meddle with a subject they had already treated – sure to incur their envy if I succeeded tolerably well, their contempt if I did not. Then, for a weak and unknown champion to throw down the gauntlet of defiance in the very teeth of Voltaire appeared too daring. The French and Italians are fond of books of criticism, but they are not so much to the taste of the English. At present the desire of most readers is to be amused with something perfectly gay and superficial. I was obliged to enter seriously into the nature of the dramatic purposes, and the character of the best dramatic writings, and by sometimes differing from the code of the great legislator in

Poetics, Aristotle, I was afraid the learned would reject my opinions, the unlearned yawn over my pages, so that I was very doubtful of the general success of my work. The booksellers who hate an author should print for himself would hardly advertise my book ...[22]

This is the thinking of a strategist, working out the enemy's positions. As a cogent statement of likely responses it proved remarkably percipient. Montagu's powerful position inhibited full-throttle attack; instead, she became the victim of a denigration that drew full support from Boswell's remarks in the *Tour to the Hebrides*. Commenting on Johnson's failure to mention Garrick in the preface to Shakespeare, Boswell instanced Mrs Montagu's high praise of the actor in her book and reported Johnson's reply as follows: 'Sir, it is fit she should say so much, and I should say nothing. Reynolds is fond of her book, and I wonder at it; for neither I, nor Beauclerk, nor Mrs Thrale, could get through it.'[23]

Elizabeth Montagu had the advantage of Johnson in terms of birth and wealth. He acknowledged her as a woman of consequence accustomed to assume leadership position and entitled to it by virtue of her innate abilities. They were never intimates (unlike Mrs Chapone, he was not inclined to admit to his own insignificance and helplessness). Mrs Montagu's consciousness of rank, her dictatorial manner, her love of holding the floor in talk was in every way a match for Johnson. She had not a deferential bone in her body, and there was never the faintest chance that her mind would be 'swallowed up and lost' in his. His tribute to her in 1784, that her conversation was 'always impregnated; it has always meaning' takes on an additional force in the context of their long acquaintanceship, for as rivals they early took each other's measure and settled for an uneasy co-existence. There was no outright quarrel, but his disparagement of her *Essay on Shakespeare* hurt; and his contempt for Lyttelton finished the friendship as far as she was concerned. Johnson seems to have felt this more acutely than she did. Boswell reports him as saying, 'Mrs Montagu has dropped me. Now, Sir, there are people whom one would like very well to drop, but would not wish to be dropped by.' His precision sums up the relationship very well. Montagu's power made it undesirable to be 'dropped' by her, but she was not a person it was always comfortable to be with.

The coldness of her manner towards Johnson was widely remarked: Horace Walpole reported that at Lady Lucan's, 'Mrs Montagu kept aloof from Johnson like the West from the East'; or, more pointedly, 'Mrs Montagu and Dr Johnson kept at different ends of the chamber, and set up altar against altar there'. Behind Mrs Montagu's public display of frozen politeness boiled a rage which might have burst the bounds of decorum.

Her worst thoughts were not shared with Elizabeth Carter but they were shared with others. Accusations of Johnson's 'envy' and 'malice' flowed from her: he was a hypocrite, a pedant, his heart was filled with hatred. His 'malicious falsehoods' were an 'odious subject'. Nevertheless, they were explicable, in her view, as an inevitable product of his physical deformities:

> I wish his figure was put as a frontispiece to his works, his squinting look and monstrous form would well explain his character. Those disgraces which make a good mind humble and complacent, ever render a bad one envious and ferocious.[24]

To be 'humble' and 'complacent' was to accept what Providence had willed in terms of personal fortune and social rank. Hers happened to be high; his were low. His 'monstrous' exterior bespoke monstrousness within, the monstrousness of the disgruntled lower orders. The truth is that Johnson's remarks about her writing, and about Lord Lyttelton's writing, were intolerable to Mrs Montagu on more than personal grounds. The superiority of his opinion in print challenged her superiority – the supe-riority of the lettered aristocracy – in the social world. The press quickly picked up the gossip and directed their attacks at Montagu.

As a young woman Montagu had been noted for her wit and intellect. Her step-grandfather was Conyers Middleton, a Cambridge intellectual with whom she spent long periods throughout her childhood, and by whom she was encouraged to listen to the conversation of the dons in the drawing-room and rehearse their arguments afterwards. With intellectual aristocratic women like the Duchess of Portland she had been friends since adolescence. Her marriage at the age of twenty-two to a man almost thirty years older than herself, the grandson of the Earl of Sandwich, raised her from the squirearchy into the nobility. She had no children after the death of little 'Punch' – an event that marked both herself and her husband. There was an additional blow the following year for Elizabeth in the sudden death of a favourite brother, Tom.

Edward Montagu was a scholar and mathematician of solitary persuasion – 'indolent' is the word used of him, though whether he was actually indolent or interested in matters other than those deemed appropriate is not clear. (More or less everybody habitually accused themselves and each other of indolence, a detail worth bearing in mind when we consider Johnson's struggle against what he thought of as his own constitutional indolence.)[25] What is clear is that Edward Montagu was content for his wife to busy herself with his affairs. Like other landowning wives, she saw it as her duty to oversee the social and material conditions of the families who worked the collieries and the estates, providing some basic education, mounting annual feasts and commenting on the happy faces at her groaning board; unlike most wives, she also managed huge capital sums and followed the fortunes of trade and finance with a close eye. When she read the newspaper it was not only for politics and gossip: 'in today's paper, there is an article, that a banker in Lombard Street will answer all bills for the Newcastle Bank. It would be very embarrassing to the coal trade if the Newcastle Bank should fail.' The management of the collieries and land increasingly fell to her, a responsibility which involved a huge business correspondence and ensured that life sometimes seemed composed of nothing more than 'grovelling cares and filthy lucre and dirty coal'.[26]

In a similar way, Hester Thrale showed an aptitude for the business side of her husband's brewery, but she took little pleasure in it. After Henry Thrale had a stroke in 1779 she feared she would have to take over, since it was 'a dreadful thing to think of a man whose brain has been injured having the care and management of such a capital as ours'. She knew what was needed: 'I must go to the Borough house this winter, and hack at the trade myself, I hate it heartily, yes heartily.'[27] She also made sure that he was re-elected MP by conducting his election campaign herself, persuading key people to go out with her to 'beg votes' and dine with 'my voters'; and though it was fatiguing she was successful. Johnson (who also habitually helped Thrale at election time) told her daughter, 'she has been very busy, and has run about the Borough like a tigress seizing upon everything that she found in her way.' She was driven by her desire to protect the wealth generated by a business which, though mostly successful, had been through difficult times, and which underpinned the life she enjoyed: leisured, literary and devoted to talk. Less straightforwardly, she was also concerned about her 'consequence'. Her 'consequence' was directly related to her wealth, but it could be undermined by too close an association with trade. She was suspicious of Mrs Montagu's motives in encouraging her to keep the brewery after Henry Thrale's death:

> Mrs Montagu has been here. She says I ought to have a statue erected to me for my diligent attendance on my compting house duties; the Wits and the Blues (as it is the fashion to call them) will be happy enough no doubt to have me safe at the brewery – out of their way.

The brewery was a 'golden millstone' round her neck and she sold it as soon as she could. Free of it, she believed she had made a bargain which would bring,

> peace and a stable fortune, restoration to my original rank in life, and a situation undisturbed by commercial jargon, unpolluted by commercial frauds, undisgraced by commercial connections ...

If there had been any rivalrous calculation in her response, Montagu accounted for it differently. Once the sale had gone through, she congratulated Thrale on being rid of 'cares and hazards words cannot express' and explained that she had feared there would be no buyer for such a large concern, hence 'I threw all my arguments in favour of a continuance of the business, thinking it indeed vain to talk on the other side'.[28]

Montagu herself, by contrast, took over complete control of land and business on her husband's death in 1775. By the time of her own death in 1800, 'Montagu Main' was the most popular coal on the market. Her bank account at Hoare & Co. had been transferred to the category reserved for institutions like Eton College. She loved what she called her 'golden showers'. 'Gold', she declared, was 'the chief ingredient in the composition of earthly happiness.'

Edward Montagu accepted that his wife would cultivate intense relationships with others, men as well as women. The couple were often domiciled in different parts of the country. Soon after their marriage, she was in Yorkshire, happily ensconced in near-solitude with her sister Sarah, both of them studiously reading and writing through the long country days and not at all sharing the view expressed by their own father, that living in the country was 'sleeping with one's eyes open'. The men Elizabeth was drawn to were of scholarly disposition like her husband, but with more love of social interaction and public affairs: Edmund Burke, Gilbert West, Benjamin Stillingfleet, Lord Lyttelton, Lord Bath. The elderly Lord Bath – a notorious gallant in his younger days – became her constant companion after they met at Tunbridge in 1760. They wrote daily. They took 'airings' to Kew and Richmond: 'we have sauntered in the chaise by the Riverside, and sometimes stopped to hear the nightingales in the hedges'. There was gossip but she faced it down, deploying her customary rhetoric of virtue and honour: he was 'amiable', her feelings for him were 'love, esteem and honour', and she held him in 'veneration' for his 'noble virtues and talents'. An old hand at politics and literature, Lord Bath guided her in the ways she might figure as a patron of influence and power. His advice was crucial in these years, when she launched herself as a serious contender for supremacy in the literary world; and when he died in 1764 she felt 'forlorn and annihilated'. Her husband tactfully stayed in London whilst she called Elizabeth Carter up to her country house in Berkshire to comfort her for the loss of what her biographer called 'the greatest attachment of her life'.[29]

Lord Lyttelton was there to supply the place of Lord Bath. He was a neighbour, having a London house in Hill Street. Like Lord Bath he was steeped in politics and literature, a man of affairs and ideas. Horace Walpole told the story of Mrs Montagu's sixteen-year-old postilion who declared, 'I am not such a child but I can guess something; whenever my Lord Lyttelton comes to my Lady she orders her porter to let in nobody else, and then they call for a pen and ink and say they are going to write history.' No doubt the sage sixteen-year-old caught something in the air, but it seems likely that writing history is exactly what they were most engaged in doing and that Mrs Montagu's interest in romance was passionately cerebral. Furthermore, that it was posited on some denial of the body. She boasted of being 'in body a saint, in mind a great sinner'. Once she aligned herself with the famously virginal Elizabeth Carter in the throwaway remark, 'You and I, who have never been in love ...', a description Hester Chapone amplified: in her opinion, expressed to Elizabeth Carter, Mrs Montagu was 'an ignoramus on this subject, as I have observed on many occasions, nor are you quite an adept. It is the only subject in the world of which I think myself a better judge than either of you.' [30]

The 'sinful' energies of mind required saintly practices of body, just as the freedoms her husband gave her required a rigid adherence to his rule. She made a great point of deferring to his wishes, displaying wifely obedience in an exaggerated form. Sometimes this inconvenienced her; at other times it was no more than a pantomime. He could be difficult, churlish and bad tempered, displaying a negativity and inability to make decisions that were probably symptoms of depression. In her management of him she stressed how she constantly strove to put the bright side of things forward. He, meanwhile, gave her literary ventures his unconditional support.

Hester Thrale adopted a similar approach with her husband. Troubled by the changes produced in Henry Thrale by his stroke, she was led to reflect on how she customarily never objected to any of his demands, nor proposed her own; she would 'never offer to cross my Master's fancy' nor 'think any occasion serious enough to excuse contradiction unless virtue, life, or fortune' were involved. The reason was pragmatic. Such a battle was one which the wife would always lose:

> It has often been my admiration to observe how many people, and particularly women, delight in contest when they know beforehand they shall be defeated; always fighting the battle with their husbands and always losing the victory; 'tis comical to see how strangely insensible they must be to refusal or rejection. Was I to propose a journey Mr Thrale would refuse to let me take; or desire a tree to be cut down or planted, and he should – as he most undoubtedly would – give me a coarse reply and abrupt negative, it would make me miserable: to have one's own unimportance presented suddenly to one's sight, and one's own qualities insolently undervalued by those who do not even pretend to possess them, is sufficiently mortifying.[31]

Both these wives were skilled in the strategies for dealing with wifely 'unimportance'. Neither sought to attack the structures which vested so much power in the person of the husband. Mrs Thrale was fierce in her denunciation of women who committed adultery, for example, wishing the Bishop of Llandaff's 'paltry' Bill against adultery (which proposed that people divorcing for adultery be prevented from marrying their adulterous lovers) was stronger:

> They should inflict some real punishment: was a woman to have her ring finger cut off, her lover would hesitate a little in marrying her I'll warrant him; and she well deserves punishment as severe as that at least for thus madly transgressing – however provoked – the great laws of both God and man.[32]

Credit lay in the management of men, and of one's own feelings and desires. Hester Thrale adored the homage she received from the many men who were close to her, and perhaps it is not accidental that this shocking entry in *Thraliana* followed a long reflection about love and friendship and about the pleasures of receiving so much male admiration that 'who can wonder that my head is turned with vanity?' Questions about love and sex proliferate in *Thraliana* from this point on (she was to become increasingly preoccupied with homosexuality), suggesting that it wasn't only her head that was moved, nor vanity the only risk. Evidently, Mrs Thrale feared she might commit adultery and wanted the laws of the land to be severe enough to stop her. She recorded Johnson's remark, 'a woman has such power between the ages of twenty-five and forty-five that she may tie a man to a post and whip him if she will'. Commentators have been interested in this unexpected exchange as a sign of Johnson's sado-masochistic impulses. They align it with his requests to her to 'confine' him – to his room, to his bed, to a post – and her reply to him, 'do not quarrel with your governess for not using the rod enough'. Mrs Thrale as dominatrix in Johnson's fantasy is convincing enough, but not the only interesting element. If we think about the remark from her point of view we can also draw another meaning from it. The kind of power Johnson referred to was a power Hester Thrale was at that time coming into knowledge and possession of: the power of a mature and fully realised sexual self. This was to cause far more disturbance in her life than Johnson's fantasies ever did.[33]

Meanwhile, the pleasures Lord Lyttelton took in Elizabeth Montagu's company do not seem to have depended on the pleasures of the bedchamber, and 'a fully realised sexual self' seems no more apt a description for her than it would be for Elizabeth Carter, or, indeed, the famous virgin queen, Elizabeth I. Mrs Montagu set great store by being known to be virtuous in circles where many were not. She mourned Lyttelton after his death in 1773 as 'the most humble and gentle of any person I ever knew. He was my instructor and my friend, the guide of my studies, the corrector of the result of them. He made my house a school of virtue to young people and a place of delight to the learned.' The closeness of her connection with Lyttelton combined with its public nature suggests that they were not lovers, though that they loved each other was not a secret. Mrs Vesey told how 'his favourite subject [was] how he loved you. I never was alone with him that he did not talk of you with adoration.' Adoration was what Montagu expressly preferred to 'hand kissing' which was 'trash'. She declared at fifty-one that even at eighteen she 'preferr'd adoration to love'. Esteem and respect were what she had aimed at, as she explained when responding to a compliment from Garrick. Had they all been young still, Garrick vowed, he would love Mrs Vesey and adore Mrs Montagu, 'kiss the hands of the Sylph, but fall at the feet of Minerva'. Montagu enjoyed the compliment and approved the distinction. She was happy to be Minerva rather than that 'system of harmonic vibrations' which was the lovable and sensitive Mrs Vesey. By being happy to have the wisdom of Minerva, she believed she had avoided becoming a 'discontented old Witch' – the fate of beauties – and had instead the pleasures of her association with 'Bards and Philosophers, and all that is distinguish'd and respectable'. The men she chose enabled her to cultivate her interior world of thought and to consolidate her position in the exterior world of affairs. Lyttelton, for example, served her socially as a husband because she went about with him in society; and one thing she mourned on his death was her loss of 'consequence'.[34]

Montagu's nervousness about venturing onto the path of authorship without the protection of friends like Lord Lyttelton and Elizabeth Carter seems largely to have been directed at the imagined responses of women. One of her dialogues in Lyttelton's *Dialogues of the Dead* particularly concerned her – that between Mercury and a modern fine lady 'for which the fine Ladies would hate me still more than they do, but I shall decline the honour of their aversion by remaining unknown'. She was also intimidated by the achievements of her clever women friends. She thought Carter's introduction to Epictetus 'one of the finest things in our language'; and the Ode by Hester Mulso which prefaced it a 'fine' one; and she feared that her works would 'make a poor figure beside theirs'. She felt more comfortable imagining herself in competition with the male scholars at the university and with lawyers who dabbled in literature: 'I shall desire not to measure my sword with the Amazons; there are some infantry at Cambridge and near the Inns of Court, with whom I can better contend.'[35]

These fearful competitive feelings in Montagu might account for some of Elizabeth Carter's headaches during the trip to Spa in 1763. Carter was subjected to elaborate teasing by her more worldly hostess, who joked with Mrs Vesey that a 'metamorphosis' had taken place when Mrs Carter discovered Greek to be a dead language and that 'French words, and a little coquetry, would do better at Spa; so with the same facility with which she translated Epictetus from the Greek into English, she translated her native timidity into French airs and French modes.' Montagu claimed that Carter spent three whole days in Brussels doing nothing but clothes shopping; and that, when they visited the nunneries, as they did in every town, this dedicated scholar expressed 'the greatest abhorrence of their strict vows, and sequestered life, with an air of libertinism extremely suited to the gayety of her dress and coquetry of her manners'. Though there was never any evidence of rouge, Mrs Montagu could congratulate herself that she 'brought Mrs Carter back a coquette' from Spa.[36]

Bringing Mrs Carter back a coquette was to make an ordinary woman of her. Such teasing projected more unease about the meanings of 'ordinary' and 'extraordinary' than about sexuality; the rhetoric of sexuality was available for jokes between women in ways that intellectual rivalry was not. Montagu had less of Carter's confident commitment to women writers per se, or to the vision of herself as one of the party, though she shared enthusiasm for particular writers such as Catherine Cockburn, whose *Works* she borrowed from Nathaniel Hooke and lent to Gilbert West. In considering whether to put her name to her own writings, her concern was whether a known identity as author would enhance or diminish her social power. Having the gifts of a Minerva, she expected admiration but doubted if she could be 'happy' – a word which in its context meant something closer to 'powerful' than, say, 'contented' or 'fulfilled':

> Extraordinary talents may make a woman admired, but they will never make her happy. Talents put a man above the world, and in a condition to be feared and worshipped, a woman that possesses them must be always courting the world, and asking pardon, as it were, for uncommon excellence.[37]

As an analysis, Elizabeth Carter might have acknowledged a partial truth here, but no more. The vision (or hope) in this revealing reflection is of being 'feared' 'worshipped' and 'above the world'. The woman with extraordinary talents might have to ask pardon because of the power she would possess. This is what 'superior parts and noble ambition' had it in them to produce, much as extravagant wealth freed one from the ghastly prospect of 'courting the world'. George Lyttelton's encouragement to Montagu – 'we will have something to be printed, something to be published, something to show the whole world what a woman we have among us!' – indicates the level at which her ambitions were pitched. Her fear of being known to have published – broadcasting her 'uncommon excellence' – was in essence a fear of losing power and lessening status. The power of rank and wealth was already hers. Sarah Scott, the sister who went (anonymously) first into print, in 1750, and who was not wealthy (not 'rich in purse & parts'), urged her to write 'for the honour of the age' as if she was indeed its presiding figure like that earlier Elizabeth, the queen whose life she studied, who also combined the highest talents with the highest rank.

5

Hannah More

When Elizabeth Montagu published her *Essay on Shakespeare* in 1769, she was able to mark a difference in the way female authors were received. In her youth (she was born in 1720) she 'should not have liked to have been classed among authors'; at fifty she drew strength from personal maturity, but also from the knowledge that the world had moved on. There was still, to be sure, 'in general a prejudice against female authors'; men were concerned to protect territory they considered rightfully theirs. Nevertheless, a woman like herself, 'amusing herself with reading books or even writing them', had ceased to be an object of comment or offence. As Johnson declared in 1770, 'all our women read now'. Many of them also wrote and published. Some of that change had been brought about by the efforts of women like Montagu, Carter and Lennox, and men like Johnson.[1]

Born in Bristol in 1745, Hannah More came of age in time to ride the crest of the bluestocking wave which was at its most brilliant between 1770 and 1785. She was to live a long life, dying at the age of eighty-eight, having lived through the reigns of four kings as well as major transformations in the social identity of the woman writer. All her books were bestsellers and she made a fortune by her writing. Not only an author, she was also a social activist: passionately anti-slavery (much of Bristol's wealth came from the hugely profitable slave trade), she urged people to boycott sugar, wrote a poem, 'The Slave Trade', and carried about a shocking picture showing the slaves crammed in the holds of ships which she brought out at tea parties. She was a reformer who sought to reform the highest and the lowest classes in society. Manners and morals, she insisted, were linked: urging the great to improve their manners, she wrote 'Strictures' on the education of girls, 'Hints' on how to form the characters of princesses, and tracts telling the poor how to lead happy and useful lives whilst being content with the station to which God had called them. Deeply religious, she was an important figure in the Evangelical movement. She became 'Saint Hannah' and in the latter part of her life renounced the social ambitions that had driven her, a vivacious young woman who made no secret of the fact that she wanted to go as far and as high as she possibly could, to 'know the great, and hear the wise'. In her youth, she very much wanted to be 'classed among authors'. The 'general' prejudice that might have worked against such a desire seems not to have troubled her. Her experiences in the 1770s show with what profusion a female author could be welcomed and rewarded in those years.[2]

The fourth of five daughters of a schoolmaster father, Hannah More was a precocious and indefatigable scribbler whose most earnest childhood wish was for a whole quire of paper of her very own – enough to write on for ever and ever. She played a favourite game in which a household chair was transformed into a carriage and her sisters were invited to ride with her to London 'to see bishops and booksellers'. Self-confident and self-assertive, she came from an entrepreneurial family: her elder sisters, Mary and Elizabeth, established a successful school for girls in 1757 which was to become famous throughout England. Hannah was herself educated there and later taught there (but not much later: like her sisters she began her didactic career early). All the sisters were involved in the school, first at Trinity Street, then in larger premises at Park Street; and they and the school were a force in Bristol cultural and political life. Their intelligence and vitality drew admiring visits not only from prospective parents but from all those interested in social improvement. Mrs Montagu reported on a 'most agreeable day with Miss Hannah More and her three sisters. They are all women of admirable sense, and unaffected behaviour, and I should prefer their school to any I have ever seen for girls.' Endorsements such as these widened the social pool from which their pupils were drawn. To the daughters of Bristol merchants and traders were added those of gentry and squirearchy. The More sisters, none of whom ever married, were able to retire on very comfortable incomes.

The school provided Hannah with a captive audience of girls for whom she wrote her first play, a pastoral drama, 'The Search after Happiness', which was acted there when she was just sixteen. 'The Search after Happiness' gave her considerable local celebrity and it went on being a staple drama text for young ladies in boarding schools for many decades afterwards. Mary Mitford recalled the 'getting up of this highly improving comedy' when she was at school in Reading in the early years of the nineteenth century. In the tradition of denying that which is most desired, Hannah's prologue to *The Search after Happiness* assured the audience:

> Simplicity is all our Author's aim
> She does not write, nor do we speak for *fame* ...

while the epilogue addressed itself humorously to men's well-known dislike of clever women. Since the play was written for, performed by and attended on its first production by an audience exclusively female, the witty epilogue in which the speaker tells the audience that verse must be given up:

> Fancy no more on airy wings shall rise,
> We must scold the maids and make the pies ...

sounds a note that is less docile than collusive, and resistant to the very knowledge it expresses, especially since the speaker goes on to say:

> Verse is a folly – we must rise above it,
> Yet I know not how it is – I love it.

Don't you love it too? it seems to ask the audience. The epilogue canters through traditional objections to writing women, laying emphasis – very pointed, considering the target audience – on how women view their scribbling sisters:

> Tho' should we still the rhyming trade pursue,
> The men will shun us, – and the women, too;
> The men, poor souls! of *scholars* are afraid,
> We shou'd not, did they *govern*, learn to read,
> At least in no abstruser volume look,
> Than the learn'd records – of a Cookery book;
> The ladies, too, their well-meant censure give,
> 'What!- does she write? A slattern, as I live –
> 'I wish she'd leave her books, and mend her cloaths,
> I thank my stars I know not verse from prose.'

The familiar opposition of books and clothes, pen and needle, surely made the audience smile in a way at once superior and complicit. The men 'poor souls' were behind the times; so were lots of women, congratulating themselves on not knowing the difference between verse and prose. How old-fashioned! The published version of this epilogue, revised later, put these attitudes in historical context. Satires on learned women might have been appropriate in the past, it declared, but not any longer: in these 'our chaster times', the learned women were 'moral Carter' and 'accomplish'd Montagu' who displayed both 'wit' and 'worth'. Female 'virtue' had been joined to female 'sense'.[3]

Poetry and drama were Hannah's passions but her intellectual appetites were strong. She was well read in Latin, French, Spanish and Italian literature, having, like Elizabeth Carter, acquired the languages herself, and she cultivated the friendship of 'men of genius' whenever opportunity arose. Scholarly men with literary interests responded to her advances. They liked her and she liked them. Dean Tucker, Dr Ford, Dr Stonehouse, Dr Langhorne were among the local intelligentsia who involved themselves in her progress; as well as James Ferguson, the astronomer, who let her check over his manuscripts before he sent them to the printer – a good way for her to acquaint herself with his ideas. When the elder Sheridan visited Bristol to give lectures on eloquence, Hannah More wrote verses in his praise. Friends (possibly her sisters) made sure the verses found their way to him and he responded appropriately, expressing a desire to meet her. They met and he was impressed with her youthful 'genius'. By these means Hannah More ensured for herself a rich supply of thoughtful, erudite men who in their conversation and correspondence provided what was essentially an informal advanced education.

At the age of twenty-three, a proposal of marriage was made to her by William Turner, a local squire much older than herself, and the guardian of two of the girls at the school. Hannah had been to stay on his estate and had written verses in praise of its beauties which he, like a lovelorn youth out of Shakespeare's comedies, had nailed up on the trees. Turner was accepted as a potential husband and plans for the marriage set in motion. But he could not go through with it and over the next six years a date was fixed three times only to be postponed. On the third occasion, Hannah More's family and friends intervened. An agreement was drawn up whereby William Turner agreed to pay damages – a lump sum and an annuity of £200 – in compensation for the humiliation he had caused. Instead of marriage to a wealthy landowner, she gained financial independence. She was able to give up teaching at the school and concentrate entirely on her writing.

In furthering her career, David Garrick was more important to Hannah More than Samuel Johnson. Her enthusiasm for drama led in the first instance to a close association with theatre circles in Bristol and Bath. (Many of the daughters of the company were pupils at the school.) She helped William Powell, the actor-manager who had previously been in Garrick's company at Drury Lane, produce plays at the Bristol Royal Theatre. She was also active in the production of her own play, *The Inflexible Captive*, which was put on in collaboration with Garrick at Bath in 1775. Garrick wrote the epilogue and Dr Langhorne the prologue. There was a gala performance attended by all the fashionable society. Her sister Sally wrote:

> All the world of dukes, lords and barons were there. I sat next to a baron and a lord. All expressed the highest approbation of the whole. Never was a piece represented there known to have received so much applause.

The *Bath Chronicle* agreed about the 'uncommon applause' and opined that it reflected 'great honor both on the authoress and her friends'.[4]

How had Hannah made the leap from schoolteacher dramatist to collaborator with David Garrick? The *Bath Chronicle* was not wrong to include her friends in the honour, for they had worked hard on her behalf. She made her first trip to London in the winter season of 1773–74 and one of her first objects was to see Garrick on stage. In this she was disappointed; he did not appear because of illness. Instead, with her sisters Sally and Martha, she made a pilgrimage to Garrick's villa at Hampton. (Forty years earlier Elizabeth Carter had made her pilgrimage, with Johnson, to Pope's villa and garden at Twickenham, and they had published their verses about plucking sprigs of laurel. Hannah also went to Pope's house: she stole two pebbles from his grotto and plucked a sprig of laurel.) Of Garrick's villa she reported back to Bristol:

> His house is repairing and is not worth seeing, but the situation of his garden pleases me infinitely. It is on the banks of the Thames; the temple about thirty or forty yards from it. Here is the famous chair, curiously wrought out of a cherry tree which really grew in the garden of Shakespeare at Stratford. I sat in it, but caught no ray of inspiration. But what drew, and deserved, my attention was a most noble statue of this most original man, in an attitude strikingly pensive – his limbs strongly muscular, his countenance strongly expressive of some vast conception, and his whole form seeming the bigger from some immense idea which you suppose his great imagination pregnant. The statue cost five hundred pounds.[5]

Later, visiting Johnson, she was to sit in *his* chair (the three-legged, broken one) in hopes of catching a 'ray of inspiration'. Meanwhile, having missed Garrick on stage, the sisters returned to London in May and saw him in *King Lear*. Hannah was overwhelmed. She wrote an ecstatic account of the production to Dr Stonehouse. Stonehouse was a wealthy, well-connected and eloquent preacher, a neighbour to the sisters and a very conspicuous and much respected figure in Bristol. His intervention had been crucial in the miserable affair of Hannah's engagement to William Turner and the subsequent settlement. He had, the previous year, sent Hannah's play, *The Inflexible Captive*, to Garrick in hopes that he might produce it in London. Garrick had declined. Stonehouse, in other words, was again acting as an intermediary. A campaign was in progress. It was no casual act on Stonehouse's part to arrange for a copy of Hannah's letter of ecstatic praise of Garrick to be sent to Garrick himself with a covering letter explaining that the writer was 'a young woman of an amazing genius.' (Nor was Hannah's letter itself a casual act.) Stonehouse informed Garrick where Hannah was staying in London, invited him to call on her – 'You would not be displeased with the interview, and I know she would take it very kindly, as she has a great desire to see you' – and entered into discussion of play-writing projects she might develop if she knew they were subjects that Garrick might be interested in.[6]

The shared and sociable nature of the endeavour is very striking. Hannah's genius, nurtured in Bristol, was a source of pride in the community. Her dreams and aspirations were personal but not private. Her confidence was in herself but also in those around her and in the wider society beyond. Special, because of her 'amazing genius', she was not set apart; rather, her 'amazing genius' made it all the more imperative that a proper place be found for her so that her talents could be put to best use for the wider social good. This was the logic that drove Hannah More's supporters.

Stonehouse's letter succeeded. The result was a friendship between David Garrick and Hannah More which rapidly ripened into intimacy – though with never a hint of sexual impropriety. After making initial contact in London, the Garricks visited the More sisters at Bristol. They were all together in Bath for *The Inflexible Captive*; and, in January 1776, Hannah and her sister Martha spent three days at Hampton as guests rather than as tourists. Martha wrote that they were settled at

> the temple of taste, nature, Shakespeare and Garrick; where everything that could please the ear, charm the eye, and gratify the understanding passed in quick succession. From dinner to midnight he entertained us in a manner infinitely agreeable. He read to us all the whimsical correspondence, in prose and verse, which, for many years, he had carried on with the first geniuses of this age. I have now seen him in a mellower light, when the world has been shaken off ... The next time we go, Hannah is to carry some of her writing; she is to have a little table to herself, and to continue her studies; and he is to do the same.[7]

By March of that year Hannah More had become part of the family. She moved into the Adelphi, accompanied the Garricks back and forth on their trips to Hampton, and helped out in a daughterly sort of way at parties. She was even admitted to gatherings usually reserved for men:

> I dined in the Adelphi yesterday. It was a particular occasion – an annual meeting, where none but men are usually asked. I was however of the party, and an agreeable day it was to me. I have seldom heard so much wit, under the banner of so much decorum.

It was all utterly agreeable, a remarkably successful conclusion to a campaign to get Hannah More of Bristol accepted as a genius worthy the metropolis:

> Mrs Boscawen came to see me the other day with the duchess, in her gilt chariot, with four footmen (as I hear), for I happened not to be at home. It is not possible for anything on earth to be more agreeable to my taste than my present manner of living. I am so much at my ease: have a great many hours at my own disposal: read my own books, and see my own friends; and, whenever I please, may join the most polished and delightful society in the world! Our breakfasts are little literary societies ...

Garrick declared that she was all the nine Muses in one, and he dubbed her 'Nine' or 'Dear Nine' accordingly.[8]

Hannah's responses to David Garrick's acting were important to both Garricks. They made sure she had the best view – 'the pit, which increases the pleasure ten-fold' – and when she developed her observations in letters to friends and family she shared the letters with them. Thus a letter might be delayed if it was full of reflections about Garrick's different parts: Hamlet, Abel Drugger, Leon, Benedict and others:

> I wrote the above two or three days ago, and intended to have sent it immediately; but happening to show it to Mrs G. she was so pleased with my remarks on *Hamlet* and the performance, that they insisted on having a copy. Though they paid my foolish letter an undeserved compliment, yet I could not refuse to comply, and not having time to transcribe it, is the reason you did not hear from me sooner.

Showing the letter to Eva Garrick meant showing it to Garrick as well: 'she', in the extract above, became 'they' without need of comment.

Hannah More's imagination was every bit as heated as Boswell's and her identifying impulses no less roused by talk of the literary giants of the earlier eighteenth century. Mrs Boscawen introduced her to Mrs Delaney. Hannah explained:

> She was a Granville, and niece to the celebrated poet Lord Lansdowne. She was the friend and intimate of Swift. She tells a thousand pleasant anecdotes relative to the publication of the *Tatler*. As to the *Spectator*, it is almost too modern for her to speak of it ... In short, she is a living library of knowledge.

Dinner with Mrs Delaney was followed by 'a very splendid assembly' at Mrs Boscawen's full of people of 'the first quality' some of whom she was able to list. Hannah More's letters from this time are full of lists. Family and friends at home were able to savour the full honour and credit they had helped her attain:

> The Duchess of Beaufort, Lady Scarsdale, her sister, Lord and Lady Radnor, Lady Ranelagh, Lady Onslow, the Bishop of Bath and Wells, Lord and Lady Clifford, Captain and Mrs Middleton, and Mrs Bouverie.[9]

As the Garricks' material prosperity testified, it was theatre which continued to offer penniless talent its best hopes of financial reward. By 1773 David Garrick could afford to pay £500 for a statue of Shakespeare, but when he first came to London in 1737 it was with Samuel Johnson, sharing a horse for the journey from Lichfield, travelling tie and ride, and with precious little in their pockets. Both were quickly recognised as outstanding talents, but only Garrick's gifts had translated into affluence. Whilst he lorded it in two commodious mansions, Johnson lived a bohemian existence in rented houses where he accommodated others as propertyless as himself. His play, *Irene*, over which he had laboured and for which he had great hopes, was not a success when it was finally staged by Garrick in 1749, though it was not exactly a failure either. It ran for nine nights, which was respectable, and made £300 in total profits for the author. Johnson appeared for his opening night in a scarlet waistcoat with gold lace and a gold-laced hat, believing some 'distinction of dress' was appropriate to an author on such an occasion. There was never to be another. Johnson's stage writing was confined to a sprinkling of prologues and epilogues for other people's plays.

Meanwhile, from the middle of the eighteenth century, there was a steady rise in productions of plays by women authors. In 1779, Mrs Thrale wrote in *Thraliana*: 'I cannot imagine why I should not write a comedy; it seems to me as if everybody could write a comedy, here is one Miss and another Miss and all the Misses writing plays.' [10] Much of this was due to Garrick. When he took over the management of Drury Lane, in 1747, he at once began to establish a new style which others, like the two George Colmans, elder and younger, John Philip Kemble and even Thomas Harris, found it convenient and profitable to imitate. No longer a byword for rapacity, the theatre manager could now play fatherly guardian and benevolent mentor. Frances Brooke, Elizabeth Griffith, Frances Sheridan, Hannah Cowley, Amelia Opie, Elizabeth Inchbald and Harriet Lee were among the better known names amongst female dramatists in the second half of the eighteenth century. Their experiences were mixed. Elizabeth Inchbald had to defend herself against a violent seduction by Thomas Harris. She pulled his hair and escaped from his house, grateful, as she explained to the company after she reached the safety of the theatre, that Harris hadn't been wearing a wig.[11] A shift had occurred, however. Hannah More came seeking fame and fortune as a dramatist and was able to fall without difficulty into the role of good daughter to Garrick. She could spend her days behind the scenes at Drury Lane without compromising her respectability – although some of the actresses in the green room were less than enthusiastic: Kitty Clive wrote to Garrick, 'Pray what is the meaning of a hundred Miss Mores purring about you with their poems and plays and romances? Send them back to Bristol with a flea in their ears.' Garrick chose instead to work closely with Hannah More on her second play, *Percy*.[12]

Throughout the writing of *Percy*, Hannah More was in constant and close communication with the Garricks. Their 'kindness and friendship' were unceasing. The play was read in progress and commented on by both, David Garrick warning her that Mrs Garrick was a severe critic:

Mrs Garrick is studying your two acts. We shall bring them with us, and she will criticise you to the bone. A German commentator (Montaigne says) will suck an author dry. She is resolved to dry you up to a slender shape, and has all her wits at work upon you.

He himself was pleased with neither the third nor the fourth act. He wrote, 'I don't think you were in your most acute and best feeling when you wrote the third act – I am not satisfied with it, it is the weakest of the four.' And later, 'I have read and studied the four – the three will do and well do – but the fourth will not stand muster – that must be changed greatly but how, I cannot yet say ...' The revisions continued. Hannah More was pragmatically aware that Garrick's involvement in her play gave her an advantage that other writers could only dream of. He urged her to employ all her wit and feeling:

Let your fifth act be worthy of you, and tear the heart to pieces, or woe betide you. I shall not pass over any scenes, or parts of scenes, that are merely written to make up a certain number of lines. Such doings, Madam Nine, will neither do for you nor for me.

When the play was completed, he wrote a prologue and epilogue for it, demanding as his fee 'a handsome supper and a bottle of claret' on the grounds that Dryden used to get five guineas a piece but that he was richer than Dryden. Hannah shared the joke with her sisters: 'We haggled sadly about the price, I insisting that I could only afford to give him a beef steak and a pot of porter; and at about twelve we sat down to some toast and honey, with which the temperate bard contented himself.'[13]

Staged in 1777, *Percy* was universally acclaimed and commercially profitable. Elizabeth Montagu, who was not a keen theatre goer, 'overcome by the universal plaudits of the first night', ordered a box for the third, sixth and ninth nights. Writing to Garrick, the worldly Kitty Clive put into words what Hannah More undoubtedly knew:

I must needs say I admire you (with the rest of the world) for your goodness to Miss More; the protection you gave her play, I dare say, she was sensible was of the greatest service to her; she was sure every thing you touched would turn into gold; and though she had great merit in the writing, still your affection for tragedy children was a very great happiness to *her*, for you dandled it, and fondled it, and then carried in your arms to the *town* to nurse ...[14]

Playing to full houses, *Percy* generated a profit of £600 for Hannah More, all carefully invested on her behalf by Garrick at the end of the run. For the published text she received £150 from Cadell and had sold 4000 copies by March 1778. As Kitty Clive's remarks make plain, all this activity was

very public. In literary circles, in theatrical circles, in the press, a close eye
was kept on celebrities much as it is today. Kitty Clive called More 'Garrick's
bantling' but from Elizabeth Montagu there was an expression of shared
pride which again alluded to the honour of her friends: 'May you ever be
the pride of your friends and wear your bays with pleasure.'

Hannah More's first meeting with Samuel Johnson took place at Sir Joshua
Reynolds's house. It followed an introduction to Frances Reynolds, the
'most amiable and obliging of women', probably facilitated by another
Bristol friend, Mrs Lovell Gwatkin. The Reynoldses were generously disposed
to help provincial talent climb and, having had Hannah and her sister to
drink tea of an evening and sup with 'a brilliant circle of both sexes [who]
would not suffer us to come away until one', they knew that the individual
she most desired to meet was Johnson. It was arranged, though Reynolds
warned her she might find Johnson in one of his moods of sadness and
silence. Far from it. He came towards her in great good humour, reciting
a verse he had memorised from her own 'Morning Hymn' as he shuffled
across the room whilst balancing a macaw of Sir Joshua's on his wrist. After
this picturesque and gratifying start, the More sisters called on Johnson at
home. Sally wrote to Bristol in great excitement describing how they felt
upon hearing that the coach had been ordered to take them 'to Dr Johnson's
very own house; yes, Abyssinia's Johnson! *Dictionary* Johnson! *Rambler's*,
Idler's, and *Irene's* Johnson! Can you picture to yourselves the palpitation
of our hearts as we approached his mansion.' Shown into the parlour and
finding it empty, it was on this occasion that Hannah 'seated herself in his
great chair, hoping to catch a little ray of his genius'.[15]

The More sisters knew how to do adulation but at the same time they
had a healthy respect for their home-grown young genius and her entitle-
ments. Hannah, after all, was the precocious child whose amusement had
always been scribbling and who adored to hear the stories of her nurse
who had lived in the family of Dryden. She was 'an ardent and intelligent
country girl who found herself suddenly introduced to the choicest society
of the metropolis', but she was an author and it was as a young authoress
that she went, looking for intellectual society and gaining her introductions.
Her youth and the 'enthusiasm', which she took care should be not only
'visible in the whole manner of the young authoress' but also 'evidently
genuine and unaffected', succeeded splendidly with Johnson, just as they
had succeeded with Sheridan, Ferguson and Garrick.

The sisters went storming the heights and Hannah's wit was the weapon.
She was the pride of her family and the pride of Bristol. No door was
barred to her. Johnson dubbed her the Hannibal of poets and it was very

much in the spirit of Hannibal conquering the Alps that she had been able
to write home in triumph:

> I had yesterday the pleasure of dining in Hill Street, Berkeley Square, *at a certain
> Mrs Montagu's, a name not totally obscure.* The party consisted of herself, Mrs
> Carter, Dr Johnson ... Mrs Boscawen, Miss Reynolds, and Sir Joshua (the idol
> of every company); some other persons of high rank and less wit, and your
> humble servant.[16]

Her social rank was low – she was, she said proudly, 'the meanest person
in the company' – but her wit placed her high. There was an unstoppable
quality about her. Back in Bristol after the summer of 1775, she set about
writing a ballad, 'Sir Eldred of the Bower', to which she added a poem, 'The
Bleeding Rock'. These she offered to the London publisher Thomas Cadell
as a combination likely to please her London friends. Cadell, anticipating
strong sales on the basis of Hannah More's excellent connections, advanced
her the handsome sum of forty guineas. Her popularity served Cadell well:
he published all her best-selling books. Medieval ballads were in vogue,
partly because of Thomas Percy's antiquarian researches, *Percy's Reliques,*
which had appeared in 1765. 'Sir Eldred' became 'the theme of conversation
in all polite circles'. Mrs Montagu congratulated the author once more for
'doing so much honour to your sex'. Johnson, characteristically, praised her
in a compliment which drew attention to her extraordinary ability (which
he, above all others, was in a position to appreciate) to find her way to the
top table. She had, he said, speaking of her as the 'parent' of her heroine,
'the beauteous Bertha', 'but one fault; which is, suffering herself to graze
on the barren rocks of Bristol, while the rich pastures of London are guarded
by no fence which could exclude her from them'.

Hannah More's letters to her sisters, and some of their letters about her
during these first summers in London in the mid 1770s, give a wonderful
picture of a young provincial confidently making her way through the 'rich
pastures' of the metropolis. With Johnson she flirted:

> I had the happiness to carry Dr Johnson home from Hill Street, though Mrs
> Montagu publicly declared she did not think it prudent to trust us together, with
> such a declared affection on both sides. She said she was afraid of a Scotch
> elopement. He has invited himself to drink tea with us to-morrow, that we may
> read 'Sir Eldred' together. I shall not tell you what he said of it, but to me the
> best part of his flattery was, that he repeats all the best stanzas by heart.[17]

Johnson enjoyed her assertiveness. A typical progress report home, after an
evening which went on until well past midnight, included: 'Dr Johnson and
Hannah, last night, had a violent quarrel, till at length laughter ran so high
on all sides, that argument was confounded in noise.' Or, in similar vein,

Hannah herself boasted, 'Keeping bad company leads to all other bad things. I have got the headache today, by raking out so late with that gay libertine Johnson.' Her active, outgoing temperament, her relish of argument combined with her eagerness to please, her comfort in the company of older men and her deference to older women, made her presence welcome in literary circles. The leading figures in bluestocking London were, by then, middle-aged and elderly. She was a bright-eyed, good-looking, good-natured young thing who also happened to be brilliant. She took advice from the Garricks about her appearance; and, though she disliked the fashion for elaborate hairstyles, she nevertheless adapted herself to wearing 'sycophancy's mask' in dressing her hair as in other things. It was a question of looking the part. Being noted by the notables was a vital ingredient of literary success. Even Hannah More's strongly principled objections to Sunday parties faded before the prospect of a glittering assembly at Mrs Montagu's, after one of which she sat down and wrote home:

> Just returned from spending one of the most agreeable days of my life, with the female Maecenas of Hill Street; she engaged me five or six days ago to dine with her, and had assembled half the wits of the age. The only fault that charming woman has, is, that she is fond of collecting too many of them together at one time. There were nineteen persons assembled at dinner, but after the repast, she has a method of dividing her guests, or rather letting them assort themselves into little groups of five or six each. I spent my time in going from one to the other of these little societies, as I happened more or less to like the subjects they were discussing. Mrs Scott, Mrs Montagu's sister, a very good writer, Mrs Carter, Mrs Barbauld, and a man of letters, whose name I have forgotten, made up one of these little parties. When we had canvassed two or three subjects, I stole off and joined in with the next group, which was composed of Mrs Montagu, Dr Johnson, the Provost of Dublin, and two other ingenious men. In this party there was a diversity of opinions, which produced a great deal of good argument and reasoning. There were several other groups less interesting to me, as they were composed more of rank than talent.[18]

She made full use of her freedom to move about amongst these groups, literally and symbolically following the impulse of her own interests; aware of the women – 'Mrs Scott, Mrs Montagu's sister, a very good writer' – and not specially attentive to the men – 'a man of letters, whose name I have forgotten'. Her work was well circulated and widely praised. At one party Garrick read aloud 'Sir Eldred of the Bower' 'with all his pathos and all his graces' so movingly that both Hannah and Mrs Garrick wept. Johnson said she was 'the most powerful versificatrix in the English language'. What her sister described as the 'adulation and kindness of the great folks here' came down in showers on Hannah More's head.

Blessed with a formidable degree of what used to be called animal high spirits, bursting with energy and drive, lavish with flattery and abounding in combative charm, Hannah More suited the military metaphors Johnson used of her. It was not her style to be retiring. Attacking, fighting, firing, conquering and vanquishing were her *forte*. To be effective, to please and to win were her objectives. She was new and she was successful. Naturally so much adulation and easy success, so much rampant self-congratulation, also produced envy. In a 1751 *Rambler* article, Johnson had mused at length on the calumny and malice which seemed to be endemic in the literary world: 'It is impossible to mingle in conversation,' he wrote, 'without observing the difficulty with which a new name makes its way into the world. The first appearance of excellence unites multitudes against it.' These multitudes, 'the envious, the idle, the peevish and the thoughtless', obstructed what they could not equal. Given that even Mrs Thrale declared, 'I think Hannah More is the cleverest of all us female wits', that the Theatre Royal, Bristol, had inscribed on its walls the legend, 'Boast we not a More?', and that her progress in the world had been manifestly far from difficult, it is easy to see that there was a good deal about Hannah More to provoke envy.

Her first appearance as the 'new name' of the day, in a public place with Johnson, gave rise to the circulation of a story which illustrates this. The encounter appeared in Boswell's *Life of Samuel Johnson* as follows – although she was not named, only alluded to as 'a celebrated lady':

> At Sir Joshua Reynolds's one evening, she met Dr Johnson. She very soon began to pay her court to him in the most fulsome strain. '*Spare me, I beseech you*, dear madam,' was his reply. She still laid it on. 'Pray, madam, let us have no more of this,' he rejoined. Not paying any attention to these warnings, she still continued her eulogy. At length, provoked by this indelicate and vain obtrusion of compliments, he exclaimed, 'Dearest lady, consider with yourself what your flattery is worth, before you bestow it so freely.' [19]

The story had by that time become public currency. Mrs Thrale had told it to Fanny Burney at breakfast at Streatham Park in 1778. The younger woman duly recorded it in her diary in the following way: Hannah More, she wrote, being introduced to Johnson,

> began singing his praise in the warmest manner, and talking of the pleasure and the instruction she had received from his writings, with the highest encomiums. For some time he heard her with that quietness which long use of praise has given him: she then redoubled her strokes, and, as Mr Seward calls it, peppered still more highly: till, at length, he turned suddenly to her, with a stern and angry countenance, and said,

'Madam, before you flatter a man so grossly to his face, you should consider whether or not your flattery is worth his having.'

In recording this anecdote, Fanny Burney prefaced it with a personally reassuring report by Mrs Thrale on Fanny's own behaviour towards Johnson. The conversation, she tells us, had begun as follows:

> 'And yet,' said Mrs Thrale, 'Miss Burney never flatters him, though she is such a favourite with him: – but the tables are turned, for he sits and flatters her all day long.'
>   'I don't flatter him,' said I, 'because nothing I could say would flatter him.' [20]

We need not doubt the sincerity of Burney's response to note that lessons were being learned in dialogues like these. Fanny's diary served her as a storehouse of very particular wisdom: it was not only Evelina who had to learn the rules about entering the world. Yet this story of Hannah More's encounter with Johnson was given very differently at the time by Hannah's sister, Sally, in one of her lively letters home to the sisters in Bristol (and through them to the wider circle of friends there who would be shown the letter). Sally More was present on the occasion and *she* observed nothing amiss. Nor did she think Hannah was engaged in anything 'indelicate' as Boswell chose to denote her 'compliments'. Rather, she saw her sister and 'the lexicographer' coming together in a mutual and agreed battle of wits. She saw them as equal participants, well-matched adversaries. In this triumphal account, Hannah More is Johnson's 'favourite', the guest most able to provide him with the calibre of wit he needed for pleasurable verbal combat:

> Tuesday evening we drank tea at Sir Joshua's with Dr Johnson. Hannah is certainly a great favourite. She was placed next to him, and they had the entire conversation to themselves. They were both in remarkably high spirits, it was certainly her lucky night! I never heard her say so many good things. The old genius was extremely jocular, and the young one very pleasant. You would have imagined we had been at some comedy had you heard our peals of laughter. They, indeed, tried who could 'pepper the highest,' and it is not clear to me that the lexicographer was really the highest seasoner.[21]

The difference between the three accounts is instructive. What Sally conveys as positive and arising from a feeling of equality – peppering highly – the others represent as negative and as the provincial's misreading of social relations: her frantic attempts at flattery, the great man's patience followed by an angry reprimand that reinstates the proper hierarchical relationship. Boswell, Thrale and Burney were all circulating secondhand anecdote and gossip. Such a story, told and retold with didactic intent, served many purposes, from the gratification of envious malice to the confirmation of personal superiority. Imbued with the ideology of female deference, the most obvious thing it taught was that a presumptuous woman needed a sure understanding of social codes. If she faltered or transgressed, in whatever way, the story would go against her; or faults and transgressions would be discovered anyhow in order to *make* the story go against her. In contrast, no sense of error or fault is present in Sally More's letter home. Her object was to promote a shared celebration. She was reporting a triumph that family and friends could recognise. Her letter resounds like a loud halloo from London to Bristol, for in Bristol they expected Hannah to achieve this sort of success.

Even more ebullient than Hannah, did Sally choose not to notice Johnson's 'stern and angry countenance'? Did she notice but conceal it from those at home? Did she simply fail to understand London social codes? All these are possible interpretations. It is also possible that 'the envious, the idle, the peevish and the thoughtless' witnessing this extraordinary scene or hearing about it later bristled at the self-confidence of these Miss Mores.

Sally had her own success, impressing Johnson with her command of autobiographical narrative. The sprightly younger sister was to write and publish two novels of her own, but she did so anonymously and they have never been traced. Sally was the 'wit' of the family while Hannah was the 'genius'; Hannah was also reliably good whilst Sally was potentially wayward – outspoken, noisy, wild. She gave Johnson the family story, a 'history' that was also a fiction like the fictions of real life and real people – *Tom Jones, Joseph Andrews, Roderick Random, Pamela, Clarissa, Amelia* – that were by then so popular. She wrote up the entire exchange in detail for those at home, giving it the quality of a dramatic performance. It is as though the spotlight falls for a moment on Sally as she speaks her lines; and then the leading character exits stage left:

After much critical discourse, he turns round to me, and with one of his most amiable looks, which must be seen to form the least idea of it, he says, 'I have heard that you are engaged in the useful and honorable employment of teaching young ladies,' upon which, with all the same ease, familiarity and confidence we should have done had only our dear Dr Stonehouse been present, we entered upon the history of our birth, parentage, and education; showing how we were born with more desires than guineas; and how, as years increased our appetites, the cupboard at home began to grow too small to gratify them; and how with a bottle of water, a bed, and a blanket, we set out to seek our fortunes; and how we found a great house, with nothing in it; and how it was like to remain so, till looking into our knowledge-boxes, we happened to find a little 'larning', a good thing when land is gone, or rather none; and so at last, by giving a little of this 'larning' to those who had less, we got a good share of gold in return; but how, alas! We wanted the wit to keep it – 'I love you both,' cried the inamorato – 'I love you all five – I never was at Bristol – but I will come on purpose to see you – what! Five women live happily together! – I will come and see you – I have spent a happy evening – I am glad I came – God forever bless you, you live lives to shame duchesses!' He took his leave with so much warmth and tenderness, we were quite affected at his manner.[22]

Johnson did go to Bristol to see them, later that same spring, 1776, when he had been on a visit to Bath with Boswell. Boswell makes no mention of it.

David Garrick died on 20 January 1779. He was sixty-one, and though he had been ill, his death came as a shock. When she received the news, Hannah wrote at once to Garrick's friend and solicitor, Albany Wallis, to know if Mrs Garrick wanted her in London:

Oh Sir! What a friend have I lost! My heart is almost broken! I have neither eaten nor slept since. My tears blind me as I write – But what is *my* loss, what is *my* sorrow? It is quite lost in the idea of what our beloved Mrs Garrick suffers . . . Ask her, dear Sir, if she will allow me to come to her – I cannot dry her eyes but I can weep with her, – I can be of no service perhaps but there is a sort of mournful consolation in the company of one who knew, who loved, who mourns, and who will forever mourn the first of men.

The answer was that she was indeed wanted. She rushed straight to London and found Mrs Garrick 'prepared for meeting me; she ran into my arms, and we both remained silent for some minutes; at last she whispered, "I have this moment embraced his coffin, and you come next".' [23]

A long period of private mourning followed. Mrs Garrick was too distressed to attend the funeral, a magnificent affair at Westminster Abbey; women did not, in any case, customarily take part in funeral rites. Hannah went in her stead. The procession of thirty-three mourning coaches draped in black, horses with black velvet saddlecloths, riders carrying black scarves and staffs, and the whole set off with black feathers and escutcheons, took two hours to go the short distance from the Adelphi in the Strand to Westminster Abbey. The streets were thronged. Then, for a year and a half afterwards, Hannah lived in virtual seclusion with the childless widow. The two women moved between the town house at the Adelphi and the country house at Hampton. They received few visitors. Both were devastated by Garrick's death. This seclusion did not prevent Hannah More from seeing her next play, *The Fatal Falsehood*, onto the stage, grief-stricken and ill though she was and apparently, so far as her sisters could tell, 'mightily indifferent about the matter'. Perhaps her indifference made her careless or perhaps she really didn't know that some parts of her play were remarkably similar to a play by another prominent woman playwright who had also been sponsored by Garrick.

On the second night of *The Fatal Falsehood*, Hannah Cowley stood up from the audience and shouted loudly, 'That's mine! That's mine!' then, according to press reports, fainted in her box. The play she believed to have been plagiarised was *Albina* which she had written some years before. In the press, a paper war followed. Hannah More reluctantly published her defence: 'I am under the necessity of solemnly asserting that I never saw, or heard, or read a single line of Mrs Cowley's tragedy, nor did I even hear she had written a tragedy till after *The Fatal Falsehood* came out.' Hannah Cowley made no outright accusation of plagiarism, but suggested that More might have been influenced by Garrick who had the script in his possession at Hampton when Hannah More was in residence at that delightful place. The only other interpretation was that 'by some *wonderful* coincidence, Miss More and I have one common stock of ideas between us'.[24]

This episode soured More's success as a dramatist. Vulgar wrangling in the press offended both propriety and piety. Her Christian values of meekness and charity, of gentle, long-suffering peacableness, were sorely tested. She was angry and scarred. Following so closely on Garrick's death, this revelation of the dark underside of celebrity marked the end of her short but successful career as a dramatist. She had said quite early on, 'when Garrick has left the stage, I could be very well contented to relinquish plays also'. The surrogate daughter buried herself at Hampton. Bonded by grief, the women drowned their sorrows in books, an activity which, from its beginnings as a survival strategy, seems to have developed into a voracious indulgence of single-minded appetite. According to Hannah More, they 'read without any restraint, as if we were alone, without apologies or speechmaking'. By the following January the benefits of this regime were clear. Hannah reported cheerfully to her sisters from Hampton:

> Here we are still, and as little acquainted with what passes in the world as though we were five hundred, instead of fifteen miles out of it ... We never see a human face but each other's ... We dress like a couple of Scaramouches, dispute like a couple of Jesuits, eat like a couple of aldermen, walk like a couple of porters, and read as much as any two doctors of either university.[25]

It wasn't until April 1781 that Eva Garrick signalled her emergence from retirement with a dinner for a select party of David Garrick's friends. Hannah More was of course present, along with Joshua Reynolds, Mrs Boscawen, Dr Johnson, James Boswell, Charles Burney and Elizabeth Carter.

This was the London inner circle and mostly they had been dining and talking and sharing life for many decades.

Solitude was agreeable but Hannah was also restless and ready for society. She made some unlikely new friends, such as Horace Walpole, a most unreligious man who addressed her as 'Holy Hannah' and 'my dear Saint Hannah'. Urbane and often outrageous, Walpole, it seemed, had licence to say anything. On sending her money, as requested, to help out a man who had been cut down alive after trying to hang himself, he wrote:

> It is very provoking that people must always be hanging or drowning themselves, or going mad, that you forsooth, Mistress, may have the diversion of exercising your pity and good-nature, and charity, and intercession, and all that beadroll of virtues that makes you so troublesome and amiable, when you might be ten times more agreeable by writing things that would not cost one above half a crown at a time. You are an absolutely walking hospital, and travel about into lone and bye places with your doors open to house stray casualties. I wish at least you would have some children yourself, that you might not be plaguing one for all the pretty brats that are starving and friendless.[26]

Stray casualties needing charity were a permanent fixture. Less successful was Hannah's venture into literary patronage. If the unfortunate episode with Hannah Cowley and the accusation of plagiarism shook her confidence, the hopes, hard work and disillusion that followed on Hannah More's 'discovery' of the milkwoman poet, Ann Yearsley, was even more bruising.

By 1784, when Ann Yearsley became More's protégée, the peasant poet, or the unlettered genius, was a recognised figure in literary culture. Almost anybody of any standing whatever in literature had a pet bard from the lower orders whom they supported in some way – a shoemaker poet, a washerwoman poet or a thresher poet. The prototype was Stephen Duck, the self-educated farm labourer taken up by Queen Caroline and promoted to yeoman of the guard in 1733. (He later committed suicide.) Becoming a patron, like building a house – which Hannah More had also done for herself in the early 1780s – was a sign of maturity in the profession. Really rich people could support many writers. Mrs Montagu seems to have imagined that her wealth could stretch indefinitely, telling James Beattie, who was under her patronage:

> Consider me always ... as the banker of the distressed; and at any time call upon me for such objects; and in all senses of the word, *I will honour your bill.* Vulgar wretchedness one relieves, because it is one's duty to do so; and one has a certain degree of pleasure in it; but to assist merit in distress is an Epicurean feast ... indulge this luxury of taste in me.[27]

Ann Yearsley had merit and distress, but helping her was no Epicurean feast. She was the milkwoman who delivered milk to the More household and who paid an annual retainer to the Mores' cook for the privilege of taking away the slops – the 'hogwash' – with which she was able to feed her pig. She was desperately poor, pregnant, had a husband of 'little capacity', an elderly mother, five children and an appetite for poetry. She was fierce, gifted, and frustrated. Hannah More was shown her poems and told about her by the cook when she returned to Bristol after spending the summer with that 'female Maecenas' and cultural patron, Elizabeth Montagu. She was excited by what she read and heard. As Johnson had told her, 'vehemence of praise' was among her faults, and she admitted, 'transcendent genius in any book or persons excites in me pleasures even to rapture'. (Johnson rebuked Mrs Thrale in similar terms: 'I know nobody who blasts by praise as you do.') Perhaps Hannah wanted some of the luxury Elizabeth Montagu could so easily indulge. She wrote at once to Montagu:

> The verses excited my attention, for, though incorrect, they breathed the genuine spirit of poetry and were rendered the more interesting by a certain natural and strong expression of misery, which seemed to fill the heart and mind of the author.[28]

The 'misery' so naturally expressed in her verse and appreciated by Hannah More's critical ear and eye ('I never met with an Ear more nicely tuned') also filled Ann Yearsley's life. She and her family were perishing and in despair, starving huddled in a stable when discovered by a passing benefactor. After making very careful enquiries about her character and discovering that she was a deserving case, 'active and industrious in no common degree ... without the least affectation and pretension of any kind', More decided to take her on as a cause. Yearsley was a genius, uneducated, and 'buried in obscurity'. Apparently this genius did not know 'a single rule of grammar'. She had 'never seen a dictionary'. The teacher in Hannah More rose up. 'I will get Ossian for her. As she has never read Dryden I have given her his Tales, and the most decent of the *Metamorphoses*.' For the next thirteen months she devoted herself to Ann Yearsley, instructing her, working with her, seeking to improve her. This meant diminishing the 'milker of cows ... feeder of hogs' elements (whilst at the same time mythicising those very terms) and replacing them with genteel qualities. In honour of her pastoral associations, Ann Yearsley now went by the sobriquet of 'Lactilla'. Four months later, Mrs Montagu was sent a new poem:

> I cannot help troubling you dear Madam with a new production of Lactilla; which I am the more impatient you should see because it betrays totally new talents, for I think you will agree with me that there is in it, wit, ease and

pleasantry; and what sounds quite ridiculous the poem appears to me to have the tone of good company, and a gentility that is wonderful in a milker of cows and a feeder of hogs.

The object exchanged between the two patrons was a composite. There was the poem itself, and there was the old Ann Yearsley along with what Hannah More hoped might be a shared vision of the new: an Ann Yearsley taught by Hannah More how to catch the 'tone of good company', a milkwoman whose words could comport themselves with 'wit, ease and pleasantry' in the finest drawing rooms of the land. (There was no finer drawing room than Mrs Montagu's at her new house, her 'palace' in Portland Square.) Hannah More's creative passions were engaged. This was a process she understood very well: how words, used with skill, could transform life. Words could produce things, if not 'showers of gold' at least the odd sprinkling. Horace Walpole was not the only one of her correspondents who became tired of hearing about it all. His impatience was directed at the shape-changing milkwoman not her enthusiastic patron. Acidly, he reminded More: 'She must remember that she is Lactilla, not Pastora, and is to tend real cows, not Arcadian sheep.'

More gave Yearsley what she herself had got from David Garrick: the benefits of experience, undivided attention, and the influence wielded by a successful practitioner. The obvious way forward – given the extent of her own network of contacts – was to raise a subscription to publish Yearsley's verse and produce for her an income. This was the simplest and most common method for the wealthy and well-connected to show their appreciation and help sustain those who had talent but no funds. Carter's *Epictetus* had been published this way; so had Johnson's *Shakespeare*. Ann Yearsley's name and genius were spread about amongst the quality. The duchesses responded; there was, after all, luxury in relieving the distress of merit. Yearsley was invited to visit at grand houses; she was sent gifts. Subscriptions poured in.

Elizabeth Montagu, also roused by 'the wondrous story of the milkwoman' and approving of verses in which 'native fire [had] not been damped by a load of learning', agreed to be co-trustee with Hannah More of the funds raised. Both brought class anxieties to the affair. Now making lists of the great names calling the milkwoman to their houses, Hannah More fretted,

> I hope all these honours will not turn her head, and indispose her for her humble occupations. I would rather have her served than flattered. Your noble and munificent friend, the Duchess Dowager of Portland, has sent me a twenty-pound bank-note for her; so I take it she will soon be the richest poetess, certainly the richest milkwoman, in Great Britain.

Mrs Montagu put the matter more disdainfully: 'a legion of little demons,' she wrote, 'vanity, luxury, idleness, and pride might enter the cottage the moment poverty vanished.'

The letters that passed between Hannah More and Elizabeth Montagu on the subject of Ann Yearsley are not pleasant to read but they are illuminating. The incomparably wealthy Montagu drew on her experience of the upward social mobility of some exceptional individuals to warn comfortably off Hannah More of the moral dangers kept at bay by poverty: vanity, luxury, idleness and pride. In sharing these thoughts, she invited More to identify with those, like herself, who had never been at risk of living in cottages and knew nothing whatsoever about poverty. But Hannah More had been, and was still, much closer to the poverty end of the spectrum than she was to the wealth Elizabeth Montagu lay lapped in. If she hadn't grown up poor she had at least known what it was like to have 'more desires than guineas'. Her life pattern had been defined by upward social mobility, a lifestyle that demanded to be monitored by attention to manners and morals, hence her own preoccupation with these matters, turned to account in didactic writings. Montagu's words had a very particular application to herself, too particular to acknowledge without collapsing the whole structure inside which Hannah More was able to spend the summer with Elizabeth Montagu and imitate her ways by becoming a literary patron.

In *Rambler* 202, Johnson identified the tendency of poets and philosophers to sentimentalise poverty. The truth about poverty, he wrote, was not 'content, innocence and cheerfulness', nor 'health and safety, tranquillity and freedom'. The cottage was not 'elysium'; it was a place of 'meanness, distress, complaint, anxiety and dependence'. Hannah More knew this, but her idealising enthusiasm combined with self-interest led her to agree that flattery not poverty was the source of moral collapse. These were the sorts of things patrons said to each other, just as they chose to ignore the advantages they received by being patrons. Charlotte Lennox had explored the psychology of the patronage relationship in her first novel, *Harriot Stuart*, emphasising that patronage was always an *exchange* of benefits, and giving to her heroine a spirited resentment and a head-tossing, door-slamming insistence on her personal dignity that was drawn according to a model first fully delineated by Johnson in his *Life of Savage*. Ann Yearsley may not have read *Harriot Stuart* but she was sure to have known about Richard Savage, who had died, after all, whilst confined for debt in Bristol gaol.

Johnson's *Life of Richard Savage* (1744) was the first such life of a struggling author and it was to have a powerful impact as the paradigmatic writer's life. It was written when Johnson was himself barely known and often without the means of shelter or food; famously, he and Savage passed the nights walking the streets of London. Johnson's strong identification with unrewarded genius permeated the text and accounts for much of its power. Savage, being in Johnson's view singular and special, was not subject to the usual social codes and rules: he was the undiscovered genius self-nursed in obscurity who knew truths others had yet to be persuaded of, full of pride and a sense of true worth denied. Johnson fully believed Savage's story of rejection by his aristocratic mother (scholars nowadays incline to view the whole story as an invention, 'brilliantly and brazenly acted out'); and he justified Savage's resentment on the grounds that he was 'a great Mind':

> The insolence and resentment of which he is accused, were not easily to be avoided by a great mind, irritated by perpetual hardships and constrained hourly to return the spurns of contempt, and repress the insolence of prosperity; and vanity surely may be readily pardoned in him, to whom life afforded no other comforts than barren praises, and the consciousness of deserving them.
>
> Those are no proper judges of his conduct who have slumber'd away their time on the down of plenty, nor will a wise man easily presume to say, 'Had I been in *Savage's* condition, I should have lived, or written, better than *Savage*'.[29]

This rhetoric and this structure of thinking were to remain important to Johnson throughout his life. Hannah More would surely not have recognised herself as embodying 'the insolence of prosperity' nor of having slept out her existence on 'the down of plenty'; but for Ann Yearsley any difference between Hannah More and Elizabeth Montagu was neither here nor there. Both women had what she wanted: freedom from privation, comfort to pursue their desires, wealth. Insolence and resentment, meanwhile, were qualities that signalled genius in those whose lives were full of 'hardships'. Given how much irritation had to be endured by great minds situated like Savage, like Ann Yearsley ('perpetual hardships', 'hourly' instances of contempt), any *lack* of resentment actually called the genius into question.

Perhaps Hannah More had the fantasy of those who start out as clients and dream of being perfect patrons in their turn.[30] Even so, she had a characteristically pragmatic end in view: 'I would rather have her served than flattered.' The focus here is not on how Yearsley might receive but on what she might be given, on what the rich were prepared to do: flattery is easy, service more demanding. Situated between the social extremes, with wealth on the one hand, utter destitution on the other, and literature the means of grace between, middling Hannah More had set herself a delicate task. It was made impossible by Ann Yearsley's refusal to act according to the rules her betters considered absolute.

The subscription edition was collected, edited, printed (by Cadell), paid for, distributed. There were over a thousand subscribers, nine of them duchesses, and a decent trawl of countesses, earls, marchionesses, bishops and bluestockings. The book was an impressive object: beautifully produced, with heavy linen paper and gilt-tooled leather covers. And, as intended, it made a profit: over £350 was left after expenses. Just as Garrick had invested her profits from *Percy*, so Hannah More invested Ann Yearsley's profits in the five per cents. There was £28 14s. for immediate spending (to clothe the family, furnish the house and pay off debts) and the rest would produce an income of £18 per annum, enough to underpin Yearsley's earnings as a milkwoman and introduce some stability and security into her life but not enough to change the essential conditions of that life. An agreement was drawn up by a lawyer. Montagu and More together had control of the money (Montagu dealt with the banking). Yearsley had, in More's opinion, already demonstrated 'the Poet's vice, want of economy': her liking for fine gauze bonnets, long lappets and gold pins betrayed her. (Savage spent extravagantly whenever money came his way.) But the real reason for keeping control of the money was to make sure that it reached the children by 'putting it out of the husband's power to touch it'.

Ann Yearsley was outraged at the refusal of her patrons to allow her to handle her own profits. 'I felt,' she wrote, 'as a mother deemed unworthy of the tuition and care of her family.' She went to confront Hannah More in person. Hannah not being at home it was the elder sisters, Mary and Elizabeth – capable women who had spent their lives making sensible decisions for themselves and their pupils – who received the raging poet, and who advised docility, gratitude, submission and good sense. Ann Yearsley demanded that they give her her money. She created a scene. Imperious and furious, she screamed and made demands; they decided she was drunk or mad. Before long, it was a public matter and once again Hannah's name was being dragged through the gutter press. Literature-loving Bristol was divided: some supported Hannah More, others Ann Yearsley. The world had moved on since 1759 when Charlotte Lennox declared in *Henrietta* that 'the world seldom espouses the part of the oppressed'; not everybody was on the side of the rich; new communities of support, new models of understanding, were coming into being. Bristol, like Birmingham and London, was a hotbed of radical thinking.[31]

By going on the attack, which Yearsley did with relish, even dragging up the story of the engagement for purposes of mockery – Hannah was a 'slighted prude' – Yearsley revealed the weaknesses of More's position. More could not speak out. To go public in response would bring her down to Yearsley's level; it was absolutely unacceptable to engage the milkwoman poet in print since such an act would narrow the crucial social space between them, the space which enabled Hannah More to look up with confidence to Elizabeth Montagu rather than down to Ann Yearsley.

Montagu advised a clean break, 'as it would be, if one had from pity fed a famished tiger'. Someone else should hand over the money. More should 'get free from any connection with this fury'. The whole affair carried the potential for 'danger and trouble'. Furies and famished tigers were not to be treated tenderly; scrapping with them was out of the question. Montagu, with her experience of managing the poor, and her cold determination to keep the upper hand nature and fortune had dealt her, spelled it out:

> I earnestly entreat you to consider how disagreeable it would be to have any contention with a milkwoman ... Your distinguished talents render you an object of envy to your own sex and of jealousy to the other. I who have several tenants who pay me rent for dairy farms am more likely to be visited by envy than a woman who milks cows herself, so that her abuse of us will be favorably received and credited.[32]

Earnest entreaty of this sort from this source could not be disregarded. To allow oneself to go being exposed as 'an object of envy' and target for public abuse was to help spread disaffection. Other objects of envy, such as Elizabeth Montagu, were 'likely to be visited'. Four years earlier, in the Gordon Riots of 1780, the wealthy had feared for the safety of their property and the Thrale brewery in Southwark had come close to being torn down by a mob.

Hannah More complained instead, endlessly, to her friends, laying out the ungrateful protégée's accusations against her (the source for much of our information). She would not leave the 'odious tale' alone. Mrs Garrick finally told her to 'shut up her feelings and throw the writing of the Trust at Mrs Yearsley's head and have done with it'. But her dealings with Ann Yearsley were too painful and difficult to be so easily dismissed. In the prefatory letter to the first edition of Yearsley's verses, More had outlined the story of her connection and explained her hopes:

> The ambition of bringing to light a genius buried in obscurity, operates much less powerfully on my mind, than the wish to rescue a meritorious woman from misery, for it is not fame, but bread, which I am anxious to secure to her.

Why did she not want to secure 'fame' for her? Surely 'fame' would lead to 'bread'? The distinction More made and held to with an intransigence that polarised observers then and has exercised scholars since was rather like the distinctions she made later when deciding what was and wasn't appropriate for the children of the poor to learn in her Sunday schools: they would be taught to read but not to write. They would be made fit for particular stations in life. Merit lay in a pragmatic recognition of what was required to maintain that station and perform the duties demanded. It meant controlling passionate desire for an imagined other life. What 'fame' actually meant – for Hannah More, for Ann Yearsley – was some access to the lives lived by those in the privileged classes. In immediate terms this might be expressed by patronage: Ann Yearsley went on to use her fame to establish what for her was a more satisfactory patronage relationship with Lord Bristol (a man as well as an aristocrat – which may have been a factor). Young Hannah More had dreamed of fame: an innocent and meritorious activity, judging by the responses of her family and friends. But fame, now, was troubling in ways that bread was not. With prosperity and status, as she sought to become a patron in her turn, her views shifted. Perhaps the envious component intrinsic to the dream of fame became awkwardly apparent to her. Fame was more of a threat to the order of society than was the charitable provision of bread. The relationship of patronage led the low to dream of being high (witness her own case). The deference culture that had rewarded her so well might be endangered by the very people it allowed to come inside. If she didn't follow Mrs Montagu's advice, Mrs Montagu might look on her with new eyes and realise she was not, after all, 'one of us'. Hannah More's loyalties were with the established order and this may explain her viciousness towards the one woman of her time who represented the repudiation of deference culture, who dedicated her books to the leaders of the French Revolution, and who claimed rights for women: Mary Wollstonecraft.

Yearsley, having nothing to lose, exploited press interest and presented her own side of the affair in the preface to the fourth edition of her *Poems on Several Occasions* (1786) and the volume that followed, *Poems on Various Subjects* (1787). She had no incentive to be tender towards her former patron. Like Richard Savage and Thomas Chatterton, that other Bristol poet whose 'great mind' was so 'irritated by perpetual hardships' that he killed himself at the age of eighteen, she felt ill-used. In broadcasting her indignation she found a ready response in the reading public. The press had a field day. The bookseller Joseph Cottle's attempt to be fair-minded – 'both parties meant well' – represented the exception in a dispute which aroused fiercely partisan responses. Ann Yearsley used the language of rights and independence in the new modern way. She declared that, since she had 'not been accustomed to your rules of polished life', she would always err in the 'polite' manner of speaking – and there is a hint of pride in the declaration which should alert us that power was building elsewhere. She could be contemptuous, she did not have to be obsequious. She could defy, she did not have to please; 'sycophancy's mask' could hang unused. On the question of money, and the absolute rule in polite society that money was never to be spoken about *at all*, she would not even try. The subject was too important, the money too vital. To More she wrote:

> You tax me with ingratitude, for why? You found me poor yet proud, if it can be called pride to feel too much humbled by certain obligations, and above submitting to servility. You helped to place me in the public eye; my success you think beyond my abilities, and purely arising from your protection; but granting this to your vanity, surely mine does not *soar*, in thinking the singularity of my situation would have secured me some success ... I cannot think it ingratitude to disown as obligation a proceeding which must render me and my children your poor dependents for ever. I have trusted more to your *probity* than the event justifies. You have led me to sign a Settlement which defrauds me of my right, and makes it ever received your peculiar gift. Your bankruptcy or death may lose it for ever, and let me ask you Miss More what security you have ever given my children whereby they may prove their claim? [33]

Hannah More's own leap by merit into the polite circles of 'the conversable world' was underwritten by the annuity from her reluctant lover and the financial security afforded by her sisters and their school. She could play by the rules of the world she found herself in. Gratitude was a currency she had used with skill. Like her poem, 'The Bas Bleu: or Conversation', addressed to Mrs Vesey:

> Vesey, of verse the judge and friend,
> Awhile my idle strain attend ...

so another poem, 'Sensibility: An Epistle', was addressed to Mrs Boscawen:

> Accept, Boscawen, these unpolish'd lays,
> Nor blame too much the verse you cannot praise.

They were poems expressing gratitude. Unlike Yearsley, she did not feel 'too much humbled by certain obligations'. When, as a young writer, she was the 'meanest' person in the company, she could announce herself 'a worm but a happy worm'. The security in poems like 'The Bas Bleu' and 'Sensibility' ('let me ask you Miss More what security You have ever given my children ...') came not from asserting her independent rights but from the celebration of an existing social formation: it was the classic role of the bard singing the honours on the assumption of sharing in them. (And perhaps it came from not having any children to worry about.) The listing of names which is so marked a feature of her letters is, in 'Sensibility: An Epistle', relentless:

O let me grateful own these friends are mine;
With CARTER trace the wit to Athens known,
Or view in MONTAGU that wit our own;
Or mark, well pleas'd, CHAPONE's instructive page,
Intent to raise the morals of the age
Or boast, in WALSINGHAM, the various power
To cheer the lonely, grace the letter'd hour;
DELANEY, too, is ours ...

These lists, whilst they celebrate, also circumscribe. They draw a boundary to dictate who is out as well as who is in. Hannah More was 'grateful' to have made the progress she made, marked as it was by the acquisition of high-ranking friends. She was skilled in deference strategies that served her well. But the lists already looked antiquated. They spoke of the past, of tight control by small well-organised groups who had vested interests to protect. Ann Yearsley knew that the combination of genius and adversity had selling power which spoke to a new community capable of giving her the support she needed: 'the singularity of my situation would have secured me some success'.

The shrewdest comment on the whole affair was made by Anna Seward, the bluestocking poet and literary critic who reigned in solitary splendour over polite society at Lichfield. She observed that Hannah More had idealised the 'muse-born wonder' and had at first naively celebrated her 'inflexible moral honesty, [and] stern uncomplaining patience, that silently endured the bitterest evils of want'. Anna Seward, on the other hand, found in Yearsley's writings no such heroism of acquiescent endurance but 'a gloomy and jealous dignity of spirit'. She went on to make the following comparison:

> Great delicacy was required in the manner of conferring obligation on a mind so tempered. Miss More's letter to Mrs Montagu, prefixed to Lactilla's first publication, struck me with an air of superciliousness towards the being she patronized; and the pride of genius in adversity revolted. So, in a similar situation, would surly Samuel Johnson have spurned the hand that, after it had procured him the bounty of others, sought to dictate to him as to its use; and that resentment, which, in *her*, is universally execrated, would, coming down to us now as a record of *his* emerging talents, have been generally excused, and probably, with whatever little reason, admired.[34]

Ann Yearsley, self-described as having 'a stubborn and a savage will', got her money. It finally came to £600. She used part of it to apprentice a son to an engraver, and part to start a circulating library at Bristol Hotwells. The bookseller Joseph Cottle, who was taking up a new generation of local poets that included Robert Southey and Samuel Taylor Coleridge, was sympathetic to her work and accepting of her pride. Over the years, she brought out more poems, a novel and a play. Literary critics nowadays are far more interested in Ann Yearsley's literary productions than they are in anything Hannah More wrote.

6

Fanny Burney

Fanny Burney barely mentions Hannah More in her diary. Dinner companions though they were, frequenters of the same social assemblies and sharing intimate friends, it is probable that they disliked each other. Certainly, there was little intimacy and the few references in the diary are negative ones. Fanny Burney records without comment but with obvious relish the opinion of a 'gay, flighty, entertaining' friend who said of Hannah More: 'I do not like her at all, in fact I detest her. She does nothing but flatter and fawn, and then she thinks ill of nobody. Don't you hate a person who thinks ill of nobody?' [1]

The word 'nobody' had a special meaning for Fanny Burney. It was to 'Nobody' that she began writing her first private journal in 1768 which began:

> To whom ... must I dedicate my wonderful, surprising and interesting adventures? – to whom dare I reveal my private opinion of my nearest Relations? The secret thoughts of my dearest friends? My own hopes, reflections and dislikes? – Nobody!
>
> To Nobody, then will I write my Journal! Since to Nobody can I be wholly unreserved – to Nobody can I reveal every thought, every wish of my heart. [2]

In this passage, a word which begins by denoting an absence – an empty space – reverses its meaning and becomes substance. Nobody becomes *a* body. Nobody is the body who can be trusted with secrets and told every thought. To read the entry about Hannah More in the knowledge that Fanny Burney had a private meaning for the word 'nobody' in her diary, that it signified her closest confidante, an extension of herself, adds and changes its meaning. In the enclosed world of the diary, written '*solely* for my own perusal', the carefully recorded malicious remark has a singular twist. Thinking ill of nobody is actually thinking ill of somebody: Fanny Burney's Nobody. It is an action we can assume to be offensive to Fanny Burney. What is opened up is the pleasure of her private triumph over Hannah More – who, in Fanny Burney's friend's opinion, thinks *she* triumphs by thinking ill of nobody – intensified for Burney by the additional pleasure of hiding her 'private opinion' and projecting her own ill thinking onto a Hannah More who remains oblivious that she has been caught thinking ill at all.

These secret pleasures and reversals, private meanings and revealed hidden thoughts, are characteristic of Fanny Burney. Extremely shy and very observant, with a powerful memory for incident and dialogue, she could recall and record not only the words people said and their gestures but the little details which revealed secrets of personality. Every bit as addicted to scribbling as Hannah More, the meaning invested in the activity was far more fraught for her. At the age of fifteen, Fanny Burney built a bonfire and burnt everything she had written. The violent destruction of poems, epic histories, plays, romances and an almost completed novel suggests a lost quantity of juvenilia to rival that of the Brontës. The underlying cause seems to have been rage at her father for introducing a much-disliked stepmother into the family, but the precipitating event was being discovered in midflow, actually writing, by her stepmother. Revelation and exposure determined her to give up the 'clandestine delight'. She 'considered it her duty to combat this writing passion as illaudable, because fruitless'.[3]

This was the explanation Fanny herself gave for lighting the bonfire and it raises several questions. First, would the activity of writing have been laudable if it bore fruit? What kind of fruit? Secondly, how far was Fanny's delight in writing dependent on its clandestine nature? Thirdly, who was she punishing or pleasing by putting to the flames 'her whole stock of prose goods and chattels; with the sincere intention to extinguish for ever in their ashes her scribbling propensity'. And lastly, by whom and for whom was the nostalgic account of the bonfire written?

Fanny Burney incorporated this story into her *Memoirs of Doctor Burney, Arranged from his own Manuscripts, from Family Papers and from Personal Recollections by his Daughter, Madame d'Arblay,* which she published in three volumes in 1832. Charles Burney had died in 1814 and in 1817, Fanny set about sorting her father's papers, which included twelve notebooks of memoirs written by himself. Of humble origin, he had lived a long life, had been a scholar and musician, working long hours as a peripatetic music-master in the houses of the wealthy, cultivating the social graces that ensured he was considered a cut above a servant. At the time that Charles Burney was apprenticed to Thomas Arne, in the 1740s, musicians had very low social prestige. Not much had changed by the time he accumulated a large family and an ever-pressing need to earn a living. So long as his days were filled, as he put it, with 'ABC-battles' with 'little Master' and 'little Miss' he remained 'a drudge amid the smiles of wealth and power'. The turning point came in the middle of his life when he saw that he could improve his social position by writing about music, and by capturing a polite literary audience, thereby transforming himself from a 'mere musician' into a 'man of letters'.

His unprecedented success earned him entry into the most distinguished intellectual circles. He had been able to introduce himself to Johnson, become an intimate of Mrs Thrale, friends with Garrick and draw to his house the 'various' and 'brilliant' society Macaulay later celebrated in an essay about his more famous daughter: 'few nobles', Macaulay observed, 'could assemble in the most stately mansions of Grosvenor Square or Saint James's Square, a society so various and so brilliant as was sometimes to be found in Dr Burney's cabin'.[4] (The use of the word 'cabin' is a brilliant touch: Burney lived in fact in perfectly substantial houses, including one in Leicester Square that had previously been the London home of Isaac Newton.) He made it his business to get to know and keep the friendship of everybody of consequence, exercising his charm, art and humour in person and in correspondence. He had traded on his wits and risen by his talents. Mrs Thrale observed that his children were keen to follow his example: 'The family of the Burneys are a very surprising set of people; their esteem and fondness for the Doctor seems to inspire them all with a desire not to disgrace him; and so every individual of it must write and read and be literary'.[5]

Fanny's concern in writing her father's *Memoir* was to make sure that his reputation as a scholar and friend of the great was confirmed. She by then was the distinguished author of *Evelina, Cecilia, Camilla* and *The Wanderer*. When she began reading through Dr Burney's papers, a prepara-tory task which was to take her three years, she was shocked and disappointed. The picture formed was not the picture she wanted to publish. It was morally offensive to her: 'peccant' was the word she used to describe material she afterwards burnt, records which in her view were so foul they 'might have bred fevers, caused infectious ill-will, or have excited morbid criticism or ridicule'. Her objective was to keep up her father's credit as a literary man. These writings 'were so unlike all that honoured writer had ever produced to the public, that not only they would not have kept up his credit and fair name in the literary world, if brought to light, but would certainly have left a cloud upon its parting ray'.[6]

Instead of editing and publishing her father's notebooks, Fanny Burney spent the next twelve years writing her own version of his life, ruthlessly cleaning up Dr Burney's character and reputation and in the process, according to one contemporary critic, glorifying her own name rather than memorialising her father. There is widespread agreement that what she produced is duller than the materials he left. She rewrote him with an eye to social and literary credit for surviving family members – money was still much-needed. She herself was part of that credit: her celebrity as an author had given lustre to the name of Burney. Paradoxically, by the 1820s when she was working on this text, to depict herself, a known female author, in the act of renouncing authorship by burning her early manuscripts at the tender age of fifteen, was entirely in keeping with the larger objective. It was a way of feeding a literary myth she had done much to create – the myth of propriety, covertness and denial – since authorial self-effacement had come to define the 'proper' woman writer. By the time Fanny Burney sifted so distressfully through Charles Burney's papers, forty years after the birth of *Evelina*, a woman writer's best hope of literary credit lay in denying that she was engaged in the activity of authorship at all.

As a young woman, Fanny Burney was fully occupied as her father's secretary and copyist. Her days were filled with literary business. At the same time, she wrote – often at night – her diary and fiction. The diary was private but she had every intention of publishing her fiction, and indeed her sense of connection to the world of print and publishing was highly developed. She was young but by no means ignorant. *Evelina* was offered to Thomas Lowndes as a proposal in 1776 before it was fully written. Her letter to him explained: 'The plan of the first volume is the introduction of a well educated but inexperienced young woman into public company ... I believe it has not before been executed, though it seems a fair field open for the novelist ...'[7]

She presented herself professionally as a novelist and had spotted a gap in the market. Once the first volume was written, she was anxious to keep her identity secret though the writing itself was not secret: her siblings – 'the laughing committee' – were in on the joke, and her brother Charles acted as her agent, going disguised through darkened streets 'muffled up ... in an old great coat, and huge hat' to deliver a manuscript that had been laboriously copied out in '*a feigned hand*' because the booksellers might otherwise recognise the handwriting of Dr Burney's daughter. Nor had her efforts at authorship been kept secret from her father. When she told him she was writing a book, his response was one of amused indulgence: 'He could not help laughing.' She adds that he asked her 'to acquaint him, from time to time, how my work went on, called himself the *père confident*, and kindly promised to guard my secret as cautiously as I could wish'. The condescension riled her, particularly as 'he forbore to ask me its name, or make any enquiries'.[8] All this when she was engaged in negotiations with publishers, up to and including monetary negotiations: she had refused the publisher's first offer of twenty guineas. She had insisted she was worth more and held out for ten guineas a volume – to which he, recognising a surefire winner, agreed.

Fanny Burney's thirty guineas for the three-volume *Evelina* is not a large sum when we consider how well the novel sold and how significant it came to be. It was also considerably less than Hannah More's forty guineas for two poems, 'Sir Eldred of the Bower' and 'The Bleeding Rock', and £600 profits on the play, *Percy;* and a great deal less than Ann Yearsley's £350 profits on the subscription edition of her poems. But it was a reasonable, businesslike price for a first-time novelist to accept from a reputable publisher.

Businesslike too was the unusually self-conscious dedicatory address to the reviewers, those 'Authors of the Monthly and Critical Reviews'. Where a novelist might thank her patrons, the author of *Evelina* mockingly thanked these gentlemen in advance for their attention, whilst emphasising her newness and novelty: she was 'without name, without recommendation, and unknown alike to success and disgrace'. Nevertheless, the writer making this debut spoke with some authority: 'Remember, Gentlemen, you were all young writers once, and the most experienced veteran of your corps, may, by recollecting his first publication, renovate his first terrors, and learn to allow for mine.'

When Charles Burney discovered his daughter's authorship of *Evelina* his reaction was to do everything he could to promote it. At Streatham he proudly let Mrs Thrale into the secret, knowing that, as a hostess who prided herself on being an arbiter of literary fashion, she would spread the word; as indeed she did, passing the first volume to Samuel Johnson as soon as she had read it. Mrs Thrale wrote in her diary:

> I was shewed a little novel t'other day, which I thought pretty enough and set Burney to read it, little dreaming it was written by his second daughter Fanny, who certainly must be a girl of good parts, and some knowledge of the world too, or she could not be the author of *Evelina* – flimsy as it is, compared with the books I've just mentioned by Charlotte Lennox, Smollett and Fielding! [9]

The celebrity of *Evelina* made Fanny a sought-after guest at Streatham Park, as Charles Burney knew it would. She made her first visit in July 1778 – 'the most *consequential* day I have spent since my birth' – and it was then that she began her intimacy with Johnson. But it was not the first time Fanny had had occasion to observe the great man. Some time before, Mrs Thrale had brought Johnson to St Martin's Street, where the Burneys lived, to view Dr Burney's library of foreign literature. Fanny noted her first impressions:

> He is, indeed, very ill favoured, – he is tall and stout, but stoops terribly, – he is almost bent double. His mouth is in perpetual motion, as if he was chewing; – he has a strange method of frequently twirling his fingers and twisting his hands; – his body is in continual agitation, *see-sawing* up and down; his feet are never a moment quiet, – and, in short, his whole person is in perpetual motion … He is shockingly near sighted, and did not, till she held out her hand to him,

even know Mrs Thrale. He *poked his nose* over the keys of the harpsichord, till the duet was finished, and then, my father introduced Hetty to him, as an old acquaintance, and he instantly kissed her. His attention, however, was not to be diverted five minutes from the books, as we were in the library; he pored over them, almost brushing the backs of them, with his eye lashes, as he read their titles; at last, having fixed upon one, he began, without further ceremony, to read, all the time standing at a distance from the company. We were very much provoked, as we perfectly languished to hear him talk; but, it seems, he is the most silent creature, when not particularly drawn out, in the World.[10]

At Streatham, Johnson teased Burney for being recognised as a wit. He approved of Dr Jebb forbidding her wine since 'he knows how apt wits are to transgress that way'. She commented, 'In this sort of ridiculous manner he *wits* me eternally'. As a wit, as a devoted admirer of David Garrick, friend of the dramatist Arthur Murphy with whom she could discuss stage-craft, and newly established pet of Dr Johnson who might be prevailed upon to usher any production into the world with a prologue, in 1779 Fanny Burney set about writing a comic play. Mrs Thrale thought a play the right next step: 'you *must* write one – a *play* will be something *worth* your time, it is the road both to honour and profit, – and *why* should you have it in your power to gain these rewards and not do it?' Sheridan had said he would accept a play from her without even reading it, so great was his confidence in her talent for lively dialogue.[11]

The young celebrity's development and future as a writer was a publicly spoken affair at Streatham, so it was not remarkable that Johnson involved himself in her plans. Like the others, he urged her on: in fact, he wanted her to take as her subject the comings and goings at Streatham Park and begin her dramatic career by writing *Streatham: A Farce*. Though surprised by this turn for the burlesque which she had not expected to find in Johnson, Fanny was not surprised to be advised: she was used to having the support of older men. (It was not only in the theatre that being fatherly and helpful to talented women became an acceptable role for men in the mid eighteenth century, often rationalised as the patriotic endeavour of helping to boost the stock of the nation's achievements in literature and the arts.) Samuel Crisp, a friend of her father's, was Fanny's 'dear Daddy'. He not only encouraged her 'scribbling', he also provided her with a room of her own at his house, Chesington Hall. This room was known between them as 'the conjuring closet', a space devoted to her writing. Staying with Crisp, she could go in there and shut the door and be undisturbed for as long as she chose – a contrast to her own home where her stepmother demanded her time and attention. 'There is no place where I more really *enjoy myself* than at Chesington', Fanny wrote. Her enjoyment was the enjoyment of pursuing her own inclinations, specifically that of writing and being treated as an author:

> All the household are kind, hospitable and partial to me; there is no sort of restraint, – everybody is disengaged and at liberty to pursue their own inclinations, – and my Daddy, who is the soul of the place, is, at once, so flatteringly affectionate to *me*, and so infinitely, so beyond comparison in *himself*, – that were I to be otherwise than happy in his company, I must either be wholly without feeling or utterly destitute of understanding.[12]

Samuel Crisp told her in no uncertain terms: 'a state of independence is the only basis on which to rest your future ease and comfort'. By this he meant the two sorts of independence she could earn by writing: financial independence; and the independent social position available through reputation. Fanny Burney's gratitude and deference to this older man who fully believed in her as a writer is as characteristic of the times as Hannah More's artistically productive, emotionally satisfying and financially rewarding relationship with Garrick. But whereas Garrick was a working professional actor-manager with a record of successful achievement behind him, Samuel Crisp was a disappointed writer; specifically, a disappointed and somewhat embittered playwright.

Accustomed to Crisp's encouragement, Fanny Burney looked to Johnson for similar services. She wanted more than a prologue from him, however. Tête-à-tête late one night after the Thrales had gone to bed, the following conversation on the subject of her comedy took place as recorded by her. In the diary, she describes herself asking him:

> 'if I should make such an attempt, would you be so good as to allow me, any time before Michaelmas, to put it in the coach, for you to look over as you go to town?'
>
> 'To be sure, my dear! – What, have you begun a comedy then?'
>
> I told him how the affair stood. He then gave me advice which just accorded with my own wishes, viz., not to make known that I had any such intention; to keep my own counsel; not to whisper even the name of it; to raise no expectations, which were always prejudicial, and finally to have it performed while the town knew nothing of whose it was ...
>
> He said he would not have it in the coach, but that I should read it to him; however, I could sooner drown or hang!
>
> When I would have offered some apology for the attempt, he stopped me, and desired I would never make any.
>
> 'For,' said he, 'if it succeeds, it makes its own apology, if not.' 'If not,' quoth I, 'I cannot do worse than Dr Goldsmith, when his play failed, – go home and cry!'
>
> He laughed, but told me repeatedly (I mean twice, which, for him, is very remarkable) that I might depend upon all the service in his power ...[13]

The play was *The Witlings*, a satirical comedy. We don't know if Johnson ever read or heard *The Witlings* once it was completed. It seems unlikely, for Charles Burney and Samuel Crisp both forcefully insisted that it was a bad play which Fanny should suppress. Fanny followed the advice of her father and 'Daddy' Crisp.

Though set in a milliner's shop, the satire of *The Witlings* is directed at the bluestocking ladies and anxious would-be literary men amongst whom Fanny spent so much of her time. Strikingly, her response to success and fame was to satirise the circles that now welcomed her in, unlike Hannah More whose poem 'The Bas Bleu' returned praise for praise, celebrating the bluestockings in effusive verse. (Although, of course, Burney's satire of literary longing and yearning for literary fame is also directed at her own obsessions.) Mrs Thrale thought she detected herself in Lady Smatter, which amused her. Others, including Fanny's father, saw in Lady Smatter too close a similarity to Elizabeth Montagu. (Whether Charles Burney saw himself in Dabler, the obsequious poet endlessly trying to please his betters, is not known.) As intellectual hostesses, Mrs Montagu and Mrs Thrale were rivals; either might well have provided part of the inspiration for Lady Smatter, but Lady Smatter is also a stereotype with a long literary pedigree.

Samuel Johnson was perfectly happy to quarrel with Elizabeth Montagu, but Charles Burney – much less securely placed – feared antagonising her (and, indeed, feared upsetting Mrs Thrale). Had Johnson been given the chance to read or hear the script, he might well have urged Fanny on. He understood the aggression that lay behind her demure social manner; and even drew vicarious pleasure from it. Fanny had imbibed from her father and Samuel Crisp certain absolutes: that strategic caution was essential, camouflage an imperative. The business of success preoccupied all of them. Social climbing was possible, was undeniably open to talent, but the way was fraught with peril; and care was required at every turn, especially when the climber was a young woman. Johnson, by contrast, encouraged her to let her aggressive impulses loose. Informed by Mrs Thrale that Mrs Montagu was due to dine with them next day, Fanny records in her diary that he

> began to see-saw, with a countenance strongly expressive of inward fun, and after enjoying it some time in silence, he suddenly and with great animation turned to me and cried, 'Down with her, Burney! – down with her! – spare her not! Attack her, fight her, and down with her at once! You are a rising wit, and she is at the top; and when I was beginning the world, and was nothing and nobody, the joy of my life was to fire at all the established wits; and then everybody loved to halloo me on. But there is no game now; everybody would be glad to see me conquered; but then, when I was new, to vanquish the great ones was all

the delight of my poor little dear soul! So at her, Burney, – at her, and down with her! [14]

The likelihood that Fanny Burney would, as Johnson urged, 'fly at the eagle' was more or less non-existent. Her witty satire is unsparing, however, in its attack on Lady Smatter, Queen Bee of the Esprit Party, who is depicted as being both ignorant and pretentious. Beaufort, Lady Smatter's nephew, tells us that she and her coterie are self-deluded dabblers: 'To a very little reading, they join less understanding, and no judgement, yet they decide upon books and authors with the most confirmed confidence in their abilities.' This is the standard accusation against literary women. It is in the tradition of the character Phoebe Clinket in Pope, Arbuthnot and Gay's play, *Three Hours After a Wedding*. Phoebe Clinket has a writing desk strapped to her back so that her maid can write down her wonderful thoughts wherever and whenever they arise. (A character in *The Witlings*, Codger, quotes Pope's line 'Most women have no character at all'.) Having no character, no real ability, no self-knowledge and no literary taste, the further accusation about such women is that they talk non-stop. In *The Witlings* there is a character called Mrs Voluble who

> will consume more words in an hour than ten men will in a year, she is infected with a rage for talking, yet has nothing to say, which is a disease of all others the most pernicious ... Her tongue is as restless as scandal, and like that, feeds upon nothing, yet attacks and tortures everything; and it vies, in rapidity of motion, with the circulation of the blood in a frog's foot.

The Witlings is a misogynist satire about which both Dr Burney and Mr Crisp had severe reservations. Mrs Thrale wrote in *Thraliana*: 'Mr Crisp advised her against bringing it on, for fear of displeasing the female wits – a formidable body, and called by those who ridicule them, the *Blue Stocking Club*.' Had it been put on it would probably have been a hit: it still reads as a funny and vivid play today. Other plays which made fun of female authors did well: George Colman's *The Separate Maintenance* featured 'a strange, ranting, crazy being' called Fustian – a playwright; and in *The Female Dramatist* the central character is the quite absurd Madam Melpomeme Metaphor. Depicting women of literary and intellectual interests as vain and stupid is one element in *The Witlings*. The play is kinder to hard-working women of the less privileged classes and it gives over the very last speech to an assertion of the need for 'self-dependence' as 'the first of earthly blessings'.

Johnson's fascination with Fanny Burney was not always comfortable for her. To be singled out by him at public gatherings meant sharing in the attention he drew by his ungainly appearance and awkward manners. He was loud and vehement, contemptuous and sarcastic; his presence could be disruptive. During her time at Streatham, Fanny Burney noted that people stopped inviting him, 'either from too much respect or too much fear'. She was sorry because she knew how he hated to be alone, and that his scolding of others did not distress *him*:

> he is well enough satisfied himself; and, having given vent to all his own occasional anger or ill-humour, he is ready to begin again, and is never aware that those who have so been 'downed' by him, never can much covet so triumphant a visitor.[15]

For all her understanding, and her pleasure in the attention he paid her, she also tried to avoid him at times because of 'the staring attention he attracts both for himself and all with whom he talks'. In the last years of his life Johnson became deafer, more short-sighted, more irritable. Fanny Burney noted that in his 'terrible severe humour' the only person he was regularly kind to was herself: 'Mrs Thrale fares worse than anybody' while 'his kindness for me, I think, if possible, still increased: he actually bores everybody so about me that the folks even complain of it'. The person he wanted to sit next to, talk with and talk about was his 'little Burney'. If she would come and tell him stories all night it would cure his sleeplessness. At Miss Monckton's assembly in 1782, after the publication of *Cecilia*, his bad temper was provoked by other guests enthusing about the latest actress, Sarah Siddons. Fanny Burney herself reports no shortage of praise for *Cecilia* from such as Edmund Burke, Edward Gibbon, Joshua Reynolds, and all the 'old wits' like the Duchess of Portland and Mrs Delaney, but Johnson coming up at last and accusing others of 'engrossing' his favourite, was in a passion:

> 'How these people talk of Mrs Siddons!' said the Doctor. 'I came hither in full expectation of hearing no name but the name I love and pant to hear, – when from one corner to another they are talking of that jade Mrs Siddons! Till, at last wearied out, I went yonder into a corner, and repeated to myself Burney! Burney! Burney! Burney!'[16]

Burney, Burney, Burney, Burney, the young woman whose name he needed to repeat, was cruel: 'her cruelty destroys my rest'. She inspired fear: 'Harry Fielding, too, would have been afraid of her; there is nothing so delicately finished in all Harry Fielding's works as *Evelina!*' Demure and apparently harmless, she was the 'little rogue' of a romance writer who 'keeps her resources to herself', a secretive artist, an original. Fascinated by the paradoxes she embodied, Johnson's aggressive feelings about literature and the literary life found an outlet in teasing and praising Fanny. Once started on the subject, orations and panegyrics would flow. Younger men could play him like an instrument, as he well knew: 'they take me in; they ... make me say something of that Fanny Burney, and then the rogues know that when I have once begun I shall not know when to leave off'. Such young men would learn that he admired her for her powers of observation, her good sense, what he called her 'discernment' and for her powers of vivid expression. One male guest was astonished to hear Johnson rate Fanny Burney even above Pope. Pope's early poem, *Windsor Forest*, was 'delightful' but it did not need the knowledge of life and manners, the 'penetration' necessary for *Evelina*. It could have been written young or old, Johnson explained: '*Evelina* seems a work that should result from long experience, and deep and intimate knowledge of the world; yet it has been written without either. Miss Burney is a real wonder.'[17]

This real wonder with her diffidence and pride, her stiffness, her gift for ridicule – 'themes of mere ridicule offer everywhere', she confided to her diary – and her watchful perception, could be provoking. Hester Thrale was certainly provoked. She noted uneasily, 'How well you know him, and me, and all of us'. Hester Thrale welcomed Fanny Burney as a close friend, rather like a younger sister, but it was clear that their life experiences, as well as temperamental differences, set them very far apart. The publicity over *Evelina* upset Fanny in a way that seemed to the older woman quite absurd, the product of a distorted egotism and self-consciousness which she pinpointed when observing that Fanny was 'a graceful looking girl, but 'tis the grace of an actress ... her conversation would be more pleasing if she thought less of herself; but her early reputation embarrasses her talk, and clouds her mind'. She told her, 'This world is a rough road' and excused her own forthrightness, her 'indelicate' sentiments, by adding

> you are twenty years old [in fact Fanny was well into her mid twenties by this time] and I am past thirty six there's the true difference. I have lost seven children and been cheated out of two thousand a year, and I cannot, indeed I cannot, sigh and sorrow over pamphlets and paragraphs.[18]

Fanny could not eat, drink or sleep for a week at the very idea that she was being discussed. Public notice was a trial. To appear as an authoress, in Fanny Burney's view of the matter, involved secrecy and shyness – much blushing, choking on biscuits and running from the room. Treasured and gloated over in privacy, any public acknowledgement of her identity as an authoress was a 'torment'. Listening to Dr Johnson praising *Evelina*, she wanted to hide under the table: 'Never did I feel so delicious a confusion since I was born!'

Mrs Thrale offered no support for these feelings. 'Is not the world full of severe misfortunes, and real calamities?' she wrote, 'and will you fret and look pale about such nonsense as this?' She was puzzled by the contrast of the sophistication of *Evelina* and the apparent innocence of its author: 'I can never make out how the mind that could write that book could be ignorant of its value.' She believed Fanny's modesty was real but it provoked her. At Streatham she called off the tormentors, observing, 'I see it really plagues her. I own I thought for awhile it was only affectation, for I'm sure if the book were mine I should wish to hear of nothing else.' Hester Thrale, nursing literary ambitions, could admit the desire. Fanny recorded these words, as she also recorded Mrs Thrale's earlier remark: 'Miss Burney looks so meek and so quiet, nobody would suspect what a comical girl she is; but I believe she has a great deal of malice at heart.' [19]

The real troubles between them began to emerge as Fanny entered into her new role, admired and feted, and, as she told her sister, Susy, 'grown a grand person, – not merely looked upon as a writer, but addressed as a critic'. Holidaying with the Thrales on the south coast in the autumn of 1779 (Mrs Thrale had almost died in August of that year, giving birth to a stillborn son), Fanny went down with flu. She stayed in bed for seven days 'with a fever', Mrs Thrale wrote,

> or something that she called a fever: I gave her every medicine, and every slop with my own hand; took away her dirty cups, spoons &c, moved her tables, in short was doctor and nurse, and maid – for I did not like the servants should have additional trouble lest they should hate her for it – and now – with the true gratitude of a wit, she tells me, that the *world thinks the better of me* for my civilities to her. It does! Does it? [20]

Both women had a sense of what was owing to their dignity, though Mrs Thrale was perhaps more aware of her own responses. If she envied Fanny her fame, she was also, then, in the less vulnerable position of reader rather than writer. She was a 'very learned lady' according to one of her guests, who 'joins to the charms of her own sex the manly understanding of ours', and who could place the 'flimsy' *Evelina* in a category apart from heavy-weight works by Fielding, Smollett and Charlotte Lennox, but who was not herself exposed to the tribulations of public comment. Unlike Fanny Burney, Mrs Thrale relished social performance, having a gift for quick repartee and a hunger for applause: 'I am not used to people that do not worship me, and of course grow very fastidious in my desire of flattery.' She recorded in *Thraliana* her reply when asked if she had never been in love: 'with myself said I, and most passionately'. It was generally acknowledged that Mrs Thrale rivalled Mrs Montagu as a talker, though she herself made the distinction that Mrs Montagu's talk was more cultivated – not in the best sense – than her own: 'Mrs Montagu's bouquet is all out of the hothouse – mine out of the woods and fields and many a weed there is in it.'[21] Brought together, the mix was impressive. Fanny Burney reported: 'Mrs Montagu, Mrs Thrale, and Lord Mulgrave talked all the talk, and talked it so well, no one else had a wish beyond hearing them.'[22]

At Streatham, with Johnson and Fanny Burney in her camp, Thrale could acknowledge Montagu as 'the first of women in the literary way' and make fun of the competition between them for pre-eminence. Receiving flattering invitations from Mrs Montagu, she and Johnson were able mockingly to boast:

> '*Your* note,' cried Dr Johnson, 'can bear no comparison with *mine*; I am *at the head of the Philosophers*, she says.'
> 'And I,' cried Mrs Thrale, '*have all the Muses in my train!*'[23]

Meanwhile, while the authorship of *Evelina* was still being guessed at, Mrs Montagu was invited to dinner so that the Streathamites could enjoy the pleasures of one-upmanship. Fanny Burney – 'I quite sigh beneath the weight of ... praise' – recorded the moment of revelation and her 'sweet, naughty' Mrs Thrale's delight. Mrs Montagu had been building her new house in Portland Square and she invited the company to see it, fixing a date well ahead:

> Everybody bowed and accepted the invite but me, and I thought fitting not to hear it; for I have no notion of snapping at invites from the eminent. But Dr Johnson, who sat next to me, was determined I should be of the party, for he suddenly clapped his hand on my shoulder, and called out aloud,
> 'Little Burney, you and I will go together!'
> 'Yes, surely,' cried Mrs Montagu, 'I shall hope for the pleasure of seeing 'Evelina'.'
> '*Evelina?*' repeated he; 'has Mrs Montagu then found out *Evelina?*'
> 'Yes,' cried she, 'and I am proud of it; I am proud that a work so commended should be a woman's.'
> Oh, how my face burnt![24]

Mrs Montagu had brought with her her young companion, Dorothea Gregory, the daughter of Dr Gregory whose book *A Legacy for Daughters* instructed women to be malleable and docile – fit qualities for the role of humble companion. Miss Gregory sat across from Fanny and 'quite stared me out of countenance ... never took her eyes off my face'. Later, when the two young women met again in Bath, Fanny found her more compatible, perhaps because by then she had herself been drawn into a similar role with Hester Thrale.

Ever since her mother's death, in 1773, Hester Thrale had felt the need for a female friend. She wrote:

'Tis so melancholy a thing to have nobody one can speak to about one's clothes, or one's child, or one's health, or what comes uppermost. Nobody but *gentlemen*, before whom one must suppress everything except the mere formalities of conversation and by whom everything is to be commended or censured.[25]

In return for the luxuries of Streatham (including intimacy with Samuel Johnson), Hester wanted Fanny's company. She was furious with Charles Burney when he called his daughter back home. She resisted Fanny's desire to retreat to Chesington Hall where her writing time was respected in a way it never was either at Streatham or in London. The struggle over Fanny's availability made manifest the deeper troubles and struggles between them which Mrs Thrale understood as difficulties in the relationship of patronage. Conferring obligations was a minefield:

Fanny Burney has been a long time from me. I was glad to see her again; yet she makes me miserable too in many respects – so restlessly apparently anxious lest I should give myself airs of patronage, or load her with the shackles of dependence – I ... dare not ask her to buy me a ribbon, dare not desire her to touch the bell, lest she should think herself injured.[26]

Recognising that Fanny Burney was proud because poor, Mrs Thrale made allowances. But it was not easy:

Mrs Byron who really loves me, was disgusted at Miss Burney's carriage to me, who have been such a friend and benefactress to her: not an article of dress, not a ticket for public places, not a thing in the world that she could not command from me: yet always insolent, always pining for home, always preferring the mode of life in St Martins Street to all I could do for her: she is a saucy spirited little puss to be sure, but I love her dearly: for all that: and I fancy she has a real regard for me, if she did not think it beneath the dignity of a wit, or of what she values more – the dignity of *Doctor Burney's Daughter*, to indulge it.[27]

Eventually she came round to preferring Fanny for her resistance, or at least she told herself she did. Fanny became one of the 'rough' characters she liked: 'her lofty spirit dear creature! has quite subdued mine; and I adore her for the pride which once revolted me. There is no true affection, no friendship in the sneakers and fawners.'[28]

These troubles worked their way into Fanny Burney's second novel, *Cecilia*, a fiction that could never be described as 'flimsy'. It is immensely long and hugely ambitious, whilst at the same time managing to be, like *Evelina*, a rattling good read. The question of a woman's dignity, what she is worth, what her credit is or what credit she owes, lies at the heart of the five volumes. In *Cecilia* Fanny Burney, a 'portionless girl' as she was prepared to admit to her sister, though she bridled if anybody else viewed her that way (not for her Hannah More's cheerfully strategic self-description: 'the meanest person in the company'), set out in quest of the limits of self-dependence in a female. Her heroine has a fortune and a name: symbolically, in other words, she is positioned where Fanny found herself after the success of *Evelina*. The plot requires that Cecilia's adventure into the world is in search of a husband who is prepared to accept her name upon marriage, or relinquish the fortune she brings with (and in) her name. As a minor, Cecilia has three guardians – three 'Daddies' – each grotesquely unsuited to the task of leading her to a satisfying and purposeful life. Apparently a privileged heiress, she is in fact unprotected and becomes the victim of a decadent and deeply unequal society.

Everybody behaves appallingly: aristocrats are snobbish and prejudiced and greedy for her money; while the middling classes are feckless spendthrifts, greedy for her money. Cecilia's sympathies go out to the workers – milliners (as in *The Witlings*, millinery being the most common trade in which women worked), builders, traders generally. The novel shows how all these workers are treated by the genteel classes: whenever they come calling to demand that their bills be paid, the cry goes up that they are abominably 'ill-bred'. The tyranny of manners allows the rich to be cruel and rapacious; and, whilst appearances are being maintained, the deserving poor, who have given their labour, are allowed to starve.

Caught up in this, Cecilia suffers; but she also learns and conveys the lessons of her suffering. She gets embarrassed but she also gets angry. She is a young woman of great resolution who wants to set the terms and live according to her own agenda. As an heiress, her place is with the ruling classes, but no amount of money can substitute for the power and rank bestowed by particular names, for the effortless superiority available to those whose families have occupied ancestral homes and owned the land for centuries. Cecilia's position is not buttressed by lineage. She wants the dignity of her own name recognised. She does not wish to be rejected by those motivated by class snobbery, by 'the powerful instigation of hereditary arrogance!' When all seems to be up between herself and the aristocrat Delvile, she exclaims, 'my family and every other circumstance is unexceptionable … Well, let him keep his name! Since so wondrous its properties, so all-sufficient its preservation'. Names mattered. The Burney name and all it represented in terms of pride, achievement and autonomy, mattered. All the portionless Burneys had grown up knowing what they had to keep at bay: the threat of a life spent drudging 'amid the smiles of wealth and power'. There was a great deal to gain and to lose.

Fanny Burney's understanding of what was gained and lost by those who traded on wit and rose by talent – what her father had done, what she found herself doing – is dramatised directly in *Cecilia* through the character of Belfield. Belfield, 'the man of genius', strives to please the great folks, believing, as his mother believed before him, that social elevation and magical transformations would follow. Belfield is confused, socially displaced, unable to make sense of his own responses: that is, his mixture of pride and sycophancy. His female relatives have been sacrificed for a fantasy of his future. Burney points the finger of blame not at Belfield but at a corrupt society that fosters such false hopes.

If Burney's father failed to respond seriously to the knowledge that she was writing her first book, he cannot be said to have made the same mistake about the second. All through the writing of *Cecilia* he harried her to get on, to write more quickly. Charles Burney was preparing his second volume of *The History of Music*. He saw the commercial advantage in both their books coming out at the same time. He was anxiously enthusiastic for his famous daughter to finish what was turning into a much longer work than she had at first envisaged. Fanny told Mrs Thrale, 'I am often taken with such fits of temper about it, that, but for my Father, I am sure I would throw it behind the fire!'. To her sister, Susan, she confessed,

> I over harass myself, and that, instead of making me write more, bothers, and makes me write less, – yet I cannot help it, – for I know my dear Father will be disappointed, and he will expect me to have just done, when I am so behind hand as not even to see land! – Yet I have written a great deal, – but the work will be a long one, and I cannot without ruining it make it otherwise.

Meanwhile, to add to the general climate of anxiety, Mr Crisp wrote warning her that she had 'so much to lose, you cannot take too much care'.[29]

The strong sense of what there was to lose had to do with family, with the credit of the Burney name: with an awareness of how much had been accumulated by Charles Burney and what could be built on it. Credit implies debt and debt implies burden. The writing of *Cecilia* was a burden, and during it Burney experienced 'trepidation and self-estrangement' partly because of the pressure to promote the family name now that she was the chief bearer of it. The story that she tells is an anxious and resentful story, a moral tale about extortion, in which the heroine's 'debt' to others is unbounded, and is paid by a remorseless stripping of her fortune and estate.[30] Cecilia's destiny is to go on giving up (this is what she owes society, this is the ethic of the fiction) while getting nothing in return; until at last even her pocket is picked and her purse stolen. When her sense of self, memory and reason are all gone she collapses, very fittingly, in a pawnbroker's shop.

Cecilia was a great success. It was much heralded and the first edition of two thousand copies sold very quickly. However, any 'self-dependence'

Fanny Burney hoped to gain in an economic sense did not materialise. The novel's grim logic of unending forfeiture was paralleled in Fanny Burney's life. Her father took upon himself all dealings with the publisher and he behaved, as she realised, in a way that was '*no wiser than myself*' in selling the copyright for £250. His concern was for the prestige and honour that came from the widest circulation of her name; he was not concerned to secure her financial independence. Place mattered more than portion in his view.

Charles Burney's ambition was fulfilled just a few years later when his daughter was offered a place at court. The offer came about through the agency of the same Mrs Delaney whom Hannah More was so excited to meet, the friend of Swift and direct link to the earlier world of literature. Mrs Delaney had a grace and favour apartment at Windsor and a pension. Through Delaney's friendship with the Queen, Fanny Burney was offered the place of Second Keeper of the Queen's Robes. It was 'a place solicited by thousands and thousands of women of Fashion and Rank' her father crowed, at once imagining on the strength of it 'organ-posts for himself, ships for James, schools, degrees, and dioceses for Charles'. Like the Belfield family in *Cecilia*, the women in the Burney family were to be sacrificed for the men. Fanny wrestled sadly with the suicidal prospect: 'I see him so much delighted at the prospect of an establishment he looks upon as so honorable ... But what can make *me* amends for all I shall forfeit?'[31]

The successful novelist was to spend five dreadful years as a servant to royalty, a servitude which began in 1786. She was estranged from Hester Thrale (her father had insisted on the separation after Thrale's marriage to Piozzi lest she be tainted by association); Samuel Crisp was dead; Johnson was dead. Immured amidst the dull pomposities of George III's court, 'a drudge amid the smiles of wealth and power', she came near to death herself. In the end it was Johnson's old friends who rescued her. The Literary Club gathered its forces, put pressure on her father, and insisted she be removed.

As the daughter of Mrs Montagu's friend, Dr Gregory, Dorothea Gregory had all the makings of the perfect humble companion – the toad-eater or 'toadling' who served and deferred. She had been groomed to it; her father had written the book. Like Fanny Burney, she came from the aspiring professional classes who had talent and energy but no inherited wealth. She was intelligent and shrewd and her manners were such that she quickly became popular in the circles Montagu introduced her into. More than that, she was efficient and capable and she served Montagu as an energetic, reliable personal assistant: a confident horsewoman, she drove Montagu on long airings or business visits between her estates, she helped organise the households (at Sandleford alone there was a staff of thirty) and she was sympathetically available for confidences. For ten years she was to Montagu 'one perfect chrysolite'; her heart had 'no flaw, no imperfection in it'.[32]

Dorothea Gregory had no literary ambitions. She enjoyed conversation and repartee, but as 'the perfection of strict truth, blunt honesty, and clear understanding' she had little patience with what seemed to her the vanities of self-creation and self display that drove Montagu. Gregory's son later explained that his mother had 'had no objections to blue stockings, providing the petticoats were long enough to conceal them'. Since ostentation was Montagu's life blood, this element in Gregory (albeit probably exaggerated by a dutiful son) was likely to prove corrosive. Her dreams did not lead her to want to emulate her mistress nor take advantage of the unique opportunities that came her way. Furthermore, she could not have been unaware of the levels of hostility Montagu evoked. Nathaniel Wraxhall describing her in 1776 catches the intense refusal of 'womanly' social codes in Montagu's style. With her gift for ruling, combined with the pleasure she took in it, she is aptly described as 'a perfect patriarch', who was successful in maintaining her prerogatives: 'a very thin velvet glove over a steel hand that successfully executed, for a time, almost incredible achievements ... a notable captain of industry and something of a domestic tyrant'. Her parties were her arena for the display and enjoyment of her thinking and talking powers:

> Her manner was more dictatorial and sententious than conciliating or diffident. There was nothing feminine about her; and though her opinions were usually just, as well as delivered in language suited to give them force, yet the organ which conveyed them was not soft or harmonious.

Wraxhall went on to complain about her excessive use of jewellery, which, though he admitted that her opinions were 'just' and properly argued, nevertheless gave him some sullen comfort: 'I used to think that these glittering appendages of opulence sometimes helped to dazzle the disputants whom her arguments might not always convince or her literary reputation intimidate.' Being at Mrs Montagu's must often have been a trial. Her ability to 'dazzle' disputants, to win the ground and carry her point, her fearless insistence on doing so on all occasions and her absolute lack of submissiveness of any kind was recorded over and over again by aggrieved individuals. The standard accusations of vanity, affectation, superficiality and the demand for flattery often seem to be obscuring more profound objections that were more troubling to raise: the brutal arrogance of a hard and vindictive ruler whose favour or ill favour was a significant matter.

For ten years Montagu and Dorothea went about like mother and daughter. They probably suggested something of a model to Mrs Thrale in her much shorter-lived attempt to bring Fanny Burney alongside. Meanwhile, Montagu had also made her nephew, Matthew, her heir. Like the head of a dynasty, she wanted to ensure the future by arranging a marriage. It wasn't her ambition to make her empire larger: in fixing on Dorothea as a wife for Matthew, she chose a portionless girl and offered to give her everything. Dorothea, however, wanted to follow her heart back to Scotland where a poor but honest and good man wanted her and where she would live an ordinary, hard-working, satisfying life. A painful break-up ensued.

Few commentators nowadays would do other than applaud Dorothea Gregory for the strength of will and firmness of purpose with which she extricated herself. Similarly, most of us would deplore Montagu's dismissal of the peasant poet, James Woodhouse, who had served as her steward for twenty years, and was left without pension or provision. Being a poet, he fought back with a portrait of her in his autobiographical poem, *The Life and Lucubrations of Crispinus Scriblerus*, where he accused her of simply wanting a bit of 'clownish wonder' about the place and patronising him to impress her friends and have a ready source of flattery on tap:

'Twas Vanity – the vainest of the Vain!
Alas! 'twas Cunning, weaving specious wiles,
With smooth expressions, and well-polish'd smiles –
False proofs of fondness and a forg'd pretence;
While hollow promise pledg'd rewards immense.

Foregoing 'rewards immense' was of course a bitter blow to the dreaming poet. The anger is understandable, but it is also formulaic. By the early 1780s, when Montagu fell out with Woodhouse, when Hannah More got into difficulties with Ann Yearsley, when Mrs Thrale was pained by Fanny Burney, and when Dorothea Gregory jumped ship, the very idea of patronage carried unacceptable meanings of servility on the one hand and tyranny on the other. The language of obligation was being challenged by a language of rights. In 1776 Giuseppe Baretti, invited to tour his native Italy as a guide to the Thrales and at their expense, had to explain to his Piedmontese brothers that there was no loss of independence involved. Did they think, he asked them, he was going

not as a companion, but as a hired servant? How could you possibly imagine that I should be so foolish as to allow myself to appear in my own country, or any other place, in a position unsuitable for one who has gained some reputation in the world as a man of letters? How is it degrading for a man of letters to permit himself to be chosen as a travelling companion by a man of wealth? Has not this been the custom in the world since the days of Maecenas, who took Horace with him on his travels? Johnson, who is looked upon as the most learned man in England and has a pension of £300 a year from his king, so far from being ashamed, regards it as an honour to accompany Mr Thrale in the very same way ... literature makes a man of letters the equal of a rich man, and gives him rank as his companion, not as his servant.[33]

It was necessary for Baretti to believe that literature made a man of letters the equal of a rich man, but Baretti's efforts to secure his existence through patronage were not ultimately successful and he ended his days in poverty. Women of letters and wealth had few examples to draw on in negotiating the protocols of the relationship and we should, perhaps, acknowledge their efforts and some of their successes. The 'female Maecenas of Hill Street', understood that money – including money bestowed on others – was 'convertible to credit and pleasure'. Handing it over could be tricky: Montagu trod very carefully when giving Carter money to buy clothes for Tunbridge. On the other hand, she was indignant when Lord Bath failed to leave their mutual friend any money on his death in 1764: it would have done him honour, she argued, to have willed Carter an annuity 'as she is so distinguished by her virtues and talents'. (Lord Bath's testamentary failings were general: he left everything to a brother he disliked, willing a derisory amount to his faithful valet. Elizabeth Montagu was deeply disappointed that a man she had loved could be so irresponsible in the posthumous distribution of the wealth in his care.) Later, Carter did receive a small annuity from Lord Bath's estate. When Edward Montagu died and Elizabeth Montagu had complete freedom to use her wealth as she chose, she also gave Carter a modest annuity which was accepted without fuss as an appropriate gift. (She gave a similar annuity to Anna Williams.) Carter readily accepted the preferment Montagu had it in her power to extend to the male members of her family – brothers and nephews – and when Montagu offered money to help out in emergency, as when a nephew's barns burned down, again Carter accepted. As far as the press were concerned Carter was under Montagu's patronage. In April 1781, Fanny Burney copied into her diary the following newspaper paragraph:

> Miss Burney, the sprightly writer of the elegant novel *Evelina*, is now domesticated with Mrs Thrale in the same manner that Miss More is with Mrs Garrick, and Mrs Carter with Mrs Montagu.[34]

In urging Fanny Burney to 'fly at the eagle' and test her wit against Elizabeth Montagu, Johnson had recalled his own early days as a writer when he was 'beginning the world, and was nothing and nobody'. By the time Hannah More and Fanny Burney came into his life he was very much somebody.

No longer the one to 'fire at all the established wits', he was himself the supreme established wit. His pleasure in the company of these young women had something to do with their youthfulness and charm, their willingness to be told and teased, petted and fondled, but it was also a measure of their brilliance. Adoring young females were not in short supply in Johnson's daily life. Eighteen of them turned up one day, 'all ready to prostrate themselves on the carpet'. They were not well received and the one who 'had an oration ready, he saved the trouble of recital, by crying out "Fiddle-de-dee, my dear!"' [35]

In Hannah More and Fanny Burney Johnson recognised a desire that went beyond prostration and prepared orations. Their interest in him, like Boswell's, contained sufficient quantities of self-interest. As women, they negotiated literary life according to different rules, but the common ground between them and Johnson was substantial: the desire to make one's mark, be noticed, talked about, in short to 'vanquish the great ones', was not confined to men. Fanny Burney might disclaim any attempt to flatter so great a man as Johnson – 'nothing I could say would flatter him' – but her homage was flattery, especially as Johnson saw through the shy exterior to the satirical observer within, telling her: 'your shyness, and slyness, and pretending to know nothing, never took me in, whatever you may do with others. I always knew you for a toadling'. [36]

By calling her a 'toadling' Johnson insisted on a truth that was there, staring everybody in the face. Fanny Burney, like Hannah More, lived and dreamt to fulfil her ambitions as a writer. In her younger days, when she first became the favourite of Johnson, she was ruthless in pursuit of this goal. She might have been 'a poor mere worm in literature' but she was a worm who had the 'approbation' of the king: 'Dr Johnson's approbation! – it almost crazed me with agreeable surprise – it gave me such a flight of spirits, that I danced a jig to Mr Crisp, without any preparation, music, or explanation ...' [37] Her spirits were excitable; and, as Mrs Thrale discovered and Johnson intimated, she also had 'a spirit' every bit as lofty as the greatest of the great ones.

Evelina was published anonymously. Fanny Burney was able to keep secret her authorship of this novel for some months, feeling that there was 'something very formidable in the idea of appearing as an authoress!' Indeed there was: some formidable women had come forward as authoresses since the middle years of the eighteenth century. Female authorship had come to be associated with heavy-weight learning, with scholarship of various kinds. It was not patriarchal disapproval which intimidated Fanny Burney: the many older men about her did nothing but applaud her literary ambitions, and she sought to please them with what she produced. Coming to maturity in the late 1770s, she was pitched into a fully formed world of female authorship dominated by intellectual women. Fanny Burney, the 'dunce' of her family whose education had been neglected, was a gifted novelist – she knew the human heart, as Mrs Thrale put it; she had an 'insight into the deepest recesses of the mind' – but she was not an intellectual.

Fanny Burney would not 'fly at the eagle'. Johnson urged on her a model of generational combat derived from his own very different experiences: 'to vanquish the great ones was all the delight of my poor little dear soul'. In the struggle for existence, those who occupied the highest perches had to be brought down: 'Down with her – spare her not – attack her!' Thus the life cycle was perpetuated; the individual was toppled but the institution survived. Fanny's reluctance to 'fly at the eagle' – her avoidance of overt competition combined with her misogyny – symbolised a willingness to undermine the status of all female authors. Some flying at the eagle was desirable, so Johnson understood, if the institutional structure was to strengthen and grow. To be an authoress 'nobody would suspect' of writing was to do no service to the formidable array of authoresses who were already in print.

For Fanny Burney and others situated as she was, 'service' was precisely the problem. Born to serve, wriggling in the obscure earth, how was the worm to vanquish? The answer Burney pursued in *Cecilia* was to make a heroism out of submission and forfeiture. The really powerful character in *Cecilia* is Mrs Delvile, a forceful and intelligent woman, whose conversation mixes 'instruction with entertainment, and general satire with particular kindness, in a manner at once so lively and so flattering', that we can imagine it was not entirely unlike the conversation of the forceful and intelligent Mrs Thrale. The men are caricatures compared to Mrs Delvile. The conflict in the novel is between the younger woman and the older woman; and, because of the conditions of Cecilia's inheritance, it is a conflict over name and family. It is about social institutions: about who brings what credit to the perpetuation of those institutions.

The first generation bluestockings understood that the institutions of female authorship needed to be nurtured and protected, hence Mrs Montagu's distribution of annuities and tendency to congratulate any woman writer who achieved anything as one who brought honour to her sex (rather like a queen bestowing medals on her subjects). But it was not at all clear what sort of institutions they imagined might be put in place beyond personal patronage.

For Johnson the issue was not gender specific: his delight in vanquishing the great ones, his violence in argument and speaking for victory – the 'downing' of others which so upset Fanny Burney and disturbed the peace of genteel gatherings – was motivated by identification with the low, with those who, through no fault of their own, had been denied advantage; as well as by the many and varied forms of rage and sadism, unhappiness and guilt he was subject to. It was also a manifestation of an older literary style, the aggressive, vituperative style of literary exchange which prevailed in the 1730s when Johnson was forming himself as a writer, when images of demolition, siege and combat were commonplace. And when there was a reiterated insistence on the need to maintain – meaning, in fact, to establish – the purity of 'real' writers against the onslaughts of the unaccredited, those armies of dung, or as Mrs Montagu put it, the 'dunghill born'.

A powerful arguer, Johnson relished mental combat. The life of a wit was a warfare upon earth, and he was ready to fight and urge others, male and female, into battle. Telling Fanny Burney to fly at Mrs Montagu was, as he knew, a joke. It amused him; he 'began to see-saw, with a countenance strongly expressive of inward fun'. Perhaps some of this private amusement had to do with contrasts that presented themselves to his mind regarding changing models of female authorship. Fanny Burney, hidden and forceful, represented the new: she was a wicked rogue who saw through the surfaces of things to the nasty underside, but she showed a meek and dutiful face to the world. She did not display aggression nor anger; she did not 'vent' resentment. She would be quiet and uncomplaining; low social origins and a desperate desire to belong made quiet uncomplaint her ticket of admission. (In *Cecilia*, Lady Honoria's high rank entitles her to rattle on and say all the dreadful things Cecilia can't possibly say but which Fanny Burney finds thinkable and pleasurable.) Open combat with one placed so much higher than herself as Mrs Montagu was out of the question; silence and reserve, shyness and slyness were her weapons.

Johnson's literary memory stretched back a long way; he may well have recalled that twenty-five years earlier he had used the image of aggressive flight when encouraging Charlotte Lennox. Full of the pride of genius, Lennox was ever ready to do combat. The level of her aggression was one reason why she was unwelcome in high bluestocking circles. In 1753 Johnson wrote to congratulate her on *Shakespear Illustrated*. In praising this work, he declared she had proved herself fit to 'fly' at Milton. *Shakespear Illustrated* was very close to Johnson's heart. He had involved himself with it from inception to completion. Samuel Richardson considered the book an attack, 'Methinks I love my Shakespeare, since this attack, better than before'. For Johnson, the attack was a satisfying demolition job. Charlotte Lennox had stamped her authority all over her subject in a way which inspired him to congratulation: 'When Shakespeare is demolished,' he wrote, 'your wings will be *full summed* and I will fly you at Milton; for you are a bird of prey, but the bird of Jupiter.' Jupiter, the sovereign divinity of the Romans, had supreme power over gods and men. Particularly associated with tempests, his weapon was the thunderbolt.[38]

Johnson derived pleasure from the idea of Lennox, like a bird of prey, demolishing the greatest names in the English literary canon. He even took some of the credit: 'I will fly you at Milton.' Her full development – 'your wings will be full summed' – required large targets. Her bad temper, indicative of the force within, was a vital ingredient. Fanny Burney, the 'toadling', hid her violence; but Johnson, who knew it in himself, found it out in her. As his relationship with Anna Williams showed, he tolerated and even enjoyed personalities whom others found difficult or unrewarding. He kept what Mrs Thrale unpleasantly described as a 'tribe' in his house, a mixed community who squabbled incessantly and whom he supported in what might be regarded as a parodic version of the patronage of the wealthy. There was Frank Barber, the ex-slave who came into his care at the age of about nine and who was educated at his expense. Barber complained about Miss Williams's authority over him; Miss Williams resented the money Johnson spent on Barber's schooling. There was Mrs Desmoulins who quarrelled with Miss Williams. (Johnson explained, 'as they can both be occasionally of service to each other, and as neither of them have any other place to go to, their animosity does not force them to separate'.) To Mrs Thrale he admitted, 'Williams hates everybody. Levet hates Desmoulins and does not love Williams. Poll loves none of them.' Nobody seems to know who Poll Carmichael was.[39]

Fanny Burney, growing up in a household at war with an unloved stepmother, where she and her siblings had a special room where they talked 'treason' to cheer themselves, knew all about spite and hate. She dedicated herself to erasing the evidence of that knowledge in her manners and, later, in her reputation. The most important thing of all was to pass as well-bred. Part of Johnson's fascination for her (as for so many others) was his apparent ability to disregard these imperatives; although, when Mrs Thrale began to rebel, it was Johnson's ill-bred behaviour, the lack of polite manners, that she instanced: he now ate his beef and pudding 'too dirtily' for her. Charlotte Lennox vented her rage, animosities, and resentments with an ill-bred freedom that associated her with the lowly tribe of Johnson's household dependents rather than with the elegant circles at Streatham Park, letting rage and spite show, instead of carefully mastering the calibrated codes for disguising them. Her husband, the apparently worthless Alexander, was 'unkind'; it is likely that he drank and probable that he was violent.

Charlotte Lennox herself was certainly violent; so much so that she ended up in the magistrates court in 1778, the year of *Evelina*, accused with her daughter and one other woman of assaulting her maid. According to the court record, Charlotte Lennox of Kensington, spinster, together with Henrietta Holles Lennox and Hannah Davis, were charged with riotously assembling to disturb the peace in the house of Nicholas Hancock where they assaulted Ann Brown, who was beaten and wounded. The charge was dropped with the prosecutor's consent, so the wounding cannot have been serious. But for Laetitia Matilda Hawkins, recalling the episode some forty years later, such behaviour aptly displayed Lennox's 'low' leanings. There was a 'want of all order and method' in her housekeeping; she lacked any 'decorum of appearance, and regularity of proceeding'. These failings were to be expected of 'a woman whom I saw in a court of justice fairly pitted against a low female servant, who had endeavoured to obtain a compensation for ill words and hard blows received from her mistress'.[40]

Sir John Hawkins, Johnson's 'official' biographer, a long-standing friend whom the publishers approached after his death to write the life that was to preface Johnson's collected works, was the original 'unclubbable' man, a member of the Ivy Lane Club in 1749, but so tight-fisted that he would not pay his share of the bill for supper because, he insisted, he didn't usually eat supper. Widely disliked for his sanctimoniousness, rigidity and fault-finding, he nevertheless inspired sufficient esteem in Johnson to be made one of the executors of his will. This gave him access to all Johnson's papers. His claim to fame as a writer and scholar rested on his *General History of the Science and Practice of Music*, which came out in five volumes in 1776 after some sixteen years of research.

In producing this massive work, soon to be overshadowed by Charles Burney's *History of Music* in four volumes beginning in 1776, Sir John Hawkins depended heavily on the services of his daughter, Laetitia, just as Charles Burney looked to the services of his daughter, Fanny. The girls functioned as amanuenses, secretaries and scribes. They copied, wrote letters, read, sorted manuscripts, listened to innumerable discussions and gave their opinions when asked. Both were also secretly writing novels. Laetitia Hawkins claimed to have written and published many volumes – all incognito – and if this is true, then her 'exertions of industry' are truly impressive since she was 'writing six hours in the day for my father, and reading aloud to my mother nearly as long'. Unlike Fanny Burney and the numerous other women who sought the 'honour' of acquaintanceship with Johnson, Laetitia Hawkins disliked him and would not by any means prostrate herself – as she put it – on his 'sooty carpet'. She took a pride in not being impressed. Others, especially women, might consider it an honour to be 'noticed' by Johnson, but as far as she was concerned, where this honour was to be found, I confess I never could discover. For myself, I can truly say, that it was a severe punishment to me to share in any of my father's visits to him, and that I never heard him say, in any visit, six words that could compensate for the trouble of getting to his den, and the disgust of seeing such squalidness as I saw no where else.[41]

There could be no 'honour' in squalor, it was 'low'; so also was Johnson's 'brutal wit', his 'concentrated explosions of contradiction', his 'rude asperity'. As Miss Hawkins candidly explained, no 'advantage' she could have gained would have induced her to risk any closer encounter: 'I was content to view him, as I would a wild beast, at a due distance, and always with a retreat in my power.' Nevertheless, the idea of advantage gnawed at her and perhaps accounts for some of the disagreeable tone in her three volumes of memoirs. Clearly, some people who were no better than she was and who were certainly less well placed than she – the daughter of one of Johnson's friends, a child who had mingled with Goldsmith and Reynolds and Garrick – *did* derive advantage from the connection. Of these, Charlotte Lennox, Johnson's 'favourite', the woman to whom he (astonishingly, in Laetitia Hawkins's opinion) 'decreed the palm of excellence in female authorship', seems to have rankled most.

Miss Hawkins made clear her distaste for what she considered Charlotte Lennox's ill-bred behaviour, but she didn't invent the episode of the assault. Charlotte Lennox did beat her servant and her servant took her to the magistrate – an interesting insight, we might note, into mistress-servant relationships towards the end of the eighteenth century. Laetitia Hawkins went to observe the trial at Hicks Hall, her father being one of the magistrates: 'it gave me an opportunity of seeing the illustrious lady, and at a safe distance'. Evidently, Charlotte Lennox was not one of the circle of friends who had come visiting at the house along with Goldsmith, Reynolds and Garrick, but her temper had been well known to the Hawkins children by repute. Laetitia Hawkins recalled how her father liked to tell the story of an enraged Charlotte Lennox,

> going in similar wrath to Mr John Payne, Johnson's and her publisher, to complain of some want of respect to her amorous story of *Harriot Stuart*. Payne was from home, and the person from whom she learnt this fact, being his aged mother, Charlotte, in that same genuine spirit which afterwards ripened into ... 'maid-fighting,' assailed the old lady with the eloquence which was intended for the son. The old crone, unused to the language of a lady who wrote books ... cried out for quarter in the moving plea that she 'knew nothing, and was a plain old woman.' Charlotte ... indignantly turned away, repeating 'Plain enough! God knows!'[42]

Most people who had dealings with Charlotte Lennox encountered this rough, aggressive element. Whether she tried to control it and failed, or whether she did not try, is hard to judge on the flimsy scraps of evidence available. And, in a sense, any answer we might come to is of less interest than the question itself. The importance of self-control – controlling emotion, behaviour, self-presentation – was fundamental to the thinking of most women writers.

Laetitia Hawkins's account of Charlotte Lennox's court appearance concludes with a series of snappish remarks, at once self-righteous and self-defensive, which refer us to Boswell's *Life of Dr Johnson* and the account there of Johnson's enthusiasm for the women he had dined with at Mrs Garrick's:

> Yet this lady was the lady 'Johnson would pit' against any whom he had subsequently known. Thanks to my perfect command over my tongue, when punished for my delinquencies by being taken to his house, *I* could have nothing to do in the question. He was indeed well acquainted with my *writing*, for my father generally made me transcribe or write from dictation, the letters at that same time sent to him.

The sense of personal affront is inescapable but the phrasing is oblique. To understand the point being made, we need to remember that Laetitia Hawkins was herself, 'a lady who wrote books'. The words are used sneeringly of Charlotte Lennox ('the language of a lady who wrote books') to suggest lack of control. Laetitia Hawkins, by contrast, congratulated herself: 'Thanks to my perfect command over my tongue ... *I* could have nothing to do in the question.' What question? And why *should* she have anything 'to do' in it? The question, apparently, is about the relative merits of the women writers Johnson had known. Thanks to her perfect command over her tongue, Laetitia Hawkins was not among the acknowledged women writers Johnson had known over whom he considered Charlotte Lennox to reign supreme, so she was not insulted by being placed below a woman she considered 'low'.

Two kinds of silence are trumpeted. There is the silence of her resentful demeanour whenever she endured the punishment of being at Johnson's house; and the secrecy or silence she maintained about her novel-writing exploits. And two kinds of self-control are applauded: the control of her disgust at her surroundings, and the control of her desire for recognition and advancement. However, the beauty of the passage (and indeed of much in these three volumes of *Memoirs*) is that both silence and self-control are here exploded. The rage of an under-noticed, over-worked daughter breaks through in the bitter play on words of the final sentence: Johnson did not know she was 'a writer' who had secretly published a novel whilst still in her teens, but he was 'well acquainted with my *writing*' since she had to slave away as her father's assistant, and Johnson had received many a letter in her hand.

Whatever grief his failures of self control caused Johnson, for others they were to become a part of his genius and the stuff of anecdote, as Anna Seward observed when drawing the comparison between Ann Yearsley and Johnson; a measure of his 'difference' from ordinary mortals whose bodies did not twitch and who could drink tea without slurping.

Much less is generally known about how women thought about their working lives as writers than is known about men. If the unspoken codes were often difficult for men, they were more so for women. Even women who had accumulated a great deal of practical knowledge from a wide range of writing and publishing ventures – Elizabeth Carter, for example, Fanny Burney and Hannah More – projected innocence rather than experience. Taken at face value as they so often have been, these self-projections are intensely misleading. When Fanny Burney concocted, with her brother Charles, the scheme that he should dress up in disguise in order to deliver her manuscript of *Evelina*, they were enacting a literal dramatisation of dynamics they understood very well: female modesty, secret writing, collusion, revelation, celebration. It was game-playing by a family of literary sophisticates.

The Burneys, under the guidance of Dr Charles Burney who was an adept at self-advancement, worked these matters better than the Hawkins family, under Sir John Hawkins. Laetitia Hawkins was furious at the unfairness of things: she lived a writer's life yet received none of the gratification of recognition. It was not until she wrote her memoirs in the 1820s, *Anecdotes, Biographical Sketches and Memoirs* (1822) and *Memoirs, Anecdotes, Facts and Opinions* (1824) that she avowed these feelings in print. By then she claimed to have published many novels. She also had a fully developed 'story' about her early ambitions, and a self-deprecatory tone full of denied feeling to relate it in. Both story and tone match so well – that is, they create so convincing a fiction – that it is difficult to reconstruct the emotional realities hidden in the telling and difficult to know where to begin asking how much, if any of it, is 'true'.

The story Laetitia Hawkins tells about her young self is shadowed by what was already a literary cliché: a young girl writes a novel in secret which is subsequently published to great acclaim. The prototype is *Evelina*, the first novel of Fanny Burney, that young girl whose early life resembled Laetitia Hawkins's, except in the matter of celebrity and fame. To read Hawkins's account through our knowledge of *Evelina* itself, and knowing what *Evelina* was able to do for Fanny Burney, is to hear the disappointment which is so resolutely denied utterance – along with all the ordinary 'facts and opinions' Miss Hawkins might have shared with posterity about her professional experiences.

Laetitia Hawkins spoke of her writing in a long footnote, apologetically (and significantly) intruded into her narrative about the visit by booksellers Strahan and Cadell to her father to ask him to write the life of Samuel Johnson. She called this autobiographical moment 'a trifling anecdote':

> Some few years previous to this time, being in want of a sum of money for a whim of girlish patronage, and having no *honest* means of raising it, I wrote a downright novel. It could do nobody any harm – indeed *I* thought it a marvellous moral performance, as it punished the culprits and rewarded the virtuous of my *dramatis personae* – but it was a temerarious undertaking, as descriptive of manners and situations of which I knew little but by hearsay. It was done in the secrecy of a coiner, my only confidential friend being my younger brother ... The manuscript was published for me by Hookham, who ... was content to remain in ignorance, and who most honorably sent me for it, twice as much as I needed, and most kindly encouraged me to proceed. I had had the good fortune to please the then taste of the readers of such works ... and though I wrote many subsequent volumes, I still preserved my incognito. I scarcely know why I acted thus clandestinely. I was certainly afraid of some displeasure, and I was ashamed of my employment; and though my father sometimes urged me to write, and wished to have introduced me into a literary correspondence, I preferred my obscurity ...[43]

Preferring obscurity is analogous to having a perfect command over one's tongue; it is the woman writer as proper lady. But built into the account is an awareness of the oddity of this logic, a hint of uncertainty about its purpose and effects. Behind the bravado of propriety is puzzlement. And well there might be, for what Laetitia Hawkins recalls – this 'temerarious undertaking' – is, indeed, a strange state of affairs: girls who want to write 'downright' novels, publishers who want to pay good money and publish them, readers who want to read them, brothers who collude and fathers who encourage.

The story follows the example of Fanny Burney so closely that some might prefer to regard it as a compensatory fantasy. Real or imagined, it is drawn according to an archetype in which secrecy and obscurity were essential ingredients in the myth about women writers, components in the story of celebrity. Unspoken questions hover in the background. How different would things have been had she had the success of Fanny Burney – so blessed with colluding siblings and an encouraging father? (Her own brother Henry's 'Poetic Trifles' can be found at the end of *Anecdotes*.) What would her life have been like had not Sir John Hawkins but Samuel Johnson been her own father? Surprisingly perhaps, this latter question actually *is* addressed, in a brooding passage of daughterly disloyalty in which Miss Hawkins claims to harbour 'no ambitious regret that I cannot boast myself the daughter of Johnson'. Johnson as a fantasy father is the father of literature; being the daughter of Johnson would be to take on the writing self without puzzlement.

Imagining herself as Johnson's daughter is a means for Hawkins to claim self-assertiveness, a quality which she identifies as necessary and recognises was wrongly beaten out of her as a child. She was, she tells us, brought up 'under "the depressing system", a system I cannot recommend, however *wholesome* it may ultimately prove. It is not *very* pleasant to fancy one's self, for perhaps nearly half one's life, utterly good for nothing.' Disapprovingly recalling this upbringing, she describes how Johnson was twice asked by a mutual woman friend, Mrs Saunders Welch, to intervene with Sir John Hawkins on the matter since it was considered to be doing her harm. Johnson would not personally interfere; but, on the second occasion, agreeing with Mrs Welch's concern, he allowed his opinion to be used in support. Thus he served the child as a higher authority than her father, but he didn't save her. The woman writing the memoirs is angry at both men.[44]

Laetitia Hawkins claimed to prefer her obscurity, and felt ashamed of her novel-writing, when so many others were celebrated and feted for the same activity. Indeed we are told, 'my father sometimes urged me to write, and wished to have introduced me into a literary correspondence'. Evidently whatever 'shame' there might be in writing, or being known as a woman with literary interests, was not shared by her father. Beginning a 'literary correspondence' was a way of going public. It was particularly useful for women, whose ways of displaying and developing their literary talents were more limited than men's. Sir John Hawkins wishing to introduce his daughter into a literary correspondence was playing his part as a dutiful father, using his connections to help set her up in the world. He knew many writers. He was well aware that many women, particularly the daughters and sisters of literary or scholarly men, had distinguished themselves by means of their writing.

Boasting that 'two thousand pages never daunted me' – meaning, presumably, that her novels ran to two thousand manuscript pages – Hawkins continued to write in secret. She implies that her secrecy meant she forfeited privileges she might otherwise have obtained, since a daughter with more significance would not have been in the difficult position of having 'no time but what I could *purloin*'. She insistently presents a picture of herself as engaged in heroic self-improving work. In addition to the novels written in purloined intervals of the working day, we are told:

I learnt Italian, and extracted from every book that came in my way; I made as
large a part of my clothes as could be made at home; I worked muslin; I learnt
botany; and I was my mother's storekeeper. Air and exercise were little thought
on.[45]

And yet she did not pursue the opportunity of self-advancement through
literary connections. The interesting possibility suggests itself that Hawkins
refused to make more of herself out of spite for her father. The hateful
'depressing system' under which she had been raised told her she was 'utterly
good for nothing' but the literary culture into which she grew as a young
woman conveyed a different message.

An established writer who agreed to correspond with an unknown conferred honour thereby, as well as providing opportunities for contact with
a wider and more influential social sphere. When Elizabeth Carter agreed
in 1749 to a literary correspondence with Hester Mulso, she rendered the
ambitious younger woman delirious with gratitude. Hester Mulso hurried
to reply:

> I cannot too soon take advantage of the kind permission dear Miss Carter has
> given me, to begin a correspondence which will afford me so much pleasure;
> and I will do it without fear, since I have as much reason to confide in her
> good-nature, as to revere her judgement. I shall still find in her that amiable
> condescension, and unreserved benevolence, which endears her conversation, and
> enhances the value of her understanding; which teaches her how to improve her
> companions without appearing to instruct them, to correct without seeming to
> reprove, and even to reprove without offending.[46]

And on and on. The flattery is never far away ('where shall we meet with
the enlivened good sense, the happy mixture of vivacity and solidity of
genius and judgement which so remarkably shines in all that Miss Carter
writes!') and should remind us of how significant such a correspondence
could be in a woman's career. In the eighteenth century, the writing life
was understood as a life transacted quite as properly in drawing-rooms and
assemblies as in the study. What went on in the privacy of the study –
reading, thinking, writing – fed into the conversation in the drawing-rooms.
Correspondence was an important link between the two. It signified more
than a spontaneous desire to 'keep in touch' with a like-minded friend or
family member. It meant more than networks of support. It defined positions
in a hierarchy – the favour of the great raised the status of the lesser – and
it afforded publicity. When Carter wrote to Montagu from the remoteness
of her house in Deal, she was employing as effective a means of keeping
herself in the public eye as an article in a leading literary journal would be
today. The letter would carry her judgement of books and events. Her views

would be circulated by proxy and carry great weight. Simply being known to be an intimate of Mrs Montagu's, to have her ear as Mrs Carter did, worked towards the same end: it was a message about the right to disseminate opinion. It was about being high not low.

Sustaining a correspondence of this sort in which the careful presentation of self is monitored and controlled over decades called for particular personal qualities. Laetitia Hawkins chose not to attempt it, and everything we know about Charlotte Lennox suggests she would have been unequal to the challenge had she tried. Lennox's methods of promoting herself, the choices she made about writing projects and, consequently, the nature of her daily working life, drew more on Johnson's example and advice than on practices such as 'a literary correspondence' which in the 1740s were definitive of a certain kind of woman writer. Carrying on a literary correspondence was an activity which existed somewhere between self-nurturing and self-promotion; it served and satisfied personal needs but also participated in the myth-making that was essential to celebrity and therefore status.

Johnson's special praise of Charlotte Lennox caused some stir when it reached public attention with the publication of Boswell's *Life of Samuel Johnson* in 1791. Fanny Burney described one acquaintance, 'eager to inquire of me who was Mrs Lennox? He had been reading, like all the rest of the world, Boswell's Life of Dr Johnson, and the preference there expressed of Mrs Lennox to all other females had filled him with astonishment, as he had never even heard her name.' Given that Fanny Burney was herself one of the 'females' demoted by this 'preference' it is not surprising to find that she was inclined to be dismissive. She commented:

> These occasional sallies of Dr Johnson, uttered from local causes and circumstances, but all retailed verbatim by Mr Boswell, are filling all sorts of readers with amaze, except the small part to whom Dr Johnson was known, and who, by acquaintance with the power of the moment over his unguarded conversation, know how little of his solid opinion was to be gathered from his accidental assertions.[47]

Aggressively polite, the passage camouflages retaliation. The effect of Burney's remarks is to diminish Charlotte Lennox by making her appear even more obscure than she was: Johnson's judgement about her was to be considered merely one of his 'sallies', not a 'solid opinion' to be taken seriously. Also diminished are Boswell and Johnson: Boswell because he could not discriminate between the serious and the frivolous, but 'retailed verbatim' what he heard; and Johnson because he was too easily swayed by 'the power of the moment'. The person elevated is Fanny Burney, one

of 'the small part to whom Dr Johnson was known', who had the acumen
to judge wisely what she heard.

In fact, one writer at least had gone into print in the years between the
dinner at Mrs Garrick's and Boswell's *Life of Samuel Johnson* with the
matter-of-fact view that the author of *The Female Quixote* was 'well known
as one of the distinguished female writers this age has produced'. Clara
Reeve, in *The Progress of Romance* (1785) took up the real issue of *The
Female Quixote*: the issue of the authority of different literary genres. She
developed Lennox's distinction between romance as a 'low' genre because
associated with women; and history and epic, because associated with men,
as 'high'. In *The Progress of Romance*, a history of prose fiction written as
a series of dialogues between two women and a man who meet to exchange
opinion and test out critical judgements on different books, it is the man
who has most to learn because he has not begun to question these assumptions. The conversations Reeve devises evoke the conversation circles
established by the earlier generation, where 'a fellow' (of either sex) gained
credit by recollecting striking passages from different books and bringing
a stock of knowledge artfully into play. *The Progress of Romance* dramatized
the bluestocking ideal.[48]

By the time Boswell was gathering materials for the *Life of Samuel Johnson*,
this ideal was already under threat. Fanny Burney was reluctant to co-operate
with him. She would not give him her letters. She had, on the whole, a
low opinion of the man she described as 'that biographical, anecdotical
memorandummer'. Boswell accosted her outside St George's chapel at
Windsor, wanting her to read over some of what he had already written
and also to give him original materials. She recorded his words as direct
speech in her diary as follows:

> 'Yes, madam; you must give me some of your choice little notes of the Doctor's;
> we have seen him long enough upon stilts; I want to show him in a new light.
> Grave Sam and great Sam, and solemn Sam, and learned Sam – all these he has
> appeared over and over. Now I want to entwine a wreath of the graces over his
> brow; I want to show him as gay Sam; agreeable Sam, pleasant Sam; so you must
> help me with some of his beautiful billets to yourself.'[49]

The condescending tone is beautifully captured, as is Boswell's assumption
that he can wheedle and bluster and charm what he wants out of her in
this charmless fashion. Her loathing for him is palpable, but she commented
only that she would not hand over her letters, those 'revered testimonies'
of the 'high honour' Johnson's kind friendship had conferred on her. In
her opinion, Boswell had made far too much public. He had revealed 'every
weakness and infirmity of the first and greatest good man of these times'.

Fanny Burney disapproved thoroughly. Frankness of this sort she considered no virtue; she was to go through her own and her family papers remorselessly, censoring, cutting and blotting with thick black ink. On one occasion when Boswell made a point of sitting next to her; she wrote: 'though his address to me was courteous in the extreme ... I felt an indignant disposition to a nearly forbidding reserve and silence. How many starts of passion and prejudice has he blackened into record, that else might have sunk, for ever forgotten, under the preponderance of weightier virtues and excellencies!'[50]

For Boswell, 'gay Sam', 'agreeable Sam' and 'pleasant Sam' with a wreath of the 'graces' around his brow was Sam amongst the women. In his eyes Fanny Burney's notes, because penned by a feminine hand, were 'little'; they were 'beautiful billets'. Sam 'in a new light' was Sam brought down to the level of the company of women. Boswell's offensive tone flattened as it sentimentalised. The women, it implied, were all the same, a twittering band twining wreaths around the ancient and honoured bard's head. Only amongst men was Sam 'grave' 'great' 'solemn' and 'learned'. For Boswell, coming into Johnson's life relatively late on and bringing his own urgent needs and preconceptions with him, this was perhaps a necessary fiction. But it is a long way from the bluestocking vision and it is a long way from what Johnson had known and lived.

Women and Writing

Polite eighteenth-century society elevated Samuel Johnson, an awkward bookseller's son from the provinces, on the grounds of merit. In the competitive world of mid eighteenth-century London, hopeful geniuses marked their progress not only by money made (sometimes especially *not* by money made) but by the notice they managed to attract. With whom you mixed, to whose gatherings you were invited, whose influence and connections you could draw on were all matters of the most pressing concern. Johnson attached due significance to being seen at the right houses and being visited by the right folk. Mrs Thrale noted that, for all his rough willingness to give and take offence, he was also careful whom he offended. He never left any company 'with impressions to his disadvantage – he valued the world's good word exceedingly – and said so – while he appeared to set it at defiance'.

Johnson made it his business to understand the rules of the elaborate overlapping systems of social rank and literary merit. Deeply conservative, his love for the system of literature, composed as it was of so many distinct parts, amounted to veneration. He respected the jobbing printer at one end of the spectrum as much as the aristocratic patron at the other, so far as each played the part as required of him. He enjoyed the company of Mr Allen, the printer, who was one of his closest friends. He famously reproached Lord Chesterfield for offering patronage when it was longer needed – for failing, in other words, to play his part in the appropriate way and keep the system secure. The *Plan* of the *Dictionary* had been addressed to Chesterfield, but Johnson had received no benefits from him during the course of the work. Shortly before publication, however, Chesterfield, to oblige the publisher, Dodsley, agreed to recommend the work – thus unwittingly giving the public the impression that he had been its patron all along. Pride and anger led Johnson to write his reprimand:

> Seven years, my Lord, have now past since I waited in your outward rooms, or was repulsed from your door; during which time I have been pushing on my work through difficulties of which it is useless to complain, and have brought it, at last, to the verge of publication, without one act of assistance, one word of encouragement, or one smile of favour. Such treatment I did not expect, for I never had a Patron before ...

The letter continued in tones of heavy sarcasm:

> Is not a Patron, my Lord, one who looks with unconcern on a man struggling for life in the water, and, when he has reached ground, encumbers him with help? The notice which you have been pleased to take of my labours, had it been early, had been kind; but it has been delayed till I am indifferent, and cannot enjoy it; till I am solitary and cannot impart it; till I am known, and do not want it. I hope it is no very cynical asperity not to confess obligations where no benefit has been received, or to be unwilling that the Public should consider me as owing that to a Patron, which Providence has enabled me to do for myself.[1]

In Johnson's eyes, Lord Chesterfield did not simply let him down personally; he offended the dignity of the profession of literature and threatened to weaken it. Chesterfield accepted the reproach and recognised the literary quality of the letter: he left it lying on his table so that all his visitors could see it. Thus the letter acquired celebrity long before it was printed in Boswell's *Life of Dr Johnson*. This, too, was an aspect of the workings of the literary system which those who were well versed in it understood.

Johnson's letter is possibly the best known of all his writings. His dictionary definition of a patron is also celebrated: 'Commonly a wretch who supports with insolence, and is paid with flattery'. To Boswell he remarked, 'We have done with patronage'. It is tempting to represent him as the embodiment of Grub Street, a man who scorned preferment and privilege and instead lived independently by literature. But he would have been the first to point out that his 'independence' was underwritten by a crown pension. Johnson lived through a major cultural transition in a century which saw a commercial nation emerging into immense power and confidence. The expansion of print and the rise of the reading public contributed to the weakening of an old social order based on rank and privilege of which patronage (not literary patronage alone) had been an essential part. Johnson did not live to see the French Revolution in 1789, nor to read or hear of Tom Paine's *The Rights of Man* in 1791 (the same year that Boswell's *Life of Johnson* appeared), nor Mary Wollstonecraft's *A Vindication of the Rights of Woman* in 1792. It is safe to say he would not have liked any of them. His reverence for rank and respect for wealth became stronger rather than weaker as he grew older; whilst he himself became more, rather than less, implicated in the system of patronage. If patronage was 'done with', this was not necessarily a development he welcomed. The relationship of protection, in which the stronger supported the weaker and from which reciprocal benefits might flow, was one he continued to approve. What he objected to was the perversion of the relationship on both sides: patrons who promised but did not produce, writers who dreamt vain and grandiose dreams and wrote nothing of any worth, or were merely idle and spiteful. The letter to Lord Chesterfield was written in the 1750s. Frequently regarded as the death knell of aristocratic control of letters, it comes into a different focus when read against Johnson's later meditations on the writing life, the *Lives of the Poets* (1779–81). In those essays there is very little criticism of patronage amidst a great deal of thoughtful discussion.

Johnson took it for granted that a writer is typically a dependent. Writers need protection, encouragement and support. With his respect for authority and zeal for subordination – 'subordination' was one of his favourite words – he saw nothing degrading in this: it represented order and harmony, a stable balance which allowed satisfaction on both sides. On a day to day basis, in exchange for protection, writers could be secretaries, translators, tutors, librarians, companions, readers. (If ever a social role presented itself as 'natural' to women, surely it is the role of the writer: dependent and subordinate, needing to please, and, when not writing, acting as secretary, translator, teacher, librarian and companion.) On a grander scale, a writer's words had the potential to confer immortality: a fine poem addressed to a patron praising his benevolence and generosity would ensure that the patron's name lived on into succeeding generations. Furthermore, for as long as the poem was admired, it would also show the good taste and critical acumen of the patron for supporting so worthy a poet.

In Johnson's *Lives of the Poets*, all the poets are men. There is no way of working out from his discussion of so many writing lives how, in his view, women writers fitted in to the system nor how the system might adapt to fit them better. Like much biography, the *Lives of the Poets* is revealing as autobiography. It can be read as a sustained backward reflection on the conditions and circumstances, the fantasies and the aspirations, that had shaped Johnson and turned him into the leading literary figure of his day. In a series of essays which are arguably his finest achievement, the man who 'knew every adventure of every book you could name almost', took a long hard look at the meaning of this knowledge and these adventures.

This engagement with the subject made it unlikely that he would include women even if the bookseller's brief allowed. The essays were biographical prefaces to new editions of the selected poets and Johnson claimed that the choice of poets had not been for him to decide. Personally, as we know, he aided and protected individuals such as Charlotte Lennox and Anna Williams in their literary labours. By writing dedications for Lennox or persuading his friends to subscribe to Williams, he helped those women to benefits available to writers regardless of sex. The women were able to operate much as men did within a system that might reward them with encourage-ment and favour, or might equally well abandon them to neglect, discouragement and wretchedness. But they were not included in the conceptual definition. A 'poet' was male. The female version was a poetess.

In his writings, Johnson returned again and again to imaginative ident-ification as the means by which we gain useful understanding. He propounded a theory of biography in a *Rambler* essay which began:

> All joy or sorrow for the happiness or calamities of others is produced by an act of the imagination that realizes the event however fictitious, or approximates it however remote, by placing us, for a time, in the condition of him whose fortune we contemplate; so that we feel, while the deception lasts, whatever motions would be excited by the same good or evil happening to ourselves.
>
> Our passions are therefore more strongly moved, in proportion as we can more readily adopt the pains or pleasures proposed to our minds, by recognising them as once our own, or considering them as naturally incident to our state of life. It is not easy for the most artful writer to give us an interest in happiness or misery which we think ourselves never likely to feel, and with which we have never yet been made acquainted.

In reading, we 'readily conform our minds', as he put it, to circumstances that can be made to seem parallel to our own. This exercise is made possible by the universal sameness of the human condition:

> We are all prompted by the same motives, all deceived by the same fallacies, all animated by hope, obstructed by danger, entangled by desire, and seduced by pleasure. (1)

Johnson's universalism offers a capacious space for women to enter in imagination, but his 'we' is, like his 'poet', male. In the lives of women, there were many happinesses and miseries with which he had never been made acquainted. To say this is to state the obvious: in cultural terms, female life and experience was not addressed with the same particularity and respect as male life and experience. For women writers, much double thinking was required. As readers of Johnson's words, they included themselves in his 'we', recognising the pains and pleasures as their own, allowing their passions to be moved and their understandings strengthened. Acknowledging the truths and admiring the sentiments he expressed, they adopted his tone and mode of thought in order to participate in his authority. Social authority was male, but cultural authority – a subtle and unpredictable force, founded on myths and fictions, entangled in desire and seduction – might be female.

Friendship with Johnson meant different things at different stages in his life. Hannah More and Fanny Burney became friends with a man whose notice of them and approbation of their writings secured their sense of having arrived inside the institution of literature. He was 'the acknowledged head of literature'; they were the new generation. His importance to them was symbolic and personal rather than professional. David Garrick was a far more important figure in Hannah More's writing life than was Samuel Johnson; and Samuel Crisp mattered more to Fanny Burney. In the earlier decades, amongst the first generation bluestockings, the picture was different. Johnson was by no means 'the acknowledged head of literature'. He was a social outsider. The meaning of friendship with Johnson changed as his position altered, a change that was intricately bound up with the expansion of print culture and the beginnings of mass readership. The writing lives of Elizabeth Carter and Elizabeth Montagu ran alongside Johnson's, more or less. As readers, writers and thinkers, they responded to many of the same pressures of social and cultural change, but they were insulated in a number of ways. They had the protection of class, wealth, family and gender. For all its frustrations, being female in a society which valued female dependency could be turned to advantage.

The bluestocking ideal, sustained by Carter and Montagu, mystified the professional element in a public literary life. It underplayed money and all elements of trade. In a rare acknowledgement of her status, Carter once admitted (no doubt with an ironic tone), 'I may make my fortune very prettily as Mrs Montagu's owl'. This she certainly did. By throwing in her lot with Montagu, by opting out of an expanding marketplace in favour of an older, aristocratic mode of literary life, she enhanced not only her own comfort and status but that of her wider family. Montagu's protection enabled Carter to escape the limitations of provincial life whilst preserving its advantages. Carter made her own mind easy, perhaps, when she assured Montagu that 'wealth, genius and reputation are all equally transformable into virtue'.[2]

This was a view Charlotte Lennox shared, except that hers was a sardonic recognition that those who had wealth tended to define the conditions of virtue. It is not perhaps surprising that towards the end of her life Elizabeth Carter – that fiercely ambitious young woman who had published two books when she was barely twenty – should pose ambition and virtue as opposites: virtue was a stable, steady, restrained and restraining force, whilst ambition 'either flies or creeps'. Too fast to be trusted or sinisterly slow, ambition was aligned with the upset of civil society that exploded in France and which it was widely feared would spread across the water to 'this favoured nation', where ' a well ordered government and equal laws' still protected the people of rank and property.[3]

Lennox's friendship with Johnson, extending across four decades, was unquestionably – as Miriam Small, Lennox's biographer put it – 'the most important single fact in Mrs Lennox's literary life'. As Carter looked to Montagu, so Lennox looked to Johnson. Throughout the 1750s she was, like him, a hard-working professional writer, living in London and in constant communication with the booksellers, securely in the public eye. She undertook a broad range of writing activities: poetry, fiction, translation, criticism, editing a periodical, and adapting and writing plays. In the 1760s she seems to have stopped publishing, though very little is known about her for most of that time except that she had a baby, a daughter, in 1765 – this was Henrietta who, thirteen years later, assisted in the assault on the maid. She also gave birth to a son, but his date of birth is not known. Having the care of two young children might account for some diminution in the volume of work she took on.

Though self-evidently a woman of independent resourcefulness, Lennox depended heavily on Samuel Johnson. This dependence, and Johnson's acceptance of it, reflected certain mid eighteenth-century assumptions about the writerly life which changed in the decades that followed. When Johnson boasted that he had 'lived more independently by literature than any man I know', his use of the word 'independence' did not imply solitary isolation. Romantic myths of the solitary genius, scribbling and starving alone in an attic, communing with the inner self, were yet to come. The social element in the business of writing still prevailed in people's ideas about it. The writer existed in a social network. Dependency and protection were understood as integral to the structure. Johnson was Lennox's mentor, well-placed to help her on in her career, either by suggesting her to booksellers for new projects or by writing the dedications to her books.

A good example of this matter of fact professional assistance can be seen in a letter from Johnson to Lennox of March 1757. Lennox had recently completed a translation from the French, the *Memoirs of Madame de Maintenon*. Johnson wrote:

> I saw last week at Mr Dodsley's a book called *Histoire des Conjurations* par P. Tertre which I told him was a good book, so far as could be judged by the title, for him to publish, and for you to translate. He seemed not to dislike the proposal, but had not then all the volumes, I think he had only the second. Now you have ended Maintenon you may perhaps think on it. I never saw it before, and saw little of it then but fancy it likely to succeed. Mr Dodsley will lend you his volume if you send for it.[4]

Other letters show that Lennox was not the easiest person to help. Exceptionally quarrelsome and imperious, with a quick temper and a sharp tongue, she displayed behaviour that most successful women writers managed to repress or conceal. According to Fanny Burney, who was repeating the words of Mrs Thrale, 'tho' her books are generally approved, nobody likes her', a fact which might be sufficient to explain why her name rarely comes up in accounts of bluestocking parties or in the correspondence of writing women. (Mrs Thrale used a similar formulation in speaking of Hannah More, whose *Percy* she dismissed as 'a foolish play': in the 1770s, according to her, 'nobody liked Miss More at Streatham'.) Illustrating her own point about Charlotte Lennox – that her books were 'generally approved' – Mrs Thrale noted in *Thraliana*:

> Was I to make a scale of novel writers, I should put Richardson first, then Rousseau; after them, but at an immeasurable distance – Charlotte Lennox, Smollett and Fielding. *The Female Quixote* and *Count Fathom* I think far beyond *Tom Jones* or *Joseph Andrews* with regard to body of story, height of colouring, or general powers of thinking.[5]

Elsewhere there are hints that Lennox did not wash often enough: an anonymous letter reports that several ladies meeting her at Mr Langton's were 'offended by her personal uncleanliness'. (When the same accusation was levelled at Christopher Smart, that he 'did not love clean linen', Johnson commented: 'and I have no passion for it'.) Even so, she was to be found at some bluestocking gatherings. She was friends with one of Garrick's leading ladies, Mary Ann Yates, and in the mid 1770s was in close communication with Garrick about *Old City Manners* which ran in November and December of 1775. In that same year, proposals for a subscription edition of her original writings were published, written by Johnson. It is likely that she made an effort to be as visible as possible to promote these ventures.

Where a subscription was being raised – a practice which involved a great deal of networking activity on the part of well-placed friends – it was customary for the author to be grateful for whatever benefits might be conferred. The etiquette demanded diffidence, discretion and modest submission. Charlotte Lennox broke all the rules: she was ungrateful, she harassed her friends, and she complained that they were doing too little. Johnson's proposals for 'A New and Elegant Edition, Enlarged and Corrected, of the Original Works of Mrs Charlotte Lennox', failed to find many subscribers. Her efforts to help it along (she was desperate for money) drew from him this reproof:

> Madam, In soliciting subscriptions, as perhaps in many other cases, too much eagerness defeats itself. We must leave our friends to their own motives and their own opportunities. Your subscription can hardly fail of success, but you must wait its progress. By telling your friends how much you expect from them you discourage them, for they finding themselves unequal to your expectation, will

rather do nothing and be quiet, than do their utmost, and yet not please. You complain of Miss Reynolds, who probably knows not three people whom she can properly solicit. Sir Joshua has made it a rule to act on these occasions only as a gentleman. When Miss Reynolds used to lay my proposals in the way of sitters, he always hid them, and undoubtedly did right.[6]

The great and the good, sitting for their portraits to Sir Joshua Reynolds, were a soft touch, but a delicate balance had to be struck. The natural affinity between Frances Reynolds, the under-noticed younger sister who was also a painter, and Samuel Johnson, whose material success as a writer fell dramatically short of Sir Joshua's success as a painter, was kept in check by Sir Joshua's ability to act 'as a gentleman'. Johnson knew where power lay, although by the mid 1770s all was not well in subscription publishing. The new and enlarged edition never materialised. Who is to say whether Miss Reynolds, goaded by Mrs Lennox and unobstructed by Sir Joshua, might not have been more effective than Dr Johnson in this instance? There is no way of telling, for both Miss Reynolds's persistence and Mrs Lennox's impatient demands were constrained by rules of gentlemanly decorum behind which the men united, even though, as Johnson explained, most of the work of raising subscriptions was done 'principally by the great ladies'.

Lennox's reputation was high enough in the late 1770s for her to feature as 'one of the most distinguished literary characters of the time' whom the Rev. William Beloe recalled meeting at Mrs Yates's house soon after he came to London. She was, furthermore, one of the nine prominent women represented in the painting by Richard Samuel, 'The Nine Living Muses of Great Britain', now in the National Portrait Gallery. Samuel's painting was exhibited in 1779 and it is an important sign of the cultural elevation, by the late 1770s, of women as productive artists and thinkers. An engraving bearing the same title had appeared in the *Ladies Pocket-Book* of 1778, suggesting that as an image it is likely to have had wide circulation. The painting depicts nine contemporary women of arts and letters as 'Muses' in the Temple of Apollo, wearing vaguely classical garb and posed appropriately: Angelica Kauffmann, the painter, is seated at an easel; Mrs Sheridan, formerly Elizabeth Linley, the singer, strums a lyre; the writers, Charlotte Lennox, Elizabeth Montagu, Hannah More, Anna Barbauld, Elizabeth Griffith, Elizabeth Carter and Catherine Macaulay stand in dignified, thoughtful fashion or sit with quills in their hands and scrolls of paper on their laps. None of these portraits was painted from life. As Elizabeth Carter observed to Elizabeth Montagu: 'to say truth, by the mere testimony of my own eyes, I cannot very exactly tell which is you, and which is I, and which is anybody else'. Carter was pleased to find herself in the picture, however, being 'just as sensible to present fame as you can be. Your Virgils and your Horaces may talk what they will of posterity, but I think it is much better to be celebrated by the men, women, and children among whom one is actually living.'[7]

In representation, the female author conveyed a dignified and thoughtful repose. In life, all was not like this: Charlotte Lennox was often tempestuous and uncontrolled. In this she was more like Johnson who, for all his belief in order, hierarchy and propriety, for all his efforts at self-government and self-control, was an uncontrolled or eccentric personality. Perhaps this accounted both for his patience with her – he acknowledged she had 'many fopperies' but insisted she was a 'great genius' – and his impatience:

> Dearest Madam: I am sorry you misunderstood me, I did not write for my books but for their names which you did not send me. I wish you would for once resolve to use any method of transacting with your friends but that of letters. You will, in whatever part of the world you may be placed, find mankind extremely impatient of such letters as you are inclined to favour them with. You can send your letters, such as the last but one, only to two sorts of people, those whom you cannot pain, and those whom you can, and surely it is not eligible either to give mirth to your enemies or to raise anger in your friends. I have no pleasure in saying this, and am glad that I have delayed beyond the time in which I might have been inclined to say more. I have no inclination to continue quarrels, and therefore hope you will again allow me, now I have vented my resentment, to be, dear Madam, your most obedient, and most humble servant, Sam. Johnson[8]

The venting of resentment by one or the other was a frequent occurrence. Another note begins, 'When friends fall out the first thing to be considered is how to fall in again ...' and ends with a postscript: 'I have not read your letter nor will read it, till I know whether it is peevish or no, for if it be you shall have it again.'

Peevish, hot-tempered, rash and proud, Charlotte Lennox was not one to suffer quietly. She preferred action to endurance. By the time of Eva Garrick's dinner in 1784 she was no longer securely in the public eye as she had been in the 1750s, but neither was she entirely out of it. Younger, but of roughly the same generation as the senior bluestockings, she mixed in circles other than the ones they frequented, and in which Johnson was regularly to be found. She was still writing and planning books, still visiting Johnson and involving him professionally in all her schemes. In the very week of the dinner she had been in contact with him about a manuscript – probably an early draft of her last novel, *Euphemia*, which eventually appeared in 1790. A letter from the 1770s survives showing how pleased she was that he had agreed to name a day when he would 'come and eat apple dumplings of my making', though as it was too early for apples he was offered gooseberry tart instead; she wanted to speak with him about matters of business. In 1780 she sought him out on a less happy occasion, as Johnson told Mrs Thrale: 'Mrs Lennox has just been with me to get a chirurgeon to her daughter, the girl that Mrs Cumins rejected, who has received a kick from a horse, that has broken five fore teeth on the upper side ... had the blow been a little harder it had killed her.'[9]

The gruesome event was a prelude to greater unhappiness. At some point in the 1780s, 'the girl that Mrs Cumins rejected' died, leaving Charlotte Lennox with a son who was rapidly going to the bad, as well as a husband who had always been a liability. With a dwindling income and declining health, her last years were full of distress. Johnson's death in 1784 removed a major source of support, though some of his surviving friends, like Bennet Langton, took on responsibility for her, and Boswell wrote proposals for a new edition of her works. In 1792 she applied for financial assistance from the recently founded Royal Literary Fund. They gave her ten guineas, and in August of the following year she wrote to them again:

> Sir, It is with great confusion that I take the liberty to importune you, who know me only by name, with this application, and my distress may be easily imagined, when it forces me to break through decorums which I always wished to observe – but I am a Mother, and see an only child upon the brink of utter ruin. Driven as he was first, to desperation by a most unnatural father, and then deserted, and left exposed to all the evils that may well be expected from the dreadful circumstances he is in – I would preserve him if I could. Alas! I do not pretend to excuse his fault, but if his story was candidly told, that fault great as it is, would with the severest judge meet compassion as well as blame. I have in vain used my utmost endeavours to mortgage the poor income I hold from a husband whose fortune I have made by the sacrifice of my own, in order to send this unfortunate youth to my relations in the United States of America, who will receive him kindly ... the last ship that will go to America till next March will sail in a week – the money for the passage must be paid before he goes on board, and the very lowest terms that are offered are out of my reach ...

What he had done is unknown, but the Royal Literary Fund gave twelve guineas for his passage. Ten years later, Charlotte Lennox was discovered to be 'in great distress for the common necessaries of life and is too ill, and now too old to be able to assist herself in any way'. She had not been out of her lodgings at a cabinet maker's in Dartmouth Street, Westminster, for three months. Compassionate activists took up her case, and the Royal Literary Fund subsidised her until her death in 1804.[10]

Just as it was not unheard of for writers in the eighteenth century to find themselves on the wrong side of the law, so it was not unusual for them to die in poverty. Extremes of high and low were as likely to be met with in a single life as in the social realm where wealth and poverty rubbed shoulders and sometimes changed places. In the meagre records available to us, Charlotte Lennox is to be found complaining, begging, displaying lurid distress and penning imperious demands, a pattern that seems more or less consistent from the successful 1750s until her impoverished old age. That large sums of money came her way seems indisputable. She herself, on the evidence of the letter to the Royal Literary Fund, considered she had made a 'fortune' for her husband by sacrificing her own; certainly, if she had not given up the chance of a pension in his favour she would have had an adequate income on a par with that of Johnson. The system of pension-giving did not in itself discriminate against women, though there were fewer candidates and it was less easy to find for women the places which often came with the pension. Whatever jobs Alexander Lennox was given in the customs house would not have been suitable for his wife.

The characteristic dependency of the writer took different forms when the writer was a woman. This was an issue which 'great ladies' like Catherine Talbot and Elizabeth Montagu addressed; and if their efforts were not always successful, they were nevertheless appreciated in some quarters. Anna Williams was thrilled with the annuity Elizabeth Montagu settled on her in 1775: it represented honourable notice as well as hard cash. Elizabeth Carter did not decline the annuity offered to her, as we have seen; and Hester Chapone made the most of the connection with Montagu which her prior friendship with Carter made possible. But none of this removed the need for other sources of income, nor of the perplexities involved in ensuring it. When Catherine Talbot mused on the poverty of Catherine Cockburn, and feared that Elizabeth Carter might end up in the same straits, her thinking verged on the political: the sexual politics of the woman writer's life stared her in the face. There were precedents for what one might do for a man. What did one do for a woman? Successful patronage had an obvious appeal for women who accepted and lived inside doctrines of subordination. It was like marriage, a bringing together of the strong and the weak, only better – whether one were dispensing patronage or receiving it. The ideal was given expression by Johnson in his life of Isaac Watts in the *Lives of the Poets*. At Abney Park, Watts found 'friendship' 'kindness' and 'attention' for thirty-six years. Watts, Johnson wrote,

> had the privilege of a country recess, the fragrant bower, the spreading lawn, the flowery garden, and other advantages, to sooth his mind and aid his restoration to health; to yield him, whenever he chose them, most grateful intervals from his laborious studies, and enable him to return to them with redoubled vigour and delight.

Such a vision must have seemed like paradise to those young women in whose veins, as Johnson put it in 'The Vanity of Human Wishes', burned the desire for fame and 'the fever of renown'. Their passions, too, were moved by the accounts they read of poets' lives. Their 'acts of the imagination' led them to identify when they read, just as men identified, and to dream that the same good things might happen to them.

Catherine Talbot canvassed a position for Elizabeth Carter as a governess to the royal princesses – idealising it as a position that was 'high' rather than 'low' and one which would give her the 'privileges' Isaac Watts enjoyed, enabling her to continue her 'laborious studies' in an atmosphere of respect and support. Carter declined. In fact, the life she made for herself – with scholarship at the centre and repose found in flowery gardens and fragrant bowers – was modelled according to the patronage ideal, especially whilst her father lived and could serve in many ways as a substitute patron: the person with whom she exchanged ideas and who provided her with social protection and status. The respect Carter was accorded at home as a scholar – customarily working, as her nephew tells us, eight to twelve hours a day at her books – invites us to think of the father-daughter relationship in this way; and it makes more sense of the evidence than the stereotypical image, that of an unmarried daughter burdened with the care of an elderly father.

Hannah More served as chaplain in the household of Eva Garrick, a startling role if we fail to take account of the way writers were brought into wealthy families as chaplains or tutors. Mrs Garrick asked her to take over the moral and spiritual welfare of the servants. 'In the evening I read a sermon and prayers to the family, which Mrs Garrick much likes.' According to Boswell, she habitually sat at the foot of the table as chaplain when there were guests. She was made chaplain by virtue of being a writer (as well as because she was deeply religious); the fact that she was a woman and that women could not be ordained seemed not to matter. (Similarly, many women wrote sermons for less gifted clergymen to deliver.) [11]

Fanny Burney, as we have seen, was given a place at court which, disastrous though it was, earned her a small but much-needed pension for the rest of her life. Although Macaulay, writing in 1840, was caustic about this 'slavery', sneering at Dr Burney who 'seems to have thought that going to court was like going to heaven', the fact is that Charles Burney had been formed in a milieu that worshipped rank. Nor did Fanny Burney cease to do so. Her third novel, *Camilla: or A Picture of Youth* was published by subscription in 1796, a method of publication which was lucrative for her because of the high-ranking connections she had made; although it did not make the three thousand guineas which literary gossip claimed, it did clear a handsome profit. She needed the money: she had married a French émigré, General d'Arblay, who had lost everything in the Revolution.

The need for protection raised questions about money, power, social organisation and social agency that spilled beyond the confines of discussion about literary merit. We should be cautious how we read the words women wrote to each other, especially where connections were being cemented or benefits exchanged. 'Friendship', 'kindness', and 'attention' were part of the currency of patronage. Accusations of coldness or withdrawal of kindness, such as were regularly directed at Elizabeth Montagu, might appear merely personal but were likely to be political: an expression of grievance or retaliation by one whose hopes had been dashed, who had failed to find or keep favour. Montagu's appetite for power and her sheer organising energy (she managed the finances of an untold number of dependents), as well as her iron will, made her an object of much highly-charged and coded feeling which used misogynist formulations to strike at her use of power. More than anybody, she set herself to support and sustain women's cultural production, wanting not only fame for herself but to raise the profile of women artists and writers; and she could be ruthless in her pursuit of this goal. She was more feared than loved, an arrangement that suited her purposes. What Fanny Burney described as her 'earnest solicitude for pre-eminence' never faltered; keeping others in check and under her rule seems at all times to have been a priority. Hers was a benevolence that laid less claim to feeling than policy. When James Barry depicted her as 'a distinguished example of female excellence' in his murals representing the 'Progress of Human Knowledge and Culture', painted for the Society of Arts, Crafts and Manufactures, he made her a central figure in 'The Distribution of the Premiums', a painting which showed her as a generous benefactor. This role was underlined by Johnson's presence in the painting, pointing approvingly at her virtuous example. Johnson – famous for his compassion for the poor – signifies feeling and points the moral, while Montagu, shown in profile, is in action, businesslike and busy.

Although she spent more time in her country house at Sandleford, where she lived her last years with her nephew and his young family, Montagu's passion for huge parties did not diminish. The magnificent rooms at Portland Square were regularly filled with mixed assemblies – too mixed for some scornful observers who also noted that the hostess, dripping with diamonds, was too old to load her flesh that way. Poverty was never likely to be a threat. Supposedly frail, she continued to be vigorously active, hampered only by failing sight. She died, at the age of eighty, in 1800.

Posthumous reputation mattered to her. Montagu took care that her life and work should be properly memorialised after her death, so that her name would live and her example go on being an influence in the world. She kept records, annotated and arranged her correspondence, and trained up her nephew, Matthew, for the task of editing and publishing her papers after her death. She had long assumed that, as a public figure, her private writings would be of interest; and she expected to be remembered for what she had achieved publicly: her support of other writers and her original *Essay on the Writings and Genius of Shakespeare.*

Elizabeth Carter's nephew, Montagu Pennington, made a minor industry out of Carter. After her death in London in 1806, he compiled, wrote and published the official biography of his aunt in two substantial volumes. Volume one told the life and volume two offered a sample of her published work. The biography was a great success and went into several editions. Pennington capitalised on this interest by reissuing his aunt's chief claim to fame, her 1758 translation of *All the Works of Epictetus.* He also edited her letters in numerous volumes: three volumes of the letters to Elizabeth Montagu, and three volumes of those to Catherine Talbot which included those to Mrs Vesey. He recognised that the demand for all these publications rested on Elizabeth Carter's celebrity as a writer. No other justification for a two-volume *Memoirs* and six volumes of letters existed. Nevertheless he made a great point of insisting that in the latter part of her life at least, Elizabeth Carter, for all her celebrity, was not *really* a writer. She was a 'high and excellent character' and thus no apology was needed for offering the public an account of her life, but she 'could hardly be considered in the light of a professed literary character'.[12]

In amputating the 'literary' and leaving only the 'high and excellent' to her character, Pennington broke apart a balance both Carter and Montagu had spent their lives maintaining, for the bluestocking ideal combined female authorship with virtue and visibility. But he can hardly be accused of misrepresentation. Authorship had changed. Elizabeth Carter, at the end of her life, did not profess a literary character in the way that – to take the example Pennington himself was drawn to – Mary Wollstonecraft professed it. In comfortable, conservative, clerical families like Carter's, there was confusion about these matters. The ground had shifted. Elizabeth Carter was embarrassed by her own past

In a comparable way, Hannah More turned her back on the fashionable literary circles of her youth, but she went on writing and was a 'professed literary character' to the end of her long and active life. As a social reformer who set up and managed a network of schools in her neighbourhood, she appropriated the power of church, state and lady of the manor. Deferred to by the many 'bishops, nobles and persons of distinction' who visited her at her Somerset home, and deploring the spread of what she considered 'violent' democratic principles, she laboured to instil piety, sobriety and acquiescence in the poor – whose hunger and ignorance she sought to alleviate but whose circumstances she did not seek to change. The friendship with Eva Garrick dwindled to an annual invitation in tribute to the memory of David Garrick, though Mrs Garrick lived on to the advanced age of ninety-eight, keeping her box at Drury Lane until the end.

Hannah More outlived all her sisters. She spent many years bedridden in an upstairs room, maintaining an enormous correspondence, preparing herself to die and lamenting her dreadful health whilst living remorselessly on. To the outrage of her friends, it transpired that her servants were taking advantage and entertaining themselves at her expense in their quarters below. They can't have cheated her very badly, however: when she died in 1833, at the age of eighty-eight, she left £30,000 in legacies to charities.

Six months after the dinner at Eva Garrick's, on 13 December 1784, Samuel Johnson died. He had spent the summer on a round of visits that must have felt like a tour of farewell. He stayed long, gloomy weeks in his home town of Lichfield, and visited Ashbourne, Birmingham and Oxford. He was ill and unhappy, swollen with the dropsy, unable to sleep, plagued with terrors and haunted by distressing thoughts. In his pained state, London represented itself to him as the one place he might yet recover his health. He wrote to Dr Brocklesby, his physician, 'The town is my element, there are my friends, there are my books to which I have not yet bidden farewell, and there are my amusements.' He returned in mid-November but by then he was barely able to get out of bed. Friends came and sat with him through long hours of breathlessness and agitation. When he could sit up he spent his time burning great masses of his papers. He knew the value that would be put on them, the use that would be made of private writings. He burnt letters, including some written to him by his mother (bursting into tears as he laid them on the fire) and he burnt the two quarto volumes in which he had written an account of his own life. Sir John Hawkins tried to steal away a little book of meditations and reflections, claiming, when Johnson spotted him, that he was only concerned to keep it safe and that a man connected with the press had been seen lurking outside.

Stories about Johnson had always had currency. After his death their value increased astronomically. He had participated in making himself a commodity.

Like Fanny Burney, the older generation of bluestockings reacted to the publicity which followed his death with tight-lipped reserve. Elizabeth Carter only learnt that he had died by reading about it in the press. She wrote to Elizabeth Montagu:

> I see by the papers, that Dr Johnson is dead. In extent of learning, and exquisite purity of moral writing, he has left no superior, and I fear very few equals. His virtues and his piety were founded on the steadiest of Christian principles and faith. His faults, I firmly believe, arose from the irritations of a most suffering state of nervous constitution, which scarcely ever allowed him a moment's ease.[13]

If her words strike us as almost chilly in their formality, and more like a public statement than a private expression of grief at the loss of a lifetime friend, that is surely because it *was* a public statement. Whatever she wrote at such a time, about such an event, was likely to find its way into print sooner or later. Authorship had become an increasingly self-conscious activity, much talked about in periodicals, and given a boost by publications like Johnson's *Lives of the Poets* and by the many anecdotes of Johnson himself.

Hester Thrale, now Mrs Piozzi, reacted differently. She set about ordering the materials she had gathered over the years – encouraged to it by Johnson, just as he encouraged Boswell – and, as we have seen, emerged as a writer with her *Anecdotes of the Late Samuel Johnson*. She edited a collection of his letters, *Letters to and from the Late Samuel Johnson*, which was the first substantial collection of his letters to be made available. She read and reread his writings. She toured Italy and produced a travel book, her *Observations*, which owed much to Johnson's own account of his travels in the Hebrides, the *Journey to the Western Islands of Scotland* – a book she considered 'one of his first rate performances. I look it over now every day'. Her relationship with him provided her with a deep foundation on which to build an authoritative literary career. Some, like Mary Wollstonecraft, argued that she merely imitated him: 'Mrs Piozzi, who often repeated by rote, what she did not understand, comes forward with Johnsonian periods'. This accusation was also levelled at Fanny Burney, whose mature prose style, as displayed in the memoir of her father Charles Burney, has an impersonal gravity that does not at all resemble *Evelina* or the early journals. Behind the accusation lay a literary politics: Wollstonecraft was declaring Johnson's day over. All those associated with him belonged to the past.

The estrangement between Fanny Burney and Mrs Piozzi was never healed. When Mrs Piozzi's edition of Johnson's letters appeared, Burney was 'pining to procure' it; she had to be grateful to the hated Mrs Schwellenberg, her immediate superior at Windsor, for a loan of an advance copy that had come into royal circles via the Bishop of Carlisle. What she read did not please her:

> With what sadness have I been reading! What scenes has it revived! – what regrets renewed! These letters have not been more improperly published in the whole,

than they are injudiciously displayed in their several parts. She has given all – every word – and thinks that, perhaps, a justice to Dr Johnson, which, in fact, is the greatest injury to his memory.[14]

Mrs Piozzi went on behaving in ways Fanny Burney could not approve. For her seventy-ninth birthday she slapped on the rouge, hired the Assembly Rooms at Bath and threw a gala ball (which she couldn't afford) for over six hundred guests. She led the dancing till the early hours. She died a few years later in 1821, after falling whilst getting into bed at an inn in Exeter. Fanny Burney recalled in her journal the older woman's learning, her 'ardent love of literature', her 'luminous' conversation, her kindness and her grace; and added that she was also 'sarcastic, careless, and daring, and therefore feared'.

Like Mrs Piozzi, Fanny Burney found happiness in marriage to a non-Englishman. Caught up in the turbulence of the French Revolution and the wars which followed, she found herself living for ten years as an exile in Napoleonic France, bringing up a son, continuing to write. In 1811 she underwent a mastectomy, an operation conducted without anaesthetics and which she survived to outlive both husband and son. She died in 1840.

Samuel Johnson could not, ultimately, protect Charlotte Lennox nor make her fortune for her. But he could endorse her commitment to the adventure of making up a life as he had made up his. His insistence in the last year of his life that she was 'superior' to the superior women who dominated the literary world is a reminder to us, among other things, of the dynamism of the culture through which these women moved. Of his women friends, Lennox was the most closely connected with Johnson's day-to-day professional life, and if she had written 'Anecdotes' or 'Recollections' or 'Memoirs' of Johnson they would have been a valuable contribution to our knowledge. Had she written her own memoirs or, like Fanny Burney, left a vivid journal or, like Montagu and Carter, been able to entrust her papers and reputation to a younger relation whose respect for her name and fame could be taken for granted; if, like Hester Thrale, she had preserved her observations in some beautiful books presented to her by her husband, we would have, perhaps, a source which would radically alter our view of the conditions of female authorship in the eighteenth century. But we have no such writings. If they ever existed they have not survived, or if they survive somewhere, they have not been discovered.

Notes

Notes to Chapter 1: At Mrs Garrick's

1. Hester Piozzi, *Anecdotes of the Late Samuel Johnson LL.D. during the Last Twenty Years of His Life*, ed. Arthur Sherbo (London and Oxford, 1974) p. 77, in which Johnson goes on to say, 'How else ... do the gamesters manage when they play for more money than they are worth?'. All authors can take comfort from the further observation, 'A man is seldom in a humour to unlock his book-case, set his desk in order, and betake himself to serious study'.

2. James Boswell, *The Life of Samuel Johnson*, Everyman edition, 2 vols (London, 1906), ii, p. 510.

3. Samuel Johnson, 'The Age of Authors', in the *Adventurer*, 115 (December, 1753), Yale edition of the *Works of Samuel Johnson*, ii, pp. 456–61; for Mary Scott see the brief but useful biography and extract from *The Female Advocate* in Roger Lonsdale, *Eighteenth-Century Women Poets* (Oxford, 1989), pp. 320–22. Lonsdale's book continues to be an invaluable source for quick biographical reference.

4. William Roberts, *Memoirs of the Life and Correspondence of Mrs Hannah More*, 2 vols (London, 1835), i, pp. 210–11.

5. Ellis, Annie Raine (ed.), *The Early Diary of Frances Burney, 1768–1778* (2 vols, London, 1889), ii, p. 212. The question of naming will arise more than once. Is the author who was christened 'Frances' but always called 'Fanny' or 'Fanni-kin', to be referred to as Frances or Fanny, and is she 'Burney' or 'd'Arblay'? Some argue that to call her 'Fanny' is a diminishment of her stature as a writer. I have chosen to do so on the grounds that this was the name by which she was known, especially in the earlier part of her life when she became friends with Johnson.

6. Boswell, *Life of Samuel Johnson*, i, pp. 242–43

7. Chauncey Tinker, *Dr Johnson and Fanny Burney: Being the Johnsonian Passages from the Works of Mme d'Arblay* (London, 1912), Introduction, p. xvii.

8. Fanny Burney, *The Early Letters and Journals*, ed. Lars E. Troide and Stewart J. Cooke (Oxford, 1994), iii, p. 5.

9. Robert Lynd, *Dr Johnson and Company* (London, 1946), pp. 13–14. In the first chapter of this short and engaging book (an excellent starting point for anybody new to Johnson studies), Lynd gives 'a catalogue of the defects of Johnson', incorporating these well-known descriptions. Apart from Boswell's *Life*, Arthur Murphy's *Essay*, and Hester Piozzi's *Anecdotes*, I have been most indebted for

biographical information about Johnson to Walter Jackson Bate, *Samuel Johnson* (London, 1984), and to Margaret Lane, *Samuel Johnson and his World* (London, 1975).

10. Arthur Murphy, *An Essay on the Life and Genius of Dr Johnson* (London, 1792), p. 124.

11. Margaret Lane, in *Samuel Johnson and his World*, is particularly good on Johnson's wife, Tetty. Copiously illustrated, this looks 'light' but is, in fact, a most thoughtful and scholarly account, a reconsideration of familiar themes which also serves as an excellent introduction for new readers.

12. Hester Piozzi, *Anecdotes*, p. 101.

13. Murphy, *Essay*, p. 3.

14. Hester Piozzi, *Thraliana*, ed. Katharine Balderston (2 vols, Oxford, 1942), i, pp. 544–45.

15. Quoted in William McCarthy, *Hester Thrale Piozzi: Portrait of a Literary Woman*, pp. 37–38.

16. Ibid., p. 39. Carter considered Thrale 'a genius of that eccentric kind which is mighty apt to be accompanied by "a plentiful lack" of common sense'. Montagu went so far as to suggest that Mrs Thrale's behaviour had shortened Johnson's life. The issue was conducted very publicly. Fanny Burney wrote to the Thrales' daughter, Queeney: 'I have heard that Mrs Montagu and Miss More have written long letters about this cruel business which are read about the town.' Later, Mrs Piozzi had plenty of opportunities to witness Hannah More's name being dragged through the press. In 1801, she asked Sophia Pennington to '*Pray* tell me how Hannah More supports *her* torrent of scurrility'.

17. Sir John Hawkins, *The Works of Samuel Johnson*, 15 vols, of which volume one is *The Life of Samuel Johnson LL.D.* (London, 1787–88), i, pp. 285–86. This account is also given in full in Miriam Small, *Charlotte Ramsay Lennox: An Eighteenth-Century Lady of Letters* (New York, 1935) pp. 10–11, and elsewhere.

18. Biographical information about the Garricks is from George W. Stone and George M. Kahrl, *David Garrick: A Critical Biography* (Carbondale, Illinois, 1979), which is also exceptionally good on his relationship with Hannah More.

19. Roberts, *Memoirs of Hannah More* (London, 1835), i, p. 149.

20. Jones, *Hannah More* (Cambridge, 1952), p. 7.

21. Hannah More, *Florio: A Tale for Fine Gentlemen and Fine Ladies; and The Bas Bleu or Conversation. Two Poems* (London, 1786). The first was dedicated to Horace Walpole, the second to Mrs Vesey.

Notes to Chapter 2: Elizabeth Carter

1. Elizabeth Sheridan, *Betsy Sheridan's Journal*, ed. William LeFanu (Oxford, 1986), p. 40. This, and the description from Fanny Burney's diary, are quoted in Judith Hawley's Introduction to Elizabeth Carter's *Epictetus* and other selected writings in volume two of *Bluestocking Feminism* (London, 1999), which is devoted to Elizabeth Carter. This 450-page volume represents the

first sustained scholarly attention Carter has received since her death in 1806. It makes available an up-to-date bibliography of manuscript sources (not very plentiful – most of the originals were destroyed) and printed works. There is a useful chronology, helpful notes, a generous selection of poems, some letters, and miscellaneous writings. Judith Hawley's editing and specialist commentary would, one feels, probably meet Mrs Carter's high standards. *Bluestocking Feminism*, in six volumes under the general editorship of Gary Kelly is the first stop for anybody interested in the writings of the bluestockings. For detailed biographical information, the only other source currently available (though considerable scholarly work is now in progress) is Sylvia Harcstark Myers, *The Bluestocking Circle* (Oxford, 1990), which has a fund of factual information. Myers trawled archival sources in the best tradition of feminist scholarship, recovering the overlooked and the under-known. Like anybody working on women writers of the period, I have made extensive use of her work. It has, however, been a struggle to resist the overall impact of her conceptualisation which, in my view, takes insufficient account of the significance of class, and class privilege, on female self-esteem. Paradoxically, I find this reinforces a condescending view of her subjects which I am sure was unintentional.

2. All biographical details are from the official biography, *Memoirs of the Life of Mrs Elizabeth Carter* (London, 1808), by Elizabeth Carter's nephew, Montagu Pennington. The Rev. Montagu Pennington (named for his godmother, Elizabeth Montagu) had been very close to his aunt. He was educated by her, travelled with her on the Continent, and lived with her. He was well aware of her views. His *Memoir* was a labour of love and pride as well as duty (although he knew he had been groomed for the task) and in its attempts to do right by her it mixes the unexpectedly revealing with earnest piety. There is a capaciousness and attention to detail which is characteristic of the period. Pennington misrepresents aspects of Carter's life, especially the earlier period – sometimes wilfully, sometimes out of ignorance – but, having read the *Memoir* several times, my respect for his achievement has grown. He was to go on editing and publishing his aunt's writings, producing new editions, keeping old ones in print, and gathering and collecting all the letters he could.

3. Robina Napier, *Johnsoniana: Anecdotes of the Late Samuel Johnson LL.D. by Mrs Piozzi and others* (London, 1884), p. 130.

4. Pennington, *Memoir*, i, pp. 447–48.

5. Thomas Birch, *History of the Works of the Learned*, July 1739.

6. Samuel Johnson's obituary notice of Edward Cave, published in the *Gentleman's Magazine* in February 1754, is the source of much of our information about his life and personality.

7. Deal County Library, Stebbing Collection. This and subsequent extracts from Dr Carter's letters are from surviving papers held here.

8. Pennington, *Memoir*, i, pp. 132–36.

9. Ibid., pp. 7, 22.

10. Ibid., p. 31.
11. For Sarah Scott, see volume 5 of *Bluestocking Feminism*. For the Ladies of Llangollen, see Elizabeth Mavor, *The Ladies of Llangollen* (London, 1973).
12. Pennington, *Memoir*, i, p. 29.
13. Ibid., pp. 43–44.
14. Edward Ruhe, 'Birch, Johnson and Elizabeth Carter: An Episode of 1738–39', *PMLA*, 73 (1958), traces the progress of the threesome during this time. He assumes, probably falsely, that many of the meetings between Birch and Carter were private. Subsequent information about Birch, Johnson and Carter and their 1738–39 involvement with the *Gentleman's Magazine* is from Ruhe and from Myers, *The Bluestocking Circle*, ch. 2, 'Elizabeth Carter's London Career'.
15. Elizabeth Rowe, *Works*, i, pp. cx–cxii. Roger Lonsdale prints the earlier version of the poem in *Eighteenth-Century Women Poets* (Oxford, 1989), p. 167.
16. See the *Life of Mrs Elizabeth Rowe* prefixed to the *Works*. Elizabeth Carter's debt to Elizabeth Rowe is discussed at more length in Norma Clarke, 'Soft Passions and Darling Themes: From Elizabeth Rowe to Elizabeth Carter', *Writing Women*, Autumn 2000.
17. Sarah Prescott deals at length with Elizabeth Rowe in *Female Authorship in Early Eighteenth-Century England* (forthcoming).
18. Biographical information from Maynard Mack, *Alexander Pope* (New Haven, 1985).
19. Myers, *The Bluestocking Circle*, p. 68.
20. Ibid., p. 63.
21. Pennington, *Memoirs*, i, pp. 161–62.
22. *A Series of Letters between Mrs Elizabeth Carter and Miss Catherine Talbot, from the Year 1741 to 1770. To Which are Added, Letters from Mrs Elizabeth Carter to Mrs Vesey, between the Years 1763 and 1787*, edited by Montagu Pennington (3rd edition, London, 1817), i, p. 281.
23. Myers, *The Bluestocking Circle*, p. 164.
24. Elizabeth Carter to Catherine Talbot, *A Series of Letters*, i, p. 85.
25. Myers, *The Bluestocking Circle*, p. 160.
26. The details are in volume 3 of *Bluestocking Feminism, Catherine Talbot and Hester Chapone*, ed. Rhoda Zuk.
27. Elizabeth Carter to Catherine Talbot, *A Series of Letters*, i, p. 291.
28. Ibid., i, p. 371.
29. *Bluestocking Feminism*, volume 2, *All the Works of Epictetus*, p. 203.
30. Pennington, *Memoirs*, p. 193. Quoted in Claudia Thomas, 'Th'instructive Moral and Important Thought', *The Age of Johnson*, 4 (1991), a thoughtful account of Carter's work on Epictetus.
31. John Doran, *A Lady of the Last Century: Mrs Elizabeth Montagu* (London, 1873), pp. 70–71.
32. *Letters from Mrs Elizabeth Carter to Mrs Montagu between the Years 1755 and 1800: Chiefly upon Literary and Moral Subjects* (London, 1817) i, pp. 19–20.
33. *Bluestocking Feminism*, volume 1, *Elizabeth Montagu*, pp. 150–51.

34. Elizabeth Carter to Elizabeth Montagu, *Letters*, i, p. 24.
35. Ibid., p. 142.
36. Ibid., p. 27.
37. Ibid., p. 154.
38. Ibid., p. 100.
39. Elizabeth Carter to Elizabeth Montagu, *Letters*. The exchange runs across several letters: see i, pp. 229–43.

Notes to Chapter 3: Charlotte Lennox

1. *A Series of Letters between Mrs Elizabeth Carter and Catherine Talbot, from the Year 1741 to 1770: To Which are Added, Letters from Mrs Elizabeth Carter to Mrs Vesey, between the Years 1763 and 1787*, edited by Montagu Pennington (3rd edition, London, 1817), i, p. 366.
2. Fielding and Richardson quoted in Miriam Small, *Charlotte Ramsay Lennox: An Eighteenth-Century Lady of Letters* (New Haven, 1935), pp. 13–14. Biographical information about Lennox, such as it is, comes from Small, where the phrase 'information is meagre' recurs and where the biographer's task was to 'piece together' as much of a connected narrative as she could from the scraps of evidence available. Subsequent research by Duncan Isles, who in 1964 discovered a cache of forty-six letters and miscellaneous items relating to Lennox, which he published as 'The Lennox Collection' in the *Harvard Library Bulletin* (1970–71), has provided a welcome addition. Small's book begins with the same moment in Boswell's *Life* that I have taken as the starting point for *Dr Johnson's Women*. In her sophisticated, 'Samuel Johnson and Four Literary Women' (unpublished thesis, Arizona State University, 1979), Gae Annette Brack also begins with the dinner. Her thesis considers Lennox, Carter, More and Burney and their relationships with Johnson. I have drawn gratefully from it.
3. Mary Wortley Montagu, *Letters* (London, 1992), p. 41.
4. Donald Stauffer uses the term 'little biographies of the bedchamber' in his useful survey, *The Art of Biography* (Princeton, 1941).
5. 'The Art of Coquetry' is printed in full in Small, *Charlotte Ramsay Lennox*, pp. 233–36.
6. Elizabeth Carter to Catherine Talbot, *A Series of Letters*, i, p. 305.
7. Roger Lonsdale, *Eighteenth-Century Women Poets* (Oxford, 1989), p. 111.
8. Elizabeth Carter to Catherine Talbot, *A Series of Letters*, i, p. 231.
9. Johnson, *Rambler*, no. 4.
10. Catherine Talbot to Elizabeth Carter, *A Series of Letters*, ii, p. 31.
11. *Bluestocking Feminism*, volume 3, *Catherine Talbot and Hester Chapone*, ed. Rhoda Zuk, p. 211.
12. Ibid., p. 216.
13. Ibid., p. 239.
14. Elizabeth Carter to Catherine Talbot, *A Series of Letters*, ii, pp. 121–22.

15. Ibid., ii, p. 46.
16. Mrs Chapone, *Posthumous Works* (London, 1807), i, pp. 34–35.
17. Elizabeth Carter to Catherine Talbot, *A Series of Letters*, ii, p. 32.
18. Catherine Talbot looked forward to the prospect of Constantia Phillips's book being read aloud in her domestic circle. Perhaps they read Laetitia Pilkington, too. Pilkington named names, inviting those who did not want their identities revealed to be sure to subscribe to her next volume. Laetitia Pilkington, *Memoirs of Mrs Laetitia Piliungton, 1712–1750: Written by Herself*, ed. A. C. Elias, Jr, 2 vols (Athens, Georgia, and London, 1997) i, p. 263.
19. Elizabeth Montagu, *The Letters of Elizabeth Montagu*, ed. Matthew Montagu (London, 1810), iii, pp. 96–97. Montagu noted that Pilkington was 'very severe on the clergy … She is very saucy about some Bishops and some Bishops' ladies … You must excuse me if I own I could not help laughing at that passage'.
20. Charlotte Lennox, *The Female Quixote* (London, 1986), ch. 11, pp. 410–21. Subsequent extracts are from this chapter unless otherwise indicated.
21. Duncan Isles, a leading authority, makes it clear that there is no foundation for this view which, by much repetition, has acquired the status of a critical orthodoxy.
22. James Boswell, *The Life of Samuel Johnson* (London, 1906), i, p. 20–21.
23. Mrs Chapone, *Posthumous Works* (London, 1807), i, pp. 108–11.
24. Samuel Johnson, *Rasselas* (Oxford Authors, *Samuel Johnson*, 1984), ch. 26, pp. 376–77.
25. Ibid., ch. 25, pp. 374–75.
26. Small, *Charlotte Ramsay Lennox*, pp. 15–17. See also the long and thoughtful reflection on Baretti's character in Hester Piozzi, *Thraliana* (Oxford, 1942), i, pp. 43–44. Baretti's biographer, Lacy Collinson-Morley, points out that Baretti was the only foreigner welcomed as an intimate in Johnson's circle. Mrs Thrale's conviction that he hated her is confirmed by Baretti's articles in the *European Magazine*, Summer 1788.
27. Small, *Charlotte Ramsay Lennox*, p. 26; Brack, 'Samuel Johnson and Four Literary Women', ch. 5.
28. Margaret Doody, in a penetrating analysis, makes this suggestion: 'Shakespeare's Novels: Charlotte Lennox Illustrated', *Studies in the Novel*, 19 (1987); see also the refreshing, 'What's So Irritating about Charlotte Lennox?' by Laura Runge, in *Gender and Language in British Literary Criticism, 1660–1790*, which explores the hostility the book aroused. Runge concludes that the 'irritation' *Shakespear Illustrated* inspired 'derives from the irritation it expresses' – a useful and generally applicable formula for Lennox, who was rarely inclined towards anything resembling 'a pose of cool critical detachment'.
29. Small, *Charlotte Ramsay Lennox*, pp. 18–19. The entire poem is printed ibid., appendix 4, pp. 239–24, with a translation on pp. 158–60.
30. Pilkington, *Memoirs of Mrs Laetitia Pilkington, 1712–1750*, ed. A. C. Elias Jr (Athens, Georgia, and London, 1997), i, p. 88. It is never explained why *twelve*

watchmen were involved, but they do help introduce a sense of an audience, making the bedchamber a scene of performance and the reader one of the voyeurs.

31. Ordering up Lennox's *The Greek Theatre of Father Brumoy* in the British Library, at the same time as her *Memoirs of the Duke of Sully*, provided me with one of those revelatory moments in scholarly life. I was completely unprepared for the lavishness of production, having, at that early stage, imbibed the idea that translation – especially if done by a woman – was 'low'. These volumes, which I needed a trolley to transport to my desk, declared both a writer and books of consequence.

32. Small, *Charlotte Ramsay Lennox*, pp. 27–28.

33. Dustin Griffin deals with this aspect of Charlotte Lennox's writing life in *Literary Patronage in England, 1650–1800* (Cambridge, 1996), pp. 203–19. Details of payment and presents that follow can be found more fully discussed there.

34. Oliver Goldsmith, 'An Enquiry into the Present State of Polite Learning in Europe', *Collected Works of Oliver Goldsmith*, ed. Arthur Friedman, 5 vols (Oxford, 1966), i, p. 314.

35. Small, *Charlotte Ramsay Lennox*, pp. 134–35.

Notes to Chapter 4: Hester Thrale and Elizabeth Montagu

1. Samuel Johnson, *Rambler*, no. 107.

2. This and all following quotes from Frances Reynolds can be found in her 'Recollections of Dr Johnson', which is collected in (ed.) Robina Napier, *Johnsoniana: Anecdotes of the Late Samuel Johnson* (London, 1884) pp. 329–47.

3. Mrs Piozzi, *Thraliana* (Oxford, 1942), i, p. 79.

4. Frances d'Arblay, *Memoirs of Dr Burney* (London, 1832), i, p. 332.

5. Arthur Murphy, 'An Essay on the Life and Genius of Dr Johnson', *The Works of Samuel Johnson*, 12 vols (ed.) Arthur Murphy (London, 1823), i, pp. 82–83. Murphy offers a 'translation, or rather imitation' of the poem, 'Know Thyself' – 'the picture for which Dr Johnson sat to himself' – which conveys a more eighteenth-century flavour than that of John Wain's. Wain's, however, is more accessible. Both Latin and English can be found on pp. 26–30 of the Oxford Authors edition of Samuel Johnson, ed. Donald Greene (Oxford, 1984).

6. The preface is in the Oxford Authors edition of Samuel Johnson, ed. Donald Greene, pp. 419–56.

7. Mrs Piozzi, *Thraliana* i, p. 445. At that first dinner, and serving as a 'bait' or excuse for the invitation to Johnson, was James Woodhouse, the 'shoemaker' poet. Perhaps he thought he might get patrons too. If so, he was disappointed; the Thrales weren't impressed by him. He was to be taken up by Mrs Montagu.

8. Ibid., p. 172.

9. Mrs Piozzi, *Anecdotes of the Late Samuel Johnson* (London and Oxford, 1974), pp. 67, 68, 159, 130.

10. Ibid., pp. 102 and 152.

11. Ibid., p. 134.

12. Ibid., p. 156.

13. Forbes, Sir William (ed.), *Life of Beattie*, 2 vols (London, 1807), ii, p. 375.

14. *Bluestocking Feminism*, volume 1, *Elizabeth Montagu* (ed.) Elizabeth Eger, pp. 170–71.

15. Ibid., p. 173.

16. Ibid., pp. 173–74.

17. Ibid., pp. 171–72.

18. Ibid., p. 174.

19. Ibid., p. 172.

20. Ibid., introduction, pp. lxxi-lxxii.

21. Mrs Chapone, *Posthumous Works* (London, 1807), i, pp. 149, 151.

22. Rene Huchon, *Mrs Montagu and her Friends* (London, 1907), pp. 147–49.

23. James Boswell, *The Journal of a Tour to the Hebrides with Samuel Johnson, LL.D.* (London, 1852), pp. 208–9.

24. John Doran, *A Lady of the Last Century: Mrs Elizabeth Montagu* (London, 1873), pp. 290–91; Reginald Blunt (ed.), *Mrs Montagu, 'Queen of the Blues': Her Letters and Friendships from 1762 to 1800*, 2 vols (London, 1923), ii, pp. 156–57.

25. The popularity of James Thomson's poem, *The Castle of Indolence* (1733) may have some bearing on this.

26. Blunt, Mrs Montagu *(London, 1923), i, pp. 147, 260–61.*

27. Piozzi, *Thraliana*, i, p. 409.

28. Ibid., pp. 436, 494, 498. The brewery was bought by the rich Quaker family of Barclay.

29. Carter breathed no word of criticism of Lord Bath. Of Mrs Vesey's 'philandering' with Laurence Sterne (a cousin of Montagu), she was thoroughly disapproving. The 'Sylph' allowed herself too many intimate chats with Sterne in her 'warm cabinet' at Bolton Row, and, worse, spent a whole night nursing him at his house when he was sick. Sterne, Carter reminded Vesey, 'by his carelessness and extravagance, has left a wife and child to starve'. There were also his 'indecent and buffoon writings' to take into account. See Blunt, *Mrs Montagu*, i, p. 193; and Carter-Talbot *A Series of Letters*, iii, p. 99. Montagu's intimacy with Lord Bath is well conveyed in Blunt, *Mrs Montagu*, i, chs 2– 4.

30. Mrs Chapone, *Posthumous Works* (London, 1807), i, pp. 180–81.

31. Piozzi, *Thraliana*, i, p. 369.

32. Ibid., p. 379.

33. Ibid., pp. 384–85.

34. Blunt, *Mrs Montagu*, pp. 277–78.

35. Ibid., p. 37.

36. Ibid., pp. 48–49.

37. Myers, *The Bluestocking Circle* (Oxford, 1990), p. 183. In 1778 Carter urged Montagu: 'Do pray rescue our Elizabeth from the nonsense which later historians have talked about her.' One of those later historians was the

indefatigable Thomas Birch who had also edited Catherine Cockburn. Montagu was by no means eager to welcome his book on Queen Elizabeth I.

Notes to Chapter 5: Hannah More

1. M. G. Jones, *Hannah More* (Cambridge, 1952), pp. 6 –7.
2. Biographical information from Jones, *Hannah More*. Unlike Carter, Montagu or Lennox, Hannah More has been the subject of considerable critical and biographical attention. Mostly this has concentrated on her social activism. For her early experiences as a writer, William Roberts's *Memoirs of the Life and Correspondence of Mrs Hannah More* (London, 1835) remains the essential text.
3. Roger Lonsdale, *Eighteenth-Century Women Poets* (Oxford, 1989), p. 325.
4. Mary Alden Hopkins, *Hannah More and Her Circle* (New York and Toronto, 1947), p. 50.
5. Roberts, *Memoirs of Mrs Hannah More*, p. 46.
6. The best account of Hannah More's progress as a dramatist is in Stone and Kahrl, *David Garrick: A Critical Biography* (Carbondale, Illinois, 1979) pp. 426–39. All quotations concerning her relationship with Garrick are from this source unless otherwise indicated.
7. Roberts, *Memoirs of Mrs Hannah More*, p. 68.
8. Ibid., pp. 68, 78.
9. Ibid., pp. 89, 92, 93.
10. Hester Piozzi, *Thraliana*, i, pp. 386–87.
11. Ellen Donkin, *Getting Into the Act: Women Playwrights in London, 1776–1829* (London, 1995) p. 112.
12. Stone and Kahrl, *David Garrick*, p. 435.
13. Roberts, *Memoirs of Mrs Hannah More*, p. 122.
14. Stone and Kahrl, *David Garrick*, p. 435.
15. Roberts, *Memoirs of Mrs Hannah More*, p. 50.
16. Ibid., pp. 52–53.
17. Ibid., p. 63.
18. Ibid., pp. 62–63.
19. Boswell's *Life of Samuel Johnson* (London, 1906), ii, p. 553.
20. Chauncy Brewster Tinker, *Dr Johnson and Fanny Burney* (London, 1912), p. 60.
21. Roberts, *Memoirs of Mrs Hannah More*, p. 54.
22. Ibid., pp. 66–67.
23. Hopkins, *Hannah More and her Circle* (New York and Toronto, 1947), pp. 89–90.
24. Ellen Donkin, *Getting into the Act* (London, 1995), ch. 3, 'The Paper War of Hannah Cowley and Hannah More', pp. 57–76. Donkin's view of the general position of female dramatists at this time is not one I share.
25. Roberts, *Memoirs of Mrs Hannah More*, p. 167.

26. Hopkins, *Hannah More and her Circle*, p. 138. See also, M. G. Jones, *Hannah More* (Cambridge, 1952), pp. 66–73.

27. *Bluestocking Feminism*, volume one, *Elizabeth Montagu*, ed. Elizabeth Eger, introduction, p. lxiv.

28. Donna Landry, *The Muses of Resistance* (Cambridge, 1990), explores More's relationship with Yearsley at great length, see pp. 16–22 and 120–185. See also Mary Waldron, *Lactilla, Milkwoman of Clifton* (Athens, Georgia, and London, 1996), ch. 3, 'The Subscription, the Quarrel and its Aftermath', pp. 48–78.

29. Quoted in Landry, *Muses of Resistance*, p. 149. Landry explores this connection in an illuminating way. She links name and nature in her remarks on the 'savage' in Ann Yearsley, and addresses the way both Savage and Yearsley exploit popular ideas of original genius.

30. See Dustin Griffin, *Literary Patronage in England, 1650–1800* (Cambridge, 1996), on the psychology of being patronised.

31. Jones, *Hannah More*, pp. 73–76.

32. Quoted in Eger, 'The Nine Living Muses' (unpublished Ph.D thesis, Cambridge, 1998).

33. Landry, *The Muses of Resistance*, pp. 154–55.

34. Waldron, *Lactilla*, pp. 76–77.

Notes to Chapter 6: Fanny Burney

1. M. G. Jones, *Hannah More* (Cambridge, 1952), p. 61.

2. *The Early Journals and Letters of Fanny Burney, 1768–91*, ed. Lars Troide et al., 3 vols (Oxford, 1988–94), i, pp. 1–2.

3. Mme d'Arblay, *Memoirs of Dr Burney* (London, 1832), ii, p125.

4. T. B. Macaulay, *Literary Essays* (London,1905), p. 250.

5. Hester Lynch (Thrale) Piozzi, *Thraliana*, ed. Katherine Balderston (Oxford, 1942), i, p. 399.

6. Kate Chisholm, *Fanny Burney: Her Life* (London, 1998), p. 273.

7. Ibid., p. 39

8. Ibid., pp. 40–42.

9. Piozzi, *Thraliana*, i, p. 329.

10. Chauncey Tinker, *Dr Johnson and Fanny Burney: Being the Johnsonian Passages from the Works of Mme d'Arblay* (London, 1912) pp. 2–3.

11. Ibid., p. 53.

12. Chisholm, *Fanny Burney*, p. 36.

13. Tinker, *Dr Johnson and Fanny Burney*, pp. 109–10. For an excellent discussion of *The Witlings*, see Margaret Doody, *Frances Burney: The Life in the Works* (New Brunswick, New Jersey, 1988), ch. 3, 'The Witlings: The Finished Comedy'.

14. Ibid., p. 68.

15. Ibid., p. 153.

16. Ibid., p. 164.

17. Ibid., pp. 112, 144.
18. Chisholm, *Fanny Burney*, p. 67.
19. Tinker, *Dr Johnson and Fanny Burney*, pp. 31–33.
20. Chisholm, *Fanny Burney*, p. 94.
21. William McCarthy, *Hester Thrale Piozzi: Portrait of a Literary Woman* (Chapel Hill, North Carolina, 1985), pp. 31–32.
22. Tinker, *Dr Johnson and Fanny Burney*, p. 6.
23. Ibid., pp. 74–75.
24. McCarthy, *Hester Thrale Piozzi*, p. 28.
25. Piozzi, *Thraliana*, i, p. 400.
26. Ibid., i, p. 443.
27. Ibid., p. 470.
28. Chisholm, *Fanny Burney*, pp. 106–7.
29. Catherine Gallagher, in *Nobody's Story* (Berkeley and Los Angeles, 1994), builds her analysis of *Cecilia*, and, indeed, of Fanny Burney, around the idea of 'universal obligation'. Her discussion has been most useful to me.
30. Macaulay is caustic about Dr Burney's role here. See Macaulay, *Literary Essays*, 'Mme d'Arblay', pp. 267–70.
31. Rizzo dubs Montagu 'a perfect patriarch' and 'captain of industry' and gives a full account of the relationship with Dorothea Gregory in *Companions Without Vows: Relationships among Eighteenth-Century British Women* (Athens, Georgia, and London, 1994), ch. 6, 'Parent and Child: Montagu and Gregory'. All the information in this section is from Rizzo.
32. Collinson-Morley, *Giuseppe Baretti* (London, 1909), p. 285.
33. Doody, *Frances Burney*, p. 107.
34. Laetitia-Matilda Hawkins, *Anecdotes, Biographical Sketches and Memoirs* (London, 1822), p. 330.
35. Tinker, *Dr Johnson and Fanny Burney*, p. 108.
36. Ibid., p. 12.
37. She objected to her friend Mrs Pitt's 'servility' in telling the Duchess of Portland she thought 'high birth preferable to all merit whatever'. Montagu claimed that she herself would 'rather be dunghill born and have transcendent merit than be an ordinary character in a very great situation'. See Reginald Blunt (ed.), *Mrs Montagu, 'Queen of the Blues': Her Letters and Friendships from 1762–1800*, 2 vols (London, 1923), i, p. 15.
38. Johnson, *The Letters of Samuel Johnson*, ed. Bruce Redford (Princeton, New Jersey), i, p. 71. The image is taken from Milton's *Paradise Lost*.
39. Tinker, *Dr Johnson and Fanny Burney*, p. 65.
40. Laetitia-Matilda Hawkins, *Memoirs, Anecdotes, Facts and Opinions* (London, 1824), pp. 70–71.
41. Hawkins, *Anecdotes*, p. 329.
42. Ibid., pp. 331–32.
43. Hawkins, *Memoirs*, pp. 156–57.
44. Ibid., pp. 218–21.

45. Ibid., p. 157.
46. Mrs Chapone, *Posthumous Works*, i, p. 18.
47. Tinker, *Dr Johnson and Fanny Burney*, p. 205.
48. *Bluestocking Feminism*, volume six, *Sarah Scott and Clara Reeve*, edited by Gary Kelly, gives the whole of *The Progress of Romance*.
49. Tinker, *Dr Johnson and Fanny Burney*, p. 202.
50. Ibid., p. 207.

Notes to Chapter 7: Women and Writing

1. Johnson, *Rambler*, no. 60, 'Biography', Oxford Authors, *Samuel Johnson* (Oxford, 1984), pp. 204–7.
2. Quoted in Elizabeth Eger, 'The Nine Living Muses' (unpublished Ph.D. thesis, Cambridge University, 1998).
3. *Letters from Elizabeth Carter to Mrs Montagu between the Years 1755 and 1800: Chiefly upon Literary and Moral Subjects*, ed. Montagu Pennington, 3 vols (London, 1817), iii, pp. 337–38.
4. *The Letters of Samuel Johnson*, ed. Bruce Redford (Princeton, New Jersey, 1992), i, pp. 150–51.
5. Hester Lynch (Thrale) Piozzi, *Thraliana*, ed. Katherine Balderston (Oxford, 1942), i, pp. 328–29.
6. Johnson, *Letters*, ii, p. 201.
7. Carter to Montagu, *Letters* (London, 1817), iii, pp. 47–48.
8. Johnson, *Letters*, v (appendix), p. 10.
9. Ibid., iii, p. 280.
10. Miriam Small, *Charlotte Ramsay Lennox* (New Haven, 1935), pp. 57–63, details Lennox's dealings with the Royal Literary Fund and gives an account of her last years.
11. M. G. Jones, *Hannah More* (Cambridge, 1952), p. 40.
12. Pennington, *Memoirs of Mrs Elizabeth Carter* (London, 1808), i, p. 440. Pennington discusses what he describes as Carter's surprising reluctance to cultivate the society of men of letters 'so much as might have been expected' and attributes it to her 'prejudice' in favour of women writers, her 'extreme partiality for writers of her own sex', p. 447. He also defends his own actions in publishing the letters by revealing that the letters to Catherine Talbot were 'all properly arranged and dated, as if for publication, by Mrs Carter herself, and the names of persons mentioned in them carefully erased'. He justifies himself and her by adding that the letters were not actually written with a view to publication – that would have been wrong, but posthumous publication was not. Ibid., i, p. 154.
13. Carter to Montagu, *Letters*, iii, p. 234.
14. Tinker, *Dr Johnson and Fanny Burney*, p. 197.

Bibliography

Ballaster, Ros, *Seductive Forms: Women's Amatory Fiction from 1684–1740* (Oxford, 1992).

Barash, Carol, *English Women's Poetry, 1649–1714* (Oxford, 1996).

Barker-Benfield, G. J., *The Culture of Sensibility* (Chicago, 1992).

Bate, Walter Jackson, *Samuel Johnson* (London, 1984).

Beloe, William, *Recollections* (London, 1817).

Blunt, Reginald (ed.), *Mrs Montagu, 'Queen of the Blues': Her Letters and Friendships from 1762 to 1800*, 2 vols (London, 1923).

Boswell, James *The Journal of a Tour to the Hebrides with Samuel Johnson, LL.D.* (London, 1852).

Boswell, James, *The Life of Samuel Johnson*, Everyman edition, 2 vols (London, 1906).

Brack, Gae Annette, 'Samuel Johnson and Four Literary Women' (unpublished thesis, Arizona State University, 1979).

Brewer, John, *The Pleasures of the Imagination: English Culture in the Eighteenth Century* (London, 1997).

Burney, Fanny (Mme d'Arblay), *Cecilia* (Oxford, 1988).

–, *Evelina* (Oxford, 1970).

–, *The Early Journals and Letters of Fanny Burney*, edited by Lars E. Troide and Stewart J. Cooke (Oxford, 1994)

-, *The Journals and Letters of Fanny Burney*, edited by Joyce Hemlow et al., 12 vols (Oxford, 1972- 84).

Chapone, Hester (née Mulso), *Posthumous Works*, 2 vols (London, 1807).

Chisholm, Kate, *Fanny Burney: Her Life* (London, 1998).

Clarke, Norma, *Ambitious Heights: Writing, Friendship, Love. The Jewsbury Sisters, Felicia Hemans and Jane Carlyle* (London, 1990).

–, 'Anna Jameson: "The Idol of Thousands of Young Ladies"', in (eds) Hilton and Hirsch, *Practical Visionaries* (London, 2000).

–, 'Soft Passions and Darling Themes: From Elizabeth Rowe (1674–1737) to Elizabeth Carter (1717–1806)', *Writing Women*, Autumn 2000.

–, 'The Cursed Barbauld Crew': Women Writers and Writing for Children in the Late Eighteenth Century', in (eds) Hilton, Styles and Watson, *Opening the Nursery Door: Reading, Writing and Childhood, 1600–1900* (London, 1996).

Clifford, James L., *Dictionary Johnson: Samuel Johnson's Middle Years* (New York, 1979).

Climenson, Emily (ed.), *Elizabeth Montagu, The Queen of the Bluestockings: Her Correspondence from 1720 to 1761*, 2 vols (London, 1906).

Collinson-Morley, Lacy, *Giuseppe Baretti* (London, 1909).

d'Arblay, Frances, *Memoirs of Dr Burney*, 3 vols (London,1832).

Demers, Patricia, *The World of Hannah More* (Kentucky, 1996).

Donkin, Ellen, *Getting into the Act: Women Playwrights in London, 1776–1829* (London, 1995).

Doody, Margaret, *Frances Burney: The Life in the Works* (New Brunswick, New Jersey, 1988).

Doody, Margaret, 'Shakespeare's Novels: Charlotte Lennox Illustrated', *Studies in the Novel*, 19 (1987), pp. 296–310.

Doran, John, *A Lady of the Last Century: Mrs Elizabeth Montagu* (London, 1873).

Eagleton, Terry, *The Rape of Clarissa* (Oxford, 1982).

Eaves, T. C. Duncan and Kimpel, Ben D., *Samuel Richardson, A Biography* (Oxford, 1971).

Edinburgh Weekly Magazine, Memoir of Charlotte Lennox, 9 October 1783.

Eger, Elizabeth, 'The Nine Living Muses of Great Britain: Women, Reason and Literary Community in Eighteenth-Century Britain' (unpublished Ph.D. thesis, Cambridge University, 1998).

–, (ed.) *Elizabeth Montagu*, vol. 1 of *Bluestocking Feminism* (general editor Gary Kelly, London 1999).

Ellis, Annie Raine, *The Early Diary of Frances Burney, 1768–1778* (London, 1889).

Ezell, Margaret, *Writing Women's Literary History* (Baltimore and London, 1993).

Forbes, Sir William (ed.), *Life of Beattie* (London, 1807).

Ford, Charles Howard, *Hannah More: A Critical Biography* (New York, 1996).

Gallagher, Catherine, *Nobody's Story: The Vanishing Acts of Women Writers in the Marketplace, 1670–1820* (Berkeley and Los Angeles, California, 1994).

Gonda, Caroline, *Reading Daughters' Fictions, 1709–1834* (Cambridge, 1996).

Greene, Donald (ed.), *Samuel Johnson: A Critical Edition of the Major Works* (Oxford, 1984).

Griffin, Dustin, *Literary Patronage in England, 1650–1800* (Cambridge, 1996).

Gross, Gloria Sybil, *This Invisible Riot of the Mind: Samuel Johnson's Psychological Theory* (Philadelphia. 1992).

Grundy, Isobel, *Lady Mary Wortley Montagu: Comet of the Enlightenment* (Oxford, 1999).

–, 'Samuel Johnson as Patron of Women', *The Age of Johnson*, 1 (1987).

–, *Women, Writing, History, 1640–1740*, edited with Susan Wiseman (London, 1992).

Halladay, Gae, and Brack, O. M., 'Johnson as Patron', in (eds) Korshin, Paul, and Allen, Robert, *Greene Centennial Studies* (Charlottesville, 1984).

Hawkins, Sir John, *The Life of Samuel Johnson LL.D.* (London, 1787).

Hawkins, Laetitia Matilda, *Anecdotes, Biographical Sketches and Memoirs* (London, 1822).

–, *Memoirs, Anecdotes, Facts and Opinions* (London, 1824).

Hawley, Judith (ed.), *Elizabeth Carter*, vol. 2 of *Bluestocking Feminism* (general editor Gary Kelly, London 1999).

Henson, Eithne, *'The Fictions of Romantick Chivalry': Samuel Johnson and Romance* (New Jersey and London, 1992).

Holmes, Richard, *Dr Johnson and Mr Savage* (London, 1994).

Hyde, Mary, *The Impossible Friendship: Boswell and Mrs Thrale* (London, 1973).

Hopkins, Mary Alden, *Hannah More and her Circle* (New York and Toronto, 1947).

Huchon, Rene, *Mrs Montagu and her Friends* (London, 1907).

Isles, Duncan, 'Johnson and Charlotte Lennox', *New Rambler*, 3, series C (1967).

Isles, Duncan (ed.), 'The Lennox Collection', *Harvard Library Bulletin*, 18, no. 4 (1970); 19, nos 1, 2 and 4 (1971).

Jones, M. G., *Hannah More* (Cambridge, 1952).

Jones, Vivien, *Women in the Eighteenth-Century: Constructions of Femininity* (London, 1990).

–, (ed.), *Women and Literature in Britain, 1700–1800* (Cambridge, 2000).

Kelly, Gary (ed.), *Bluestocking Feminism: Writings of the Bluestocking Circle, 1738–1785*, vols 1–6 (London, 1999).

Kelly, Gary (ed.), *Sarah Scott*, vol. 5, *Bluestocking Feminism*, general editor, Gary Kelly (London, 1999).

Knellwolf, Christa, *A Contradiction Still: Representations of Women in the Poetry of Alexander Pope* (Manchester, 1998).

Landry, Donna, *The Muses of Resistance: Laboring-Class Women's Poetry in Britain, 1739–1796* (Cambridge, Massachusetts, 1990).

Lane, Margaret, *Samuel Johnson and his World* (London, 1975).

Langbauer, Laurie, 'Romance Revised: Charlotte Lennox's *The Female Quixote*', *Novel*, 18 (1984).

LeFanu, William (ed.), *Elizabeth Sheridan, Betsy Sheridan's Journal: Letters from Sheridan's Sister, 1784–1786 and 1788–1790* (Oxford, 1986).

Lennox, Charlotte (née Ramsay), *Henrietta*, 2 vols. (London, 1758).

–, *Poems on Several Occasions: Written by a Young Lady* (London, 1747).

–, *Shakespear Illustrated*, 3 vols (London, 1753).

–, *Sophia*, 2 vols (London, 1762).

–, *The Female Quixote*, edited by Margaret Dalziel (Oxford, 1970).

–, *The Greek Theatre of Father Brumoy*, 3 vols (London, 1759).

–, *The Lady's Museum*, 2 vols, 11 numbers (London, 1760–61).

–, *The Life of Harriot Stuart: Written by Herself*, edited by Susan Howard (New Brusnwick, New Jersey and London, 1995).

–, *The Memoirs of the Duke of Sully* 3 vols (London, 1756).

Lonsdale, Roger (ed.), *Eighteenth-Century Women Poets: An Oxford Anthology* (Oxford, 1989).

Lynd, Robert, *Dr Johnson and Company* (London, 1946).

Macaulay, Thomas, *Literary Essays* (London, 1905).

Mack, Maynard, *Alexander Pope* (New Haven, 1985).

Mavor, Elizabeth, *The Ladies of Llangollen* (London, 1973).

Maynardier, Gustavus, *The First American Novelist?* (Cambridge, Massachusetts, 1940).

McCarthy, William, *Hester Thrale Piozzi: Portrait of a Literary Woman* (Chapel Hill, North Carolina, and London, 1985).

Moers, Ellen, *Literary Women* (London, 1978).

Montagu, Matthew (ed.), *The Letters of Mrs Elizabeth Montagu*, 3 vols (London, 1810).

Montagu, Mary Wortley, *Letters* (London, 1992).

Murphy, Arthur, *An Essay on the Life and Genius of Dr Johnson* (London, 1792).

–, (ed.) *The Works of Samuel Johnson*, 12 vols (London, 1823).

Myers, Sylvia Harcstark, *The Bluestocking Circle: Women, Friendship and the Life of the Mind in Eighteenth-Century England* (Oxford, 1990).

Napier, Robina (ed.), *Johnsoniana: Anecdotes of the Late Samuel Johnson LL.D. by Mrs Piozzi, Richard Cumberland, Bishop Percy and Others: Together with the Diary of Dr Campbell and Extracts from that of Madame d'Arblay* (London, 1884).

Pennington, Montagu (ed.), *A Series of Letters between Mrs Elizabeth Carter and Miss Catherine Talbot, from the Year 1741 to 1770. To Which are Added, Letters from Mrs Elizabeth Carter to Mrs Vesey, between the Years 1763 and 1787*, 2 vols (London, 1808).

–, *Letters from Mrs Elizabeth Carter to Mrs Montagu between the Years 1755 and 1800. Chiefly upon Literary and Moral Subjects*, 3 vols (London, 1817).

–, *Memoirs of the Life of Mrs Elizabeth Carter, with a New Edition of her Poems, to Which are Added some Miscellaneous Essays in Prose, Together with her Notes on the Bible, and Answers to Objections Concerning the Christian Religion*, 2 vols (London, 1808).

Phillips, Constantia, *An Apology* (London, 1749).

Phillips, Patricia, *The Scientific Lady: A Social History of Women's Scientific Interests, 1520–1918* (London, 1990).

Pilkington, Laetitia, *Memoirs of Mrs Laetitia Pilkington, 1712–1750: Written by Herself* (ed.) A. C. Elias, Jr, 2 vols (Athens, Georgia, and London, 1997).

Piozzi, Hester Lynch (Thrale), *Anecdotes of the Late Samuel Johnson LL.D. during the Last Twenty Years of His Life*, ed. Arthur Sherbo (London and Oxford, 1974).

–, *Letters to and from the Late Samuel Johnson, LL.D.: To Which are Added Some Poems Never before Printed*, 2 vols (London, 1788).

–, *Observations and Reflections Made in the Course of a Journey through France, Italy and Germany*, ed. Herbert Burrows (Ann Arbor, Michigan, 1967).

–, *Thraliana*, edited by Katharine Balderston (Oxford, 1942).

Prescott, Sarah, *Female Authorship in Early Eighteenth-Century England* (forthcoming).

Reddick, Allen, *The Making of Johnson's Dictionary, 1746–1773* (Cambridge, 1990).

Redford, Bruce (ed.), *The Letters of Samuel Johnson* (Princeton, New Jersey, 1992).

Reynolds, Myra, *The Learned Lady in England, 1650–1760* (Boston, 1920).

Ribeiro, Alvaro and Basker, James (eds), *Tradition in Transition: Women Writers, Marginal Texts and the Eighteenth-Century Canon* (Oxford, 1996).

Richardson, Samuel, *Clarissa*, 8 vols (London, 1748–49).

Richetti, John, *The English Novel in History, 1700–1780* (London, 1999).

Rizzo, Betty, *Companions Without Vows: Relationships among Eighteenth- Century British Women* (Athens and London, 1994).

Roberts, William (ed.), *Memoirs of the Life and Correspondence of Mrs Hannah More* (London, 1835).

Ross, Deborah, 'Mirror, Mirror: The Didactic Dilemma of the Female Quixote.' *Studies in English Literature*, 27 (1987).

Rowe, Elizabeth, *The Miscellaneous Works in Prose and Verse*, edited by Theophilus Rowe (London, 1739).

Ruhe, Edward, 'Birch, Johnson and Elizabeth Carter: An Episode of 1738–39', *PMLA*, 73 (1958).

Runge, Laura, *Gender and Language in British Literary Criticism, 1660–1790* (Cambridge, 1997).

Sejourne, Philippe, *The Mystery of Charlotte Lennox, First Novelist of Colonial America* (Aix-en-Provence, 1967).

Small, Miriam Rossiter, *Charlotte Ramsay Lennox: An Eighteenth-Century Lady of Letters* (New York, 1935; reprint, Hamden, Connecticut, 1969).

Spacks, Patricia Meyer, 'The Subtle Sophistry of Desire: Dr Johnson and *The Female Quixote*', *Modern Philology*, 85 (1987–88).

Jane Spencer, *The Rise of the Woman Novelist: From Aphra Behn to Jane Austen* (Oxford, 1986).

Stauffer, Donald, *The Art of Biography in Eighteenth-Century England* (Princeton, 1941).

Stone, George Winchester, Jr, and Kahrl, George M., *David Garrick: A Critical Biography* (Carbondale, Illinois, 1979).

Thomas, Claudia, 'Samuel Johnson and Elizabeth Carter: Pudding, Epictetus, and the Accomplished Woman', *South Central Review* (1992).

–, 'Th'instructive Moral and Important Thought': Elizabeth Carter Reads Pope, Johnson, and Epictetus', Paul Korshin (ed.), *The Age of Johnson*, 4 (1991).

Thrale, Hester, see Piozzi.

Tinker, Chauncey Brewster, *Dr Johnson and Fanny Burney: Being the Johnsonian Passages from the Works of Mme d'Arblay* (London, 1912).

Tobin, Beth Fowkes (ed.), *History, Gender, and Eighteenth-Century Literature* (Athens, Georgia, 1994).

Janet Todd, *The Sign of Angellica: Women, Writing and Fiction, 1660–1800* (London, 1989).

Turner, Cheryl, *Living by the Pen: Women Writers in the Eighteenth Century* (London, 1992).

Uglow, Jenny, *Hogarth: A Life and a World* (London, 1997).

–, *Dr Johnson, His Club and Other Friends* (London, 1998).

Waldron, Mary, *Lactilla, Milkwoman of Clifton: The Life and Writings of Ann Yearsley, 1753–1806* (Athens, Georgia and London, 1996).

Williams, Carolyn, 'Poetry, Pudding, and Epictetus: The Consistency of Elizabeth Carter', in Alvaro Ribeiro and James Basker (eds), *Tradition in Transition: Women Writers, Marginal Texts and the Eighteenth-Century Canon* (Oxford, 1996).

Zuk, Rhoda (ed.), *Catherine Talbot and Hester Chapone*, volume 3, *Bluestocking Feminism*, general editor Gary Kelly (London, 1999).

Index

Bold type indicates main or substantial sections. SJ = Samuel Johnson